The Elaine Massacre
and Arkansas

Other books written or edited by Guy Lancaster

Racial Cleansing in Arkansas, 1883–1924:
Politics, Land, Labor, and Criminality

Bullets and Fire:
Lynching and Authority in Arkansas, 1840–1950

To Can the Kaiser:
Arkansas and the Great War
with Michael D. Polston

The Elaine Massacre and Arkansas

A Century of Atrocity and Resistance, 1819-1919

Edited by
Guy Lancaster

Little Rock, Arkansas

Contributors:
Richard Buckelew
Nancy Snell Griffith
Matthew Hild
Adrienne A. Jones
Kelly Houston Jones
Cherisse Jones-Branch
Guy Lancaster
Brian K. Mitchell
William H. Pruden III
Steven Teske

The Butler Center for Arkansas Studies
Central Arkansas Library System
100 Rock Street
Little Rock, Arkansas 72201
www.butlercenter.org

June 2018
Hardcover: ISBN 978-1-945624-11-7
Paperback: ISBN 978-1-945624-07-0

Manager: Rod Lorenzen
Cover and book design: Michael Keckhaver
Copyeditor: Ali Welky

This book was funded in part by a grant from the
Black History Commission of Arkansas.

Front cover image courtesy of the Butler Center for Arkansas Studies.

Library of Congress Cataloging-in-Publication Data
Names: Lancaster, Guy, 1976- editor. | Butler Center for Arkansas Studies.
Title: The Elaine Massacre and Arkansas : a century of atrocity and resistance, 1819-1919 / edited by Guy Lancaster.
Description: Little Rock, Arkansas : Butler Center Books, [2018] | Includes bibliographical references and index.
Identifiers: LCCN 2018014417| ISBN 9781945624070 (pbk. : alk. paper) | ISBN 9781945624117 (hardcover : alk. paper)
Subjects: LCSH: Arkansas--Race relations--History. | African Americans—Civil rights--Arkansas--History. | Elaine Race Riot, Elaine, Ark., 1919. | African Americans--Arkansas--History. | African American farmers--Arkansas--History.
Classification: LCC E185.93.A8 E43 2018 | DDC 305.8009767--dc23 LC record available at https://lccn.loc.gov/2018014417

Butler Center Books, the publishing division of the Butler Center for Arkansas Studies, was made possible by the generosity of Dora Johnson Ragsdale and John G. Ragsdale Jr.

Printed in the United States of America

Table of Contents

Acknowledgements

Anyone who commits to writing about the Elaine Massacre today owes a significant debt of gratitude to Grif Stockley, whose groundbreaking work on the subject, the 2001 book *Blood in Their Eyes*, forced discussion and reconsideration of what happened in Phillips County in 1919 into the mainstream. Grif's historical research and writing arose from the same longstanding commitment to justice that has typified his life and career, and he has been more than just a professional influence in my life—he has been a friend and a source of constant encouragement in navigating the darker corners of Arkansas and American history.

As editor of this volume, I would like to thank all of those whose work appears herein. Scholars today—be they based at universities, archives, or libraries—face frequent demands for their time and energy, and I am truly fortunate to have a group like this willing to be so generous with their abilities. Rod Lorenzen of Butler Center Books eagerly embraced this book concept and led the way in bringing it to fruition, while David Stricklin, director of the Butler Center for Arkansas Studies at the Central Arkansas Library System, and Bob Razer, Archie House Fellow at the Butler Center, ensured that I had the time and resources to work on this volume. This project was also the recipient of the Curtis Sykes Memorial Grant from the Black History Commission of Arkansas, and we appreciate this generous financial support.

I must also thank Pat Rowe, who reached out to the Encyclopedia of Arkansas many years ago to share with us images taken by her grandfather at the time of the Elaine Massacre. Some of these are published for the first time in this book.

Finally, I have to thank Anna, my wife, who puts up with a great deal of my ranting, rambling, complaining, theorizing, and despairing. I only hope that I offer her something worthwhile in return.

Preface

Grif Stockley

There was a time and not so long ago when historians threw up their hands and declared that the evidence of a massacre in Phillips County in 1919 was too conflicting to reach any conclusions—especially about what had caused such a bloodbath or who was at fault. Over the years, to those who believed that many horrible acts of violence had been committed beginning the night of September 30, it would seem as if the profession could hide indefinitely behind phrases such as "beyond historical inquiry." With the approaching centennial anniversary of what is *now* generally referred to as the "Elaine Massacre," it might seem as if the historian's day has finally come, and all will be explained and tallied. However, the truth is that we will likely never identify precisely the number of African American men, women, and children who were murdered, who they were, the names of their murderers, or what was taken from them. It appears too late for that kind of courage, honesty, and integrity.

Yet what is occurring in the field of historical research in the present era must be applauded and encouraged because it is unlike anything that has come before in Arkansas. In the introduction to this volume of essays, editor Guy Lancaster cogently explains that the massacre in Phillips County in 1919 must be understood as representing a "continuum of history," and remain in its proper context—"that it be presented not as singular, not as unique, not as an atrocity *sui generis*, without equal in the legacy of white supremacy in the United States." If it still appears beyond their reach to give names to all victims and perpetrators, the approach taken in this volume of essays, *The Elaine Massacre and Arkansas: A Century of Atrocity and Resistance, 1819–1919*, confronts the reader with incontrovertible documentation that Arkansas's racial history in the previous century was filled with acts of violence, rape, and murder of African Americans as well as other devastating manifestations of white supremacy. We can be optimistic about the future of scholarship in this area in part due to the diverse array of researchers—black and white, men and women—who have contributed to this volume. If the details of the Elaine Massacre, for the moment, remain beyond our grasp, at least the broader institution of white supremacy itself no longer lies outside the field of historical inquiry.

Introduction

Guy Lancaster

It seems to me imperative…that historians and social scien-
tists pay closer attention to the moment of violence and try in
some way to represent it in their writings. There are at least two
reasons for this. First, the moment of violence, and suffering,
tells us a great deal about our condition today. Secondly, the
experience of violence is in crucial ways constitutive of our
"traditions," our sense of community, our communities and our
history.
——Gyanendra Pandey, "In Defense of the Fragment"[1]

With the establishment of a relationship of oppression, violence
has *already* begun.
——Paulo Freire, *Pedagogy of the Oppressed*[2]

On the night of September 30, 1919, a group of African
Americans, many of them sharecroppers, met at a church
in Hoop Spur, located three miles north of the town of
Elaine in southern Phillips County, Arkansas. They were attending a meeting of the Progressive Farmers and Household Union
of America, and their aim was to obtain better payments for the
crops they were growing for local white planters. Knowing that
such union activity put them at risk for violence, those attending the meeting stationed armed guards outside the church. What
happened next remains the subject of speculation, but a shootout
ensued between these guards and three individuals who had
parked near the church. The shootout left W. A. Adkins, a white

---

[1] Gyanendra Pandey, "In Defense of the Fragment: Writing about Hin-
du-Muslim Riots in India Today," *Representations* 37 (Winter 1992): 41.
[2] Paulo Freire, *Pedagogy of the Oppressed: 30ᵗʰ Anniversary Edition* (New
York: Continuum, 2000), 55.

security officer for the Missouri Pacific Railroad, dead, and Charlie Pratt, a white deputy sheriff, wounded. Almost immediately, local whites began spreading rumors that African Americans were organizing an "insurrection" to kill all the white people in Phillips County. By the next morning, the sheriff had gathered a posse to arrest members of the union, and as many as 1,000 armed whites were beginning to flood into the county, some from nearby locations in Arkansas but some also crossing the river from Mississippi. That same morning, county leaders telegraphed Governor Charles H. Brough to request that troops be sent to the area, and Brough quickly ordered 500 soldiers from Camp Pike into Phillips County; the governor even accompanied them to the area to oversee their actions. Although the troops were meant to keep the peace and to prevent the sort of violence being perpetrated by these armed white mobs, some newspaper and anecdotal reports indicate that the soldiers participated in the massacre now going on in southern Phillips County. Although the exact number of African Americans killed remains unknown, the Elaine Massacre destroyed countless black lives in Arkansas and, as part of the so-called Red Summer of 1919, was but one event in a national wave of violence undertaken to shore up white supremacy in the United States.

This book arises from a collaborative effort to commemorate the centennial of the massacre by the Butler Center for Arkansas Studies at the Central Arkansas Library System, the Arkansas State Archives, and the University of Arkansas at Little Rock's Center for Arkansas History and Culture. While many organizations and individuals are undertaking a variety of commemorative projects taking place on the ground in Phillips County, we seek to add to these efforts by placing the massacre within a broader context of Arkansas history. Prior to Grif Stockley's 2001 monograph *Blood in Their Eyes: The Elaine Race Massacres of 1919*, the event had not attracted much scholarly and popular attention, especially compared with the more urban race riots of the Red Summer of 1919. Since that time, the profile of the event has grown. For example, Robert Whitaker's 2008 book *On the Laps of Gods: The Red Summer of 1919 and the Struggle for Justice That Remade a Nation* reached a wider audience than had earlier studies of the massacre, while the Equal Justice Initiative's inclusion of an estimated death toll for the massacre in its 2015 report, *Lynching in America: Confronting the Legacy of Racial Terror*, led to national attention for Phillips County, which topped EJI's list of counties with the highest numbers of lynchings, totaling 245, or almost five times the number as the next county on this list.[3] In the midst of this increasing focus upon the Elaine Massacre, it is imperative that the event not be taken out of its proper context—that it be presented not as singular, not as unique, not as an atrocity *sui generis*, without equal in the legacy of white supremacy in the United States, but rather as representing a continuum of history. The resistance to exploitation that led the Progressive Farmers and Household Union of America to organize in the deepest, deadliest Arkansas Delta had roots in a long tradition of black collective organizing, as did violence, both official and vigilante, against black independence efforts, which was used with spectacular force in the decades leading up to the Elaine Massacre.

The Elaine Massacre and Arkansas therefore aims to provide this crucial context by looking at the event primarily through the lens of the century that preceded it. Kelly Houston Jones opens this book by taking us back to Arkansas's territorial and early statehood years to illustrate how slavery served as the foundational environment in which white suspicion of black activism and independence was institutionalized. Whites in Arkansas may have been relatively complacent regarding the stability of their regime, but news of challenges to white supremacy regularly appeared in state and local newspapers. Phillips County, in particular, hosted

---

[3] Equal Justice Initiative, *Lynching in America: Confronting the Legacy of Racial Terror*, 3rd edition, https://lynchinginamerica.eji.org/report/ (accessed January 9, 2018).

a significant slave economy, and white readers would have regularly encountered media reports of runaway slaves along the Mississippi River, tales of escaped slaves joining "lawless" groups in Indian Territory, periodic rumors of slave unrest, and confirmed reports of slave rebellions in other states. Although whites dismissed the possibility of black political consciousness, this media and cultural environment set the stage for the violent backlash to black independence during and after the Civil War.

Nancy Snell Griffith's chapter follows up the work of Jones by illustrating how the idea of "insurrection" shaped the white response to black collective mobilization in the years following the Civil War. The emancipation of African Americans, combined with their later campaigns for full citizenship, created a suspicion among whites that black people had intentions to mobilize violently against whites, perhaps even undertake a war of extermination, in revenge for the evils of slavery. The rhetoric of "insurrection" colored much of Reconstruction, but even long after Reconstruction, racial conflict was regularly attributed to blacks' desire to revolt against the established order or to engage in wholesale murder. Griffith examines how large-scale collective violence from 1883 to 1904 was justified by reference to fears of insurrection, even when the precipitant for the violence was nothing of the kind. Long before the Elaine Massacre, atrocities were predicated upon the necessity of putting down imagined insurrections.

What happened in Phillips County in 1919 has been described using a number of terms. As noted above, the Equal Justice Initiative ranks the dead as victims of lynching, while accounts from around the time of the event typically employed the phrase "race riot" to designate the nature of the phenomenon. Grif Stockley's use of the word "massacre," with its connotations of military action, has gained fairly wide acceptance, but some have even employed the term "genocide" to describe the event, thereby invoking the specter of the international "crime of crimes" and bringing down upon the head of Arkansas, and the nation entire, a significant measure of moral opprobrium. But what do these various terms actually mean? Does any particular designation more accurately represent the nature of the event than another? Guy Lancaster and Richard Buckelew attempt to answer this question by examining the current state of scholarship with regard to these categories. What they find is that there is no perfect label to describe what happened in Phillips County but, rather, that each one of these terms, as they are employed by scholars, helps to reveal certain qualities about the nature of large-scale racial violence as perpetrated in the United States.

The Elaine Massacre was not only representative of the level of violence white Arkansans and Americans were willing to employ to suppress black economic independence, but it was also representative of the long, indwelling tradition of both resistance and collective uplift in Arkansas. Matthew Hild looks at the history of labor activism, both black and white, within the Arkansas Delta in the latter half of the nineteenth century, starting with the work of former slave Bryant Singfield through movements such as the Grange, Agricultural Wheel, and Knights of Labor, highlighting the oft-overlooked efforts of sharecroppers and tenant farmers to achieve some measure of independence. These efforts came during an era, and in an area, of intense opposition to unionization, a time and place when the plantation elite was riding high and loath to part with any of its power and privilege. In Arkansas, at least, the twentieth century has long been viewed as the watershed for agricultural labor organizing, no doubt due to the outsized influence of the Southern Tenant Farmers' Union upon the scholarship, but Hild demonstrates that the spirit of collective struggle was present in the fields of the Arkansas Delta long before.

Complementing Hild's analysis is a chapter by Adrienne A. Jones, who focuses upon black fraternal organizations as sites of collective uplift and resistance to oppression. Jones takes the reader through such organizations as the Prince Hall Masons and the Mosaic Templars of America, groups that provided important services and opportunities for socialization for their constituencies and thus fostered a true sense of collective identity. Jones illustrates how such fraternal organizations prefigured, and perhaps even directly inspired, the Progressive Farmers and Household Union of America, which in many respects operated like a fraternal organization, with its own secret rituals and the like. Scholars have often overlooked the importance of ritual in such "secular" organizations, but as Stefan Arvidsson, a historian of religion, observed, the ritual and motifs of fraternal groups can help to advance political ideas and create community bonds, for "ideologies and religions not only spread, and convince, through their clear analyses, well-argued proofs, and sharp logic. No, they win as many adherents through an appeal to feelings, by waking up hope and giving a shape to anger."[4]

Following Jones's chapter, Steven Teske presents a brief biography of Scipio Jones, who not only represents a black middle class that was greatly invested in these fraternal and social organizations, but who also regularly fought to protect African Americans from mob violence, deploying every tool at his disposal. Jones also played an outsized role in the events following the Elaine Massacre through his legal defense of the twelve men who had been sentenced to death for allegedly engaging in insurrectionary activities. As the Elaine Massacre has gradually entered broader American historical consciousness, the figure of Scipio Jones has risen in stature accordingly.

As Cherisse Jones-Branch observes, the scholarship to date on the Elaine Massacre focuses largely upon the actions of men; women's roles, on both sides of the violence, have largely been overlooked. Jones-Branch offers a corrective to this view, reveal-

---

[4] Stefan Arvidsson, *Morgonrodnad. Socialismens stil och mytologi 1871–1914* (Lund: Nordic Academic Press, 2016), 13 (translation from the Swedish by Guy Lancaster).

ing, for example, how black Arkansas women participated in the broader national work for civil rights and economic independence through a variety of women's organizations, as well as how black women were among the founding members of the Progressive Farmers and Household Union of America. Indeed, several were there at the union meeting on the night of September 30, 1919, when a firefight precipitated the violent series of events now known as the Elaine Massacre, and one of the most important figures following the violence was noted anti-lynching activist Ida B. Wells-Barnett. Jones-Branch follows the work of these women before, during, and after the massacre, revealing a part of the story that has for too long been overshadowed by an outdated focus upon men.

Some of the enduring mysteries surrounding the Elaine Massacre relate to how, exactly, the violence unfolded; which people were members of the Progressive Farmers and Household Union; and what was the ultimate death toll. Brian K. Mitchell works to map out future lines of inquiry in his chapter through the consideration of three primary sources that have come to light: letters to and from Governor Henry Allen of Kansas, who refused to extradite union founder Robert L. Hill; the minutes of the inaugural convention of the Arkansas Department of the American Legion, some of whose members participated in the violence; and the Phillips County Indictment Book, which reveals the names of those who were indicted for crimes relating to the massacre. These sources open up intriguing new avenues of research for future scholarship on the details of the actual violence as well as the broader state of affairs in Phillips County at the time.

Finally, William H. Pruden III looks beyond the time frame of 1919 with the U.S. Supreme Court case of *Moore v. Dempsey*, which arose from legal proceedings challenging the outcome of trials following the Elaine Massacre—trials that resulted in the death penalty for black defendants accused of committing violence. This case was the first in a series that expanded the mean-

16

ing of due process over the twentieth century. As Pruden reveals, the case set a precedent for increased federal authority, giving defendants access to federal courts on the basis of a denial of constitutional rights by lower court rulings. Thus did *Moore v. Dempsey* lay some of the legal groundwork for the civil rights movement of the twentieth century, inspiring organizations like the National Association for the Advancement of Colored People (NAACP) to pursue a litigation-based approach for securing the rights of African Americans. The Red Summer of 1919 may have visited ghastly violence upon African Americans across the United States, but the legal work of dedicated people in Arkansas and the nation at large following that outbreak of atrocity made a significant crack in the wall of oppression.

Chapter 1

White Fear of Black Rebellion in Antebellum Arkansas, 1819–1865

Kelly Houston Jones

Whites feared and resisted blacks' collective attempts to defy exploitation long before the terrorism at Elaine in 1919. The control of black labor enriched generations of white Arkansans, an advantage that landowners remained eager to protect. And while American slavery began as an economic institution, over time it increasingly took on the added function of race control by creating a caste of black men and women. Thus, when bondspeople resisted the labor demands of slavery or worked together to undercut the system, they also challenged white supremacy itself. Despite the fact that slaveholders took measures to guard against slaves' rebellion, whites as a whole remained somewhat complacent, and thus the resistance of slaves during the Civil War caught many by surprise. No slave rebellions have been documented in Arkansas, but the specter of rebellion haunted the South, and newspaper stories of rebellions in other states, both verified and unverified, received wide coverage. This chapter, therefore, considers accounts of black resistance that whites would have learned of in the news during the territorial period through the Civil War, paying special attention to the stories whites consumed regarding violent and/or collective rebellion. Although the antebellum runs of many newspapers have not been preserved in their entirety, newspaper records nonetheless provide some insight into the information that white communities in the young slave state of Arkansas received regarding their safety and security against black resistance. Readers of the papers may not have shared the editors' sensationalized view of events, but we can use their coverage to get a feel for the level of urgency whites felt when it came to the security of white supremacy in Arkansas. The coverage reveals the ebb and flow of white apprehensions regarding where Arkansas was situated, how it was connected to larger national political conversations (exhibited in a growing militant abolitionism), and, eventually, white anxieties associated with the outbreak of the Civil War.

One hundred years before whites massacred African Americans at Elaine in reaction to attempted labor activism, the potential to exploit black labor influenced the political debate over the creation of Arkansas Territory. The Old Southwest, as the region was known then, had been growing quickly, and the "second slavery"—chattel slavery devoted to producing commodities in huge quantities, quickly developing the economies of areas that before had been peripheral—was on its way to Arkansas (then part of the greater Missouri Territory). Although subsistence farming would remain the norm for Arkansans for several years (only about 1,600 enslaved people resided in the territory by 1820), Arkansas's potential as a cotton empire shone brightly enough that, as Missouri worked toward breaking off for statehood, Arkansas also petitioned to organize as a slave territory. Protecting slavery in the territory opened the floodgates for whites to pour into Arkansas (with their enslaved workers) to carve out the freshest parts of cotton kingdom, a process already underway in Mississippi, parts of Missouri, and western Alabama. By 1830, enslaved people made up fifteen percent of Arkansas Territory's total population of about 30,000. Although the *Arkansas Gazette* probably overstated the situation when it heralded cotton as the staple of the territory in 1825—celebrating hundreds of bales from several counties being shipped to New Orleans or sold for cash at Arkansas Post—the cash crop was beginning to take hold. As it did, whites in Arkansas would become increasingly committed to controlling valuable black labor with violence.[1]

By the time Arkansas became a state (specifically, a slave state) in 1836, some stories warning of black uprisings had reached Arkansas, and, more importantly, white southerners had had time to react to the United States' most well-known slave rebellion. In spring 1830, Arkansans got word that an "insurrection"—implying the involvement of slaves—had taken place in Louisiana, forty miles north of New Orleans, in which twelve whites were killed and U.S. troops were employed to put down the rebellion. Newspaper editors admitted that the details were murky, adding, "We did not learn what number of negroes had raised."[2] But one of the slave South's most important turning points occurred in August 1831, when a man named Nat Turner organized an uprising of fellow slaves in Southampton County, Virginia. He gathered a party eventually numbering more than fifty fighters on horseback, killing white families from household to household, beginning with Turner's own oppressors. Leaving nearly sixty whites dead, Turner's revolt horrified white southerners, who were especially dismayed by the fact that most of the whites killed were women and children. Turner's effectiveness as a leader, and the ability of the rebels to coordinate quickly, prompted Southern leaders to enact state laws and local ordinances meant to hedge the abilities of enslaved people to organize future rebellions, such as restricting group activity (religious gatherings, among others) and criminalizing slaves' literacy. Men and women held in slavery learned lessons from Nat Turner's revolt, too. While black southerners

[1] Anthony E. Kaye, "The Second Slavery: Modernity in the Nineteenth-Century South and the Atlantic World," *Journal of Southern History* 75 (August 2009): 627, 632; Donald P. McNeilly, *The Old South Frontier: Cotton Plantations and the Formation of Arkansas Society, 1819–1861* (Fayetteville: University of Arkansas Press, 2000), 13–15, 33; S. Charles Bolton, *Arkansas, 1800–1860: Remote and Restless* (Fayetteville: University of Arkansas Press, 1998), 25; U.S. Bureau of the Census, Fourth Census of the United States, 1820, Schedule of Free Population, Schedule of Slave Population, Fifth Census of the United States, 1830, Schedule of Free Population, Slave Population.
[2] *Arkansas Times and Advocate*, May 12, 1830.

kept up their communication networks and clandestine subversive Christianity, a hard lesson from the aftermath of Nat Turner's rebellion was that the cost of attempted collective resistance was high. Many slaves who had nothing to do with Nat Turner were murdered by hysterical white Virginians who sought to stamp out the conspiracy in is aftermath. White backlash was deadly, and slaves' cooperation against slave conspirators could have its rewards.[3]

Shortly before Arkansas's statehood, a suspected slave conspiracy was brutally extinguished by an angry mob closer to home. In Madison County, Mississippi, in June and July 1835, an incident historian Walter Johnson calls "The Panic of 1835" erupted about 150 miles from Phillips County, Arkansas. Whites near Beattie's Bluff and Livingston, Mississippi, acted on rumors that slaves there had been planning a revolt, violently coercing confessions of conspiracy that probably revealed more about whites' fears than blacks' secrets. The "committee of safety" lynched those they deemed guilty—sixteen enslaved people and seven white men (one of whom was a slaveholder)—after holding abbreviated "trials." The hysteria created a witch hunt for whites who did not conform to the ever-constricting racial code of the cotton kingdom. Finally, a hint by one of the men, before his execution, that the supposed conspirators might have had a connection with the notorious outlaw John Murrell "sent a tremor of fear up and down the Mississippi Valley."[4]

---

[3] David Brion Davis, *Inhuman Bondage: The Rise and Fall of Slavery in the New World* (New York: Oxford University Press, 2006), 208–209; Steven Hahn, *A Nation under Our Feet: Black Political Struggles in the Rural South from Slavery to the Great Migration* (Cambridge, MA: Belknap, 2003), 41–51. For slave resistance in Arkansas generally, see Kelly Houston Jones, "'A Rough, Saucy Set of Hands to Manage': Slave Resistance in Arkansas," *Arkansas Historical Quarterly* 71 (Spring 2012): 1–21.

[4] Walter Johnson, *River of Dark Dreams: Slavery and Empire in the Cotton Kingdom* (Cambridge, MA: Belknap, 2013), 46–57. For a detailed account of the conspiracy and executions, see Joshua D. Rothman, *Flush Times and Fever Dreams: A Story of Capitalism and Slavery in the Age of Jackson* (Athens: University of Georgia Press, 2012), 91–153.

Murrell's name made headlines all over the Old Southwest for "slave-stealing," which he was convicted of in a trial in western Tennessee in 1834. As Johnson put it, "If there was a white man who embodied the uncertainties and fears that lurked behind the bright-white tide of cotton and profit that flowed down the Mississippi River in the boom years of the 1830s, his name was John Murrell." Murrell, a vagabond and "negro stealer," was a common subject in the newspapers of Arkansas and beyond. He was said to have stolen horses and spirited away enslaved people, crimes horrific enough to frontier whites, but the added legend that he attempted to organize a large-scale slave revolt (according to the booklet Virgil Stewart wrote about him) solidified Murrell's place as a true boogeyman of the Mississippi Valley. Readers found it especially easy to believe that bandits like Murrell roamed Arkansas's side of the river; from the earliest days of white settlement there, Arkansas suffered from a reputation for lawlessness, which newspapermen attempted to counteract by praising the industry and civilization of the young region. Referred to as the "morass," swampy eastern Arkansas, specifically the area across the river from Memphis, held a reputation in the 1830s and 1840s for lawlessness. Runaway slaves found that the morass could provide decent cover, at least temporarily, and the river could carry them quickly away.[5] While the Mississippi River created wealth for white Arkansans and represented cotton kingdom's most important commercial riverine interstate highway, its environs also harbored whites' fears—resistant African Americans.

While Murrell represents the fear whites associated with the untamed swamps of the Mississippi River, their anxieties about Indian Territory denoted the instability they associated with what they saw as their wild western border. In August 13, 1841, the

[5] Rothman, *Flush Times and Fever Dreams*, 34; Johnson, *River of Dark Dreams*, 57, 144–150; Larry D. Ball, "John A. Murrell," *Encyclopedia of Arkansas History & Culture*, http://www.encyclopediaofarkansas.net/encyclopedia/entry-detail.aspx?entryID=3566 (accessed January 16, 2018).

Southern Shield of Helena reprinted an account from the *St. Louis Argus*, with the caveat that it was probably exaggerated but may have some grains of truth. The story declared that a band of 600 "Indians, negroes, and mongrels" lurked west of Arkansas, camping and hunting buffalo. According to the article, this group would have included runaway slaves from Florida, those who had absconded from area whites, and some slaves who had escaped from native groups like the Choctaw and Cherokee, along with some Indians. They built a fort, from which they raided the Choctaw and took cattle, chickens, and grain. The Choctaw could not hope to overtake them, according to the account, and appealed for help from Fort Gibson. The report claimed that three companies went out to the site, reviewed the outlaws' fortifications, and gathered reinforcements and cannon from Fort Towson. The force scattered the fugitives, capturing some of them. The paper declared, "This decisive blow will give security to that exposed portion of our frontier and convince the refugee negroes and Indians that our dragoons may not be trifled with." The *Shield* editors doubted the details of the story but accepted and transmitted the general theme of the report—that Arkansans existed under the real threat of Native Americans and African Americans uniting forces.[6]

Readers of Arkansas newspapers often consumed stories that perpetuated the wild and lawless reputation of western Arkansas, Indian Territory, and points west (like Texas), including accounts of individual Native Americans murdering whites, scuffles between whites and Native Americans, or murderous thieving multiracial bands wreaking havoc. Groups of free blacks posed special threats, according to these reports. In August 1850, for instance, whites in Phillips County read in the *Shield* about a "negro town" in Indian Territory made up of runaway slaves from Arkansas, Louisiana, and the Creek tribe. The article declared, "It

[6] *Southern Shield*, August 13, 1841.

should be broken up...the troops at Fort Smith, instead of being removed, ought to be increased" to protect the security of white man's country in Arkansas. The account claimed that 100 of the blacks had been arrested but did not provide details.[7]

Similarly, the movement of black Seminole with runaway slaves from Arkansas and Texas in the 1850s put white Arkansans ill at ease. Wild Cat, a major leader in the later years of the Second Seminole War, led a multiracial band of Seminole out of Indian Territory and through Texas into Mexico. Reports claimed that Wild Cat's group numbered as many as 1,800 and included a large cohort of runaway slaves from Arkansas. Possibly exaggerating, the newspapers reported, "The greater part of these runaways have escaped from Arkansas; but at least 500 are, it is said, fugitives from Texas." In Mexico, Wild Cat was said to have used "negro warriors" to raid the Comanche. The black maroons in Wild Cat's forces, historian William Kerrigan explained, "possessed too much real power to be considered subservient or dependent" on their Indian comrades. The nonwhite coalition to the Southwest continued to fascinate and disconcert white Arkansans into the 1850s.[8] In the minds of many, Arkansas was pinned between a river valley rife with fugitive slaves and slave "stealers" to the east, and a western border where runaway slaves and Native Americans banded together to stage threats to law and order.

Black people to their west with power and weapons made Arkansas whites uneasy, but blacks with power and resources at home presented a more immediate problem for those seeking to protect white supremacy. Whites in Arkansas, as in the rest of the South, remained uneasy with the presence of free blacks in their

---

[7] *Southern Shield*, July 23, 1842, June 18, 1841, August 13, 1853, August 17, 1850.

[8] Kenneth W. Porter, *The Black Seminoles: History of a Freedom-seeking People* (Gainesville: University Press of Florida, 1996), 36, 102; *Southern Shield*, September 27, 1851; William T. Kerrigan, "Race, Expansion, and Slavery in Eagle Pass, Texas, 1852," *Southwestern Historical Quarterly* 101 (Jan. 1998): 283, 292.

neighborhoods, especially if those black families thrived. Prosperity among free families of color worked against "the white man's most exalted racial beliefs," as historian Ira Berlin put it. The existence of free families of color contradicted the premise on which slavery had long been based—that blacks were not capable of taking care of themselves and needed white instruction. By succeeding, they implied a resistance to white dominance, and their presence exhibited an alternative reality to enslaved people. In fact, in 1836 in Chicot County, Arkansas, an apparently free black man named Bunch even attempted to vote. When the election judges turned him away, he reportedly "took umbrage," and a fracas ensued, during which he stabbed Dr. Albert W. Webb multiple times. In response, local citizens swiftly lynched Bunch.[9] As time passed, whites in Arkansas and other parts of the South increasingly sought to expel free blacks or enslave them.[10]

Whites' worries in the 1840s sometimes revealed this particular distrust of free blacks and their influence on enslaved populations. In July 1841, more than 20,000 people gathered in St. Louis to witness the executions of one enslaved man and three free black men who had reportedly robbed a "counting house," killing two men who worked there and setting fire to the building, a story that surely horrified whites downriver in Arkansas.[11] The next month, the *Shield* of Helena, Arkansas, ran a report by the *Memphis Appeal* recounting the murder of a white policeman at the hands of an enslaved man in New Orleans. The story decried the frequency of attacks on whites at the hands of slaves and free blacks, blaming the prevalence of free blacks in New Orleans, as well as the "familiarity" with which whites and "creoles" treated

[9] Nancy Snell Griffith, "Chicot County Lynching of 1836," *Encyclopedia of Arkansas History & Culture*, http://www.encyclopediaofarkansas.net/encyclopedia/entry-detail.aspx?entryID=12544 (accessed January 12, 2018).
[10] Ira Berlin, *Slaves without Masters: The Free Negro in the Antebellum South* (New York: Pantheon, 1974), 321, 343 (quotation), 344.
[11] Thomas C. Buchanan, "Rascals on the Antebellum Mississippi: African American Steamboat Workers and the St. Louis Hanging of 1841," *Journal of Social History* 34 (Summer 2001): 797.

African Americans.[12] They recommended that the laws concerning free blacks be enforced more strictly.

It may be that whites' heightened worry of free blacks or their cooperation with enslaved people was exacerbated by the scares brought on by the election of 1840. In June 1840, readers of the *Shield* learned of a "riot" in New Orleans related to the presidential contest. The report claimed that abolitionists, energized by supporters of candidate William Henry Harrison, had stirred up the slave population. Whites were often quick to blame unidentified Southern white abolitionists or other agitators when they did not understand or could not accept the idea of black resistance, often claiming that black slaves could not organize themselves without outside, white help. There is evidence to suggest, however, that slaves in parts of the South did in fact interpret Harrison's campaign as anti-slavery and believed that his election might foretell the end of the institution. Historian Steven Hahn has shown that slaves across the rural South used widespread rumor networks to craft their own political understandings of current events, which may have occurred in summer 1840.[13]

Whites in Phillips County began officially watching free blacks more closely in the early 1840s. In spring 1841, the city of Helena, a small but quickly growing town (with 614 inhabitants by 1850), saw fit to review its slave patrol ordinance, which provided for compensation for those working the patrol and imposed a fine on those who refused to serve on the patrol when appointed. But the ordinance left the issue of compensation fairly loose, and when it came to the frequency of patrols, the ordinance simply decreed that the detachment was to be called up when needed. "Whenever it is deemed necessary," the council was to commission a captain of the patrol, who would then select up to five people to serve. The ordinance directed that the "Council may direct from time to time,

---

[12] *Southern Shield*, August 13, 1841.
[13] *Arkansas State Democrat and Helena Commercial Advertiser*, June 12, 1840; Hahn, *A Nation under Our Feet*, 59.

and shall visit all parts of the town, and all negro quarters and other places SUSPECTED of unlawful assemblage of slaves." The
wording of the updated slave patrol ordinance overall indicates a
heightened sense of awareness of the need to keep a close eye on
the slave population, but it does not suggest alarm. Patrols in Helena, at least officially, were not planned regularly, but were ready
to be activated in the event that whites became nervous about their
security.[14] The following spring, the town passed a new ordinance
regarding free people of color. "Free negroes or mulattoes" were
ordered to provide the alderman with proof of their free status and
pay the town's clerk fifty cents for the privilege.[15]

Readers of the *Shield* received an abundance of grisly stories in
July 1842, like the report of an enslaved man in Fayette County,
Tennessee, who killed an overseer with a hoe. In Gibson County,
located in northwestern Tennessee, it was reported that three runaway slaves broke into the house of a widow with the last name
Kelly and raped her before hitting her in the head with a hatchet.
She survived and dragged herself to the neighbors' house. The
following alarm sent "hundreds" of area whites into a frenzy to
capture the three men. A posse shot one of the men, but he escaped. The *Shield*'s copied report included the prayer, "May just
and revenging Heaven aid them in their search." By the time the
Shield got the story, one of the men had been captured and gave
the name of his accomplice as John, a man who had fled the Smith
farm near Covington, Tipton County. If this was not enough to
raise the eyebrows of the *Shield*'s white readers, they could scan
down the same issue's page for a story from the Natchez *Courier* called "Atrocious Murders & Outrages" in which an enslaved
man named Joseph from Louisiana had joined Enoch, a runaway
from New Orleans, who murdered a man named Mr. Harrington.

---

[14] *Southern Shield*, July 9, 1841; Steven Teske, "Helena-West Helena,"
Encyclopedia of Arkansas History & Culture, http://www.encyclopediaofar-
kansas.net/encyclopedia/entry-detail.aspx?entryID=950 (accessed January
16, 2018).
[15] *Southern Shield*, April 9, 1842.

The men took his daughter, a young woman, into the woods; the account insinuates that the men raped her. A young woman described as a "mulattress" named Margaret was with them, and, according to the account, she convinced them to spare the lives of the white women present. Joseph and Enoch were also said to have killed another man, Mr. Todd, and "carried off" his wife and child. By the time the story ran in the *Shield*, Joseph and Margaret had been captured, and although Enoch had escaped, he was wounded, and whites may have hoped to catch up with him. A group of white men brutally lynched Joseph after he confessed to the crimes. They chained him to a tree and started a fire around him. Joseph screamed as the fire grew and managed to break the chains holding him, so the men shot him and threw his body into the fire.[16] Accounts of black men (and women) running away from slavery and attacking whites made for dramatic reading, to be sure, but may have also reminded whites in Phillips County that white supremacy ultimately had to be protected with violence.

The tension between enslaved and enslavers continued as cotton cultivation expanded in Arkansas and Phillips County. By the time of the 1850 census, 2,291 enslaved people resided in Phillips County, out of a total population of nearly 7,000, meaning that one-third of the county's population was held in chattel slavery. This proportion would only grow over time as the cotton boom of the 1850s increased the profits whites could enjoy from the exploitation of black labor in Phillips County. By 1860—the last census before the Civil War—8,941 black Arkansans labored there, more than in any other county in Arkansas. By that time, the enslaved population represented sixty percent of the overall population (14,877) of the county. This staggering growth provides a measure of the explosion of the importance of slave-grown cotton agriculture in the area and its human cost. The county's class of

---

[16] *Southern Shield*, July 2, July 25, 1842.

large slaveholders included George W. Johnson of Spring Creek township, John A. Craig and Gideon Pillow of St. Francis, John T. Jones of Planters, and Thomas Gist and Jeptha Bowdoin of Richland. The majority of enslaved people in the county lived on plantations, and these expanded as black men and women were forced to clear new acreage. Within a decade, slaves of John T. Jones grew in number from twenty-two to sixty-two and improved 2,150 acres in a decade. Their toil produced an abundance of cotton, then the United States' most valuable export. Trade in cotton amounted to the largest chunk of the world's economy in the first half of the nineteenth century.[17]

Some idea of the experiences of those enslaved laborers in Phillips County can be found in Works Progress Administration (WPA) interviews of the 1930s, although most of the information relates to the post–Civil War period. Nearly 100 people were held by John T. Jones, who had brought slaves with him to Arkansas from Virginia, including Shepherd Rhone's parents, Katie and Daniel Rhone, who were born in Richmond and Petersburg, respectively. James Gill remembered being sent out to Phillips County with his parents and other enslaved people by Tom White, an Alabama planter who looked to profit off the fresh fertile ground in Arkansas, as his acreage in Alabama was "near wore out," according to Gill. The group traveled to Arkansas via Memphis by train and steamboat, shepherded by James (Jim) Lynch, an overseer who would continue to manage the place. Gill and his family worked White's farm about fifteen miles downriver from Helena, a place Gill described as "thick with canebrakes." White

---

[17] U.S. Bureau of the Census, Seventh Census of the United States, 1850, Schedule of Free Population, Schedule of Slave Population, Eighth Census of the United States, 1860, Schedule of Free Population, Schedule of Slave Population; Johnson, *River of Dark Dreams*, 10; McNeilly, *Old South Frontier*, 49. For tables on slave populations in Arkansas's counties, see Carl H. Moneyhon, "Slavery," *Encyclopedia of Arkansas History & Culture,* http://www.encyclopediaofarkansas.net/encyclopedia/entry-detail.aspx?entry-ID=1275 (accessed January 16, 2018) and McNeilly, *Old South Frontier*, 132–136.

came out to look over the place a few times per year. Slaves on the White place shared news and family with those on the Casteel plantation.[18]

Memories of slavery in Phillips County recorded by the WPA offer a kaleidoscope of experiences: privation, separation, connection, faith, family, travel—and, always, *work*. Building, clearing, cleaning, cooking, sewing, chopping, picking—work. If work remains a ubiquitous theme in formerly enslaved people's accounts, whites' attempts to control that labor is almost as abundant a motif. Black men and women remembered both organized and spontaneous efforts to keep black bodies on the farms and plantations where their labor was desired, and recalled brutal whippings to keep those bodies at profitable tasks.[19]

Thus, when enslaved people deprived white slaveholders of their value and labor—in Phillips County and beyond—they hit whites right in the wallet and threatened the security of the system overall. The Mississippi River was rife with people who fled from farms and plantations all over the Mississippi Valley. People who escaped from enslavement contradicted the whole purpose of slavery and threatened white supremacy. Recapturing them was risky for whites, as they might meet violent resistance from the absconded.[20] The abundance of runaways on the loose described in newspapers' many runaway slave advertisements probably seemed routine to white readers. Stories of runaways killing whites, like those described above, however, must have made readers significantly more nervous. We can only imagine how whites consuming news would have taken the reports of

[18] George Lankford, *Bearing Witness: Memories of Arkansas Slavery, Narratives from the 1930s WPA Narratives* 2nd ed. (Fayetteville: University of Arkansas Press, 2006), 287, 271, 273.
[19] Lankford, *Bearing Witness*, 260–261, 265, 279, 285, 289, 291, 298.
[20] S. Charles Bolton, *Fugitives from Injustice: Freedom-Seeking Slaves in Arkansas, 1800–1860* (Omaha, NE: National Park Service, 2006); Kelly Houston Jones, "Chattels, Pioneers, and Pilgrims for Freedom: Arkansas's Bonded Travelers," *Arkansas Historical Quarterly* 75 (Winter 2016): 329–330; Johnson, *River of Dark Dreams*, 126–150.

runaways breaking out of the Mississippi Valley's jailhouses, as when a man named Olmstead, about twenty-five years old, broke out of the jail in St. Francis County with two white men (Hugh C. Casteel and Harlin Robinson) in August 1849. Readers of the *Shield* probably began to further question the reliability of St. Francis County's jailhouse in July 1853 when three runaways who had been captured and held in St. Francis County sawed through a bolt on the iron door hinge and broke free.[21]

The specter of violence clung to slaves' truancy and long-distance flight because attempts to retake black men and women always held the potential for a fight. Yet individual acts of violent resistance by slaves that *did not* involve a showdown with posses or patrols may have alarmed whites significantly more, even when the events did not seem to indicate a larger conspiracy. In Phillips County, the decade of the 1850s began with the murder of one enslaver and a retaliatory lynching. Two men had fled Henry Yerby's plantation about two months before his dead body was found hidden under a pile of logs near his house. Whether a coincidence or because their slaying of Yerby emboldened them, the two men emerged from the woods just as whites were burying the dead man properly. The men were immediately suspected of the murder, although they claimed their innocence. After questioning them and two other enslaved men on the Yerby place, whites became satisfied that the two returned fugitives had killed Yerby, and they hanged them in retaliation.[22]

As the 1850s wore on and the boom in cotton picked up its dizzying pace, whites in Phillips County could count on stories of slave "outrages" from near and far to feature in the pages of their local papers, like that of the four men who killed their enslaver, Thomas M. Bingiman, near Grenada, Mississippi (southeast of

---

[21] *Southern Shield*, January 5, 1850, July 9, 1853.

[22] Kelly Houston Jones, "'Doubtless Guilty': Lynching and Slaves in Antebellum Arkansas," in *Bullets and Fire: Lynching and Authority in Arkansas, 1840–1950*, edited by Guy Lancaster (Fayetteville: University of Arkansas Press, 2018), 20.

Helena). Two were jailed, and two were lynched by a mob.[23] In spring 1850, an enslaved man in DeSoto Parish, Louisiana, south of Shreveport, when faced with a whipping, stabbed an overseer thirty-six times before slitting his own throat.[24] Papers reported on the rape of a white woman by a black man in Savannah, Georgia, in May 1852.[25] In summer 1853, Arkansans became aware of a supposed slave insurrection plot in New Orleans, although the *Washington Telegraph* assured readers that the rumors did not indicate a true threat.[26] In April 1852, readers of the *Shield* must have cringed to read about a "favorite servant" named Lewis killing James Burroughs of Louisiana by hitting him in the head with an axe.[27] Overseers may have experienced some jitters after learning of Andy, who killed an overseer east of Memphis a few months later.[28] Arkansas's "mistresses" could have been especially horrified to read of young black woman's retaliation in North Carolina. The woman, "in the employ of" the family of Virginia Frost, grabbed a gun and shot Frost dead after being "reproved for insolence."[29] Editors persisted in sharing such accounts despite the fact that, in October 1854, the editor of the *Shield* declared, "We are not in the habit of noticing the fights, and outrages, which too frequently occupy the local columns of city newspapers." In the same week, the *Arkansas State Gazette and Democrat* also declared that it was unwilling to print grisly murders and such "for the reason that we believe it has a demoralising [*sic*] influence."[30]

The fall of 1856 proved especially worrisome for slaveholders across the South. Readers of the October 25, 1856, issue of the

---

[23] *Southern Shield*, March 13, 1852.
[24] *Southern Shield*, May 11, 1850.
[25] *Southern Shield*, May 22, 1852.
[26] *Washington Telegraph* (Arkansas), July 6, 1853.
[27] *Southern Shield*, April 3, 1852.
[28] *Southern Shield*, July 30, 1853.
[29] *Southern Shield*, October 20, 1855.
[30] *Southern Shield*, October 20, 1854; *Arkansas State Gazette and Democrat*, October 27, 1854.

Shield learned of threats both far away and closer to home. In Alabama, nine black men who had been hiding in a swamp were said to have ambushed a wagon of white men. The white men survived and escaped from their attackers, but one lost three fingers trying to protect himself from being stabbed. Whites would also have read that in Union County, Arkansas, a rebellion plot by enslaved people had been discovered. The plan was to have been implemented on the day of the presidential election, because white men would have been away from their homes on that day. Some enslaved people were "taken up and made to confess," and they implicated accomplices up to twenty miles away. Among the co-conspirators were said to have been white men who were run out of town. The story also claimed that the plot reached all the way to Texas and, had it not been extinguished, would have been "one of the most bloody massacres in the whole annals of insurrections." Whites who believed the account may have sighed in relief that the plot had been foiled.[31]

But rumors of insurrections continued to surface, and the tension lingered through December. In November, Phillips County whites became alarmed by some unspecified menace by slaves. Just a few days before Christmas, the *Shield* reported a vague threat of a slave plot in Assumption Parish, Louisiana, that was interrupted but would have been "disastrous." And in Gallatin, Tennessee, four bondspeople implicated in a plot there had been hanged.[32] It is impossible to know for sure how much truth there was to these supposed plots, but it is clear that whites in late 1856 were spooked. The December issue of the *Shield* addressed the surge of rumored "servile insurrections," explaining that in some instances it seemed that something truly had been afoot, and that fortunately whites worked against "the fiendish plans concocted by the misguided and ignorant blacks." For example, the Iron

---

[31] *Southern Shield*, October 25, 1856.
[32] *Southern Shield*, December 20, 1856; *Washington Telegraph*, January 7, 1857

Works uprising of Tennessee and Kentucky could have "assumed a very serious aspect" if it had not been extinguished. The editor believed that errant, abolitionist whites were behind enslaved people's thoughts of rebellion, and explained that whites who encouraged uprisings only made life more difficult for enslaved people, who would be happy with their lot otherwise: "The Southern blacks, when properly treated, are doubtless the happiest and best contented serfs or vassals upon earth, and any attempt to improve their condition by force of arms can only result detrimental to them." This point of view is representative of what slaveholders generally believed about their work force. However complacent Phillips County whites may have been, the *Shield* did recommend a bit more vigilance:

> Whether or not there was really anything contemplated by the negroes of this county [Phillips], as was reported about the first of November, we are unable to say; yet it would not be amiss for slaveholders, and other citizens, during the approaching holydays, to carefully notice their movements. When negroes are permitted to come into town, they should in every instance be provided with a pass, stating the time allowed to stay, and during the week the County Court and town authorities should keep up a patrol, composed of prudent men. These precautions may to some seem unnecessary, but no harm is likely to result from their observance, whilst they might be of great benefit.

The editor's warning is significant. The recommendation of a regular slave patrol in Helena suggests that there had not been a consistent patrol in town lately.[33]

Some white Arkansans responded to their fears of slave rebellion toward the end of 1856 by trying to eliminate those whom they perceived as a major part of the threat—free blacks. The *Gazette and Democrat* railed against the failure of the "free negro

---

[33] *Southern Shield*, December 20, 1856.

bill" that would have required free black men and women to leave the state or face enslavement. The measure would make Arkansas safer by reducing the threat of slave rebellions, the paper argued, explaining that black families living free were sure to "demoralize" enslaved people and "incite" them to rebel.[34]

What whites looking to prevent slave unrest failed to understand, however, was blacks' own understandings of the terrain of struggle. The timing of the fall 1856 disturbances was not random or designed by free blacks. That year, the Republican Party—a new political party with free-labor ideology at its core and the prevention of slavery's spread as a priority—fielded its first presidential candidate, John C. Fremont. Enslaved people across the South understood the Republicans as a threat to the institution of slavery, and many grew restless believing that if Fremont were victorious, their liberation would follow. After his defeat, hope remained for those who were sure the Republicans would prevail in the next presidential contest and initiate their freedom.[35]

The year 1859 was tense locally and across the country. In the years just before the Civil War, apprehensions related to slavery embroiled the nation and put Southern whites on the defensive. Whites in Arkansas viewed slaves and abolitionists with more suspicion than ever before. In late summer 1859, an enslaved man named Calvin in Richmond Township, Phillips County, killed J. W. Carpenter's overseer, named Robert Bickers, by striking his head with an axe. Calvin hid in a barn loft until hunger forced him to venture out. According to the story, other slaves spotted him, leading to his capture. An angry white mob claimed that Calvin often suffered from an "alienation of mind," which might lead to his acquittal in a legal trial, and so determined to take matters into their own hands. They allowed him to talk to a couple of ministers, and then hanged him on August 17 near the place where he had slain Bickers. His body was left to hang for a day, as a

[34] *Arkansas State Gazette and Democrat*, December 27, 1856.
[35] Hahn, *A Nation under Our Feet*, 59–60.

message to other enslaved people who might contemplate violent resistance. That same year, Arkansas successfully passed a law to remove free families of color, although not all free blacks had evacuated the state by 1860.[36]

Later in 1859, slaveholders all over the South learned in horror that militant abolitionist John Brown had launched a failed attempt to stir up a slave rebellion by raiding the federal arsenal in Harper's Ferry, Virginia (now West Virginia), on October 16. After two days, the effort was stamped out by federal troops. The *Arkansas State Gazette*'s reporting of the crisis expressed pleasure that Brown failed to rally enslaved people to his side. To white southerners, the incident provided evidence of Northern designs against slavery. The editor painted a vivid picture of destructive extremist northerners seeking a violent slave uprising. In 1859, then, whites in Arkansas seemed to be more fearful of Northern abolitionists, free blacks, and the Republican Party than of the people they held in bondage in their own communities.[37]

The "Texas Troubles" during summer and fall 1860 seemed to confirm Southern whites' fears, causing the biggest slave revolt panic in the South since Nat Turner's revolt. Mysterious spontaneous fires broke out across northern Texas, one of which partially destroyed Dallas, creating paranoia that spurred vigilante groups to lynch at least thirty black and white Texans in a frenzy to stamp out what they were certain was an abolitionist plot.

The terror spread to whites in Arkansas. Arkansans became suspicious of whites passing through from northern Texas, afraid they might have been involved in the troubles there. Camden vigilantes gathered a posse to capture Henry A. Marsh, a white man

---

[36] *Daily Courier and Union* (Syracuse, NY), September 5, 1859; Orville W. Taylor, *Negro Slavery in Arkansas*, reprint edition (Fayetteville: University of Arkansas, 2000), 108; Billy D. Higgins, "Act 151 of 1859," *Encyclopedia of Arkansas History & Culture*, http://www.encyclopediaofarkansas.net/encyclopedia/entry-detail.aspx?entryID=4430 (accessed January 12, 2018).
[37] Davis, *Inhuman Bondage*, 291–292; *Arkansas State Gazette*, November 12, 1859.

who was accused of having abolitionist newspapers sent to Camden and of having connections to the Texas conspiracy. They pursued him to Memphis and brought him back to Camden. He was jailed for a few days, along with another white man, A. W. Keen. Authorities eventually let the men go and ordered them to leave the state, along with two men of the theater and "some Dutch Pedlar."

Still, white Arkansans' most immediate fear seems to have been of white abolitionists, not the slave population. White Arkansans' perception of Abraham Lincoln's election in fall 1860 has to be understood in the context of the Texas Troubles. While enslaved people who had been able to get information about the presidential election hoped that Lincoln was the abolitionist that whites' feared he was, white slaveholders were convinced that the rise of the Republican Party meant that the federal government sanctioned what they saw as the abolitionist conspiracy. Thus, the demise of slavery was imminent unless they took action.[38] As recorded in the WPA slave narratives, Adrianna Kerns explained that her mother viewed Lincoln as a savior—in a story that recalls ancient legends of kings who circulate among their people in disguise, Lincoln reportedly "went through the South as a beggar and found out everything. When he got back, he told the North how slavery was ruining the nation."[39]

Ironically, when their states seceded, Southern whites ushered in exactly what they feared—large-scale black rebellion against exploitation. People fled from farms and plantations in Arkansas and all over the South in droves as soon as the Civil War started, without waiting for the Emancipation Proclamation.[40] Helena be-

---

[38] Donald E. Reynolds, *Texas Terror: The Slave Insurrection Panic of 1860 and the Secession of the Lower South* (Baton Rouge: Louisiana State University Press, 2007), 84–86; Donald E. Reynolds, "Texas Troubles," *Handbook of Texas Online*, https://tshaonline.org/handbook/online/articles/vetbr (accessed January 16, 2018).

[39] Hahn, *A Nation under Our Feet*, 65–66; Lankford, *Bearing Witness*, 102.

[40] Thomas DeBlack, *With Fire and Sword: Arkansas, 1861–1874* (Fayetteville: University of Arkansas Press, 2003), 60; Hahn, *A Nation under Our*

came a center for those seeking freedom early in the war. When Union general Samuel Curtis's army arrived there, so did crowds of slaves who had been following the army—"like a magnet," as one historian described the attraction of slaves to Curtis's lines in search of freedom and protection. This area of eastern Arkansas remained a draw for runaway slaves, and freedpeople's settlements multiplied. On January 1, 1863, the Emancipation Proclamation went into effect, and slaves continued to flock to the Union army. And once the United States began accepting African American troops, more than 5,000 of Arkansas's slaves joined the Union side.[41] Knowing the danger of keeping slaves so near the Mississippi River within close proximity to Union soldiers, planters along the river often forced enslaved people to the interior of the state. Countless others were forced out of the state, usually to Texas, with masters seeking to get them as far from Union lines as possible. One estimate surmised that approximately 150,000 slaves had crossed the Red River by the middle of the war. In addition to protecting their investments, masters wanted to escape the horrors they believed would accompany the freedom of black people.[42]

Black men and women of Phillips County faced difficult and dangerous choices as the war raged. It was crucial for bondspeople to decide when to stay put and when to strike out. As recorded in a WPA slave narrative, James Gill remembered how enslaved people on the White and Casteel places in Phillips County exchanged news during the war—an important tool for navigating

Feet, 68–69.

[41] Mark K. Christ, *Civil War Arkansas, 1863: The Battle for a State* (Norman: University of Oklahoma Press, 2012), 104; Steven L. Warren, "Black Union Troops," *Encyclopedia of Arkansas History & Culture*, http://www.encyclopediaofarkansas.net/encyclopedia/entry-detail.aspx?entryID=5135 (accessed January 16, 2018).

[42] Carl H. Moneyhon, *The Impact of the Civil War and Reconstruction on Arkansas: Persistence in the Midst of Ruin* (Fayetteville: University of Arkansas Press, 2002), 115; Lankford, *Bearing Witness*, 48; DeBlack, *With Fire and Sword*, 93, 97; *Tri-Weekly Telegraph* (Houston, TX), October 7, 1863; *Arkansas True Democrat*, April 15, 1863.

wartime slavery. Gill said that several enslaved people absconded with the mules and took off to Helena. James and Mary, his mother, had stayed. Ella Johnson recalled that her father, Jack Burkes, ran away to join the Union war effort and that her mother worked at a couple of different farms until the war ended, when she brought her children to Little Rock. Daniel Rhone was forced to go with the John T. and Caroline Jones's son Tom as a "bodyguard" in the Confederate effort, remembering "my father stuck with him till peace declared—had to do it."[43]

Slaveholders tried desperately to keep the institution alive as slaves and Union forces worked to destroy it. One Union officer wrote from Helena describing the reluctance of white Arkansans to let go of the institution as late as December 1863:

> It is said that the state of Arkansas is ready to come back into the Union. It is not true. Every slaveholder sticks to the institution as his only hope for fortune, respectability and means of living. The non-slaveholders are afraid of negro equality and feel as savage a hostility to the <u>Race</u> as animals that by nature devour each other. In my vicinity a few of the slaveholders contrive to live on their plantations, and feed and clothe their negroes though [they] produce nothing, in the hope that slavery will be restored, while the greater portion of them have removed their slaves to the southwest part of the state, or into Texas, Mississippi, and Alabama. No one yet submits to the idea of its abolishment.[44]

Confederate Arkansas crumbled in the spring of 1865, and the Trans-Mississippi South officially surrendered to the United States on June 2, 1865.[45] Slavery's legacy cast a long shadow over

[43] Lankford, *Bearing Witness*, 273, 275, 287–288.
[44] Brig. Gen. Buford to Hon. Sec. of War, December 11, 1863, District of Eastern Arkansas, series 4664 (Letters Sent), vol. 37/96, District of Arkansas, pp. 240–242 (#80, 1863), Records of U.S. Army Continental Commands, Record Group 393, National Archives and Records Administration.
[45] Jeannie M. Whayne, et al., *Arkansas: A Narrative History*, 2nd ed. (Fayetteville: University of Arkansas Press, 2013), 203–204.

Phillips County, Arkansas—a shadow that still loomed by the time of the Elaine Massacre of 1919. Throughout the period leading up to the Civil War and during the war itself, Arkansas whites feared bands of runaway slaves along the Mississippi River, dreaded the thought of slaves joining "lawless" groups in Indian Territory, took seriously the periodic rumors of slave unrest while brushing off the possibility of a worthwhile black political consciousness, remained remarkably complacent in the stability of white supremacy, and, in the final contest, were defeated by a mass rebellion of African Americans who remained loyal the United States. These feelings persisted after the war. When a WPA interviewer wrote that African American workers in Phillips County in the mid-1930s had become "restless and dissatisfied with their lot and a general discontent prevailed among them…and the landowners were faced with a…very serious Negro question that threatened the peace and welfare of the county," the interviewer could have easily been describing the terrain of struggle twenty years earlier, or even eighty years earlier.

Both white fear of black rebellion and black activism were born under slavery. The lessons learned and sacrifices made by those generations of African Americans laid the foundation for the political activity of 1919. But just as black men and women passed down a collective political consciousness, so, too, did whites pass down a tendency to react with brutality when people of color put up resistance to their exploitation.[46]

---

[46] Lankford, *Bearing Witness*, 293; Hahn, *A Nation under Our Feet*, 1–10.

Chapter 2

In Defense of White Hegemony: Fear of Insurrection as a Cause of Mass Lynchings in Arkansas, 1883–1904

Nancy Snell Griffith

While the 1919 Elaine Massacre claimed the most victims of any instance of collective anti-black violence in Arkansas, there were earlier incidents in the state that involved extreme racial animus and resulted in numerous casualties. The events considered in this chapter occurred from 1883 until 1904, preceding the Elaine Massacre. Like the situation in Elaine, these incidents were seemingly rooted in the fear that African Americans, who outnumbered whites in many counties, were organizing to demand the land, equal pay, and voting rights that were promised them during Reconstruction. What whites really feared, however, was that disenchanted African Americans would rise up into full-blown insurrection. This idea of insurrection was used by whites to justify large-scale violence against blacks.

The Roots of White Fear

Fear of black insurrection has been evident in America since the colonial days. Any assembly of blacks was seen as a threat. As early as 1680, the Massachusetts Bay Colony passed "An Act for Preventing Negro Insurrections," which declared that "the frequent meeting of considerable numbers of negro slaves under pretence [*sic*] of feasts and burials is judged of dangerous consequence."[1] What is now the state of Arkansas was first under French rule as part of Louisiana. In 1724, the French enacted the

---

[1] Kermit L. Hall, *American Legal History* (New York: Oxford University Press, 2005), 54, online at http://www.ub.unibas.ch/tox/ID-SLUZ/000595614/PDF (accessed January 25, 2017).

Code Noir, or black code, which prohibited slaves owned by different masters from gathering "in crowds either by day or night, under the pretense of a wedding, or for any other cause."[2]

While there were apparently no slave revolts in what is now Arkansas, other insurrections across the United States kept the idea fresh in the Southern planter's mind. The most significant insurrections to occur before the French ceded the Louisiana Territory to the United States in 1803 were the Stono Rebellion (South Carolina, 1739), the New York City Rebellion (1741), and Gabriel's Conspiracy (Virginia, 1800). The German Coast Uprising occurred in nearby Louisiana in 1811.

After the Louisiana Purchase, Arkansas became a U.S. territory and began enforcing its own black codes. Slave patrols, intended to catch any wandering slave, were instituted in 1825. During this period, there were two more noteworthy acts of resistance: Denmark Vesey's planned uprising (Charleston, South Carolina, 1822) and Nat Turner's Rebellion (Virginia, 1831). According to the laws of Arkansas Territory, codified in 1835, any slave leaving his or her master's plantation was required to have a pass. No slave was ever to be armed. Slaves were once again prevented from gathering in groups. According to the law: "To prevent the inconvenience arising from the meetings of slaves," visiting slaves were not to stay more than four hours without specific permission from their master or overseer. Masters were punished if they allowed more than five slaves other than their own to remain on the plantation. Any slave who conspired to rebel would be charged with a felony, and if found guilty would "suffer death and be utterly excluded all benefit of clergy."[3]

Arkansas became a state in 1836 and passed its first slave laws in 1837. A slave was required to have a permit to leave his or her master's plantation and, lacking such a permit, could be appre-

[2] "Louisiana's Code Noir," BlackPast.org, http://www.blackpast.org/primary/louisianas-code-noir-1724 (accessed July 24, 2017).
[3] Laws of Arkansas Territory (Little Rock: J. Steele, 1835), 520–524.

hended by any citizen and taken before a justice of the peace. Likewise, it was lawful for whites to apprehend all slaves engaged in "riots, routs, unlawful assemblies and seditious speeches," and take them before a justice of the peace. Sheriffs, coroners, or constables who learned of any such activities were to suppress them.[4] As the population of Arkansas grew and the economy became more dependent on cotton, the number of slaves increased; the fear of insurrection grew along with the slave population.

While there appear to have been no significant slave insurrections in Arkansas, the newspapers of the day published many reports of rumored uprisings. According to the *Fort Smith Herald*, in November 1856, slaves and free blacks devised a plan to capture the U.S. Army arsenal in Little Rock.[5] In February 1858, the *New York Times* reported that twenty-three slaves in Fayetteville "attacked two settlements, killing twenty-three persons, burning houses and killing cattle." This rumor was quickly debunked. Apparently, some slaves recently brought to Arkansas from Missouri had nothing to do, and their master allowed them to wander the neighborhood. A "weak-headed old lady" saw them, was frightened, and went to a nearby settlement to spread the news "that the negroes had 'riz' and were on their march towards the settlement." It took only an hour to disprove her account.[6] Historian Georgia Lee Tatum reported on an alleged insurrection in Monroe County in June 1861, in which the slaves called for "the murder of all whites and in the case of resistance, the women and children were also to be killed." Whether or not this was true, the result was the

---

[4] Arkansas General Assembly, *Revised Statutes of the State of Arkansas: Adopted at the October Session of Said State, A.D. 1837* (Boston: Weeks Jordan, 1838), 732–735, online at https://books.google.com/books/about/Revised_Statutes_of_the_State_of_Arkansa.html?id=ohxEAAAAYAAJ (accessed January 25, 2017).

[5] Joseph E. Holloway, "Slave Insurrections in the United States: An Overview," http://slaverebellion.org/index.php?page=united-states-insurrections (accessed May 2, 2017).

[6] "Rumored Negro Insurrection in Arkansas," *New York Times*, February 6, 1858, p. 1; "The Reported Negro Insurrection in Fayetteville, Ark., a Hoax," *New York Times*, February 23, 1858, p. 3.

arrest of several slaves and the hanging of two men and one girl.[7]

Following the Emancipation Proclamation in 1862, Union forces were authorized to enlist freed slaves in their cause. In response to Lincoln's address, the *Arkansas Gazette* noted that one of the three intentions of this decision was to "induce negro insurrections." Noting the Union's "murderous malice," the *Gazette* asserted that "arming negroes, as soldiers or otherwise, or doing any thing to incite them to insurrection is a worse crime than the murder of any one individual."[8] Outrage about this policy led to a refusal by Confederate forces to take blacks as prisoners of war and resulted in massacres of black soldiers and freed blacks across the South, including on the battlefields of Marks' Mills and Poison Spring in Arkansas. The feeling was that such treatment of blacks would serve to remind them of their place in a society where whites were dominant.[9]

The Civil War ended the institution of slavery in the United States, but the fear of black insurrection did not end with it. In "Why is the Negro Lynched?," Frederick Douglass asserts that during Reconstruction, the main reasons African Americans were lynched in the South were allegations of "Negro conspiracies, Negro insurrections, Negro schemes to murder all the white people, Negro plots to burn the town and to commit violence generally."[10] In 1865, a German man named Carl Schurz, commissioned by President Andrew Johnson to travel through the South and report on conditions there, found that former slave owners were complaining about the "insubordinate spirit of their colored laborers," which they saw as a sign of impending insurrection.

---

[7] Georgia Lee Tatum, *Disloyalty in the Confederacy* (Chapel Hill: University of North Carolina Press, 1934), 38.

[8] "Lincoln's Proclamation: Retaliatory Steps Necessary," *Arkansas Gazette*, October 11, 1862, p. 2.

[9] Gregory J. W. Urwin, "We Cannot Treat Negroes…as Prisoners of War: Racial Atrocities and Reprisals in Civil War Arkansas," *Civil War History* 42 (September 1996): 193–210.

[10] Frederick Douglass, "Why is the Negro Lynched?" (Bridgewater, England: J. Whitby and Sons, 1895), 12.

Reports of imminent insurrections were rife in many parts of the South, but when such reports were investigated by the military, "they uniformly found them unwarranted by fact. In many instances...such apprehensions were industriously spread for the purpose as serving as an excuse for further persecution." Schurz asserted that such fears on the part of whites arose "from their troubled consciences, which are accusing them of the many cruel acts perpetrated against their former slaves."[11] In a letter to Schurz, Joseph Warren, the Mississippi State Superintendent of Education, noted that religious and other gatherings of freedmen were particularly concerning to whites: "The white people also fear, or affect to fear, that opposition to their plans, and even insurrection, will be hatched at the meetings of colored people....From this source arise the occasional reports of intended insurrections; and these reports are intended, often, to cause the prevention of meetings, at which the colored people may consult together, and convey information important to them."[12]

During 1865, American newspapers stoked additional fears of insurrection while describing the black rebellion in Jamaica. A Pennsylvania newspaper, reporting on this uprising, noted that in places where people of African descent made up the majority of the population, they would "continuously outrage the whites." Describing blacks as savage and barbarian, the report maintained that "whatever civilization they attain is derivative and artificial. Hence, when they get started there is none amongst them to cry shame, or beg the others to desist, but the entire mass become infuriated and unites in pursuing their victims with unrelenting hatred."[13]

[11] Carl Schurz, "Report on the Condition of the South," 39th Congress, Senate, ex. Doc. 1st session no. 2, pp. 34–35, 85, online at http://www.wwnorton.com/college/history/give-me-liberty4/docs/CSchurz-South_Report-1865.pdf (accessed April 12, 2017).
[12] Schurz, "Report on the Condition of the South," 130.
[13] "A Negro Rebellion," *Columbia Democrat and Bloomsburg General Advertiser* (Bloomsburg, PA), November 25, 1865, p. 2.

There were also widespread rumors about an insurrection closer to home. Many freedpeople expected that the Freedmen's Bureau would divide land in the South into forty-acre plots to be granted to former slaves. Instead, the Freedmen's Bureau of the Eastern District of Arkansas was irritated with African American preachers who were "teaching the people that they should, of right, own every foot of soil," rather than acquainting them with "sound practical truths." As landowners began to negotiate contracts with their black laborers that fall, they noticed "an unusual stir…and a great deal of passing to and fro at night and congregating at certain out of the way places," leading whites to fear an imminent rebellion by armed blacks.[14]

A number of newspapers reported on a rumored insurrection scheduled for between Christmas 1865 and New Year's.[15] Reports from Mississippi, dated November 23, 1865, indicated that the citizens of Ripley became suspicious about African Americans making frequent visits to LaGrange, Mississippi. Two local citizens gained the confidence of the supposed plot's ringleaders and reported that African Americans had organized a conspiracy "extending from the Mississippi River to South Carolina, and that an insurrection was contemplated about Christmas." Supposedly, the plan was almost complete, and had it not been exposed, it would "have resulted in the horrors of San Domingo and Jamaica in the Southern States."[16] There were also rumors about a Christmas uprising in Pine Bluff.[17]

---

[14] Steven Hahn, "'Extravagant Expectations' of Freedom: Rumour, Political Struggle and the Christmas Insurrection Scare of 1865 in the American South," *Past & Present* 157 (November 1997): 132, 151–152, online at http://africanamericanhistorysp2014.voices.wooster.edu/files/2014/01/extravagant-expectations.pdf (accessed April 12, 2017).
[15] *Evening Star* (Washington DC), October 25, 1865, p. 4; "Virginia Items," *Alexandria Gazette* (Alexandria, VA), December 14, 1865, p. 2; "Telegraphic: From Richmond," *Cleveland Daily Leader*, December 23, 1865, p. 3.
[16] "A Negro Insurrection in Mississippi Apprehended—Arrest of Disaffected Blacks, &c, &c," *The Spirit of Democracy* (Woodsfield, OH), December 6, 1865, p. 2.
[17] "Report of the Joint Committee on Reconstruction, at the First Session,

In the end, despite the widespread rumors, nothing happened. On December 28, the *New York Times* reported that responses to their inquiries on the Christmas insurrection indicated no disturbances in Petersburg, Norfolk, and Richmond in Virginia or Raleigh and Wilmington, North Carolina. Indeed, several of these localities reported that Christmas week was more peaceful than usual.[18] Tongue firmly in cheek, the Washington (Arkansas) *Evening Star* declared that Southern alarmists had predicted unrest primarily because "the negroes were going about the country looking black."[19]

There is one account of an incident of mass lynching in Pine Bluff in March 1866. At the time, due to the presence of both a contraband camp (a camp for escaped or Union-freed slaves), and a home farm (colony for former slaves) in Jefferson County, African Americans made up over seventy percent of the county's population. The alleged incident is detailed in only a single letter and has not yet been corroborated elsewhere. The letter was sent by a freedman named William Mallett to Congressman Thaddeus Stevens of Pennsylvania, a longtime opponent of slavery and a member of the Joint Committee on Reconstruction. According to Mallett, the trouble started when some "rebs" got into a dispute with some freedmen. Things seemed to have calmed down, but that night "the Negroes Cabbens [*sic*] were seen to be on fire." The next morning, Mallett went to inspect the conflagration and found "Negro Men Woman and Children...hanging to trees all round the Cabbins [*sic*]." That night, these same "rebs" burned down "a fine African Church which cost the Freed Man about $5000."[20]

Whether this incident happened or not, it serves to illustrate the fears of white southerners after the Civil War. These African

Thirty-ninth Congress" (Washington DC: U.S. Government Printing Office, 1866), 70.
[18] "The Negro Uprising," *New York Times*, December 28, 1865, p. 4.
[19] Untitled, *Evening Star* (Washington DC), February 8, 1866, p. 4.
[20] Papers of Thaddeus Stevens, Vol. 2, April 1865–August 1868, p. 152.

Americans were apparently prosperous. They had a community and had enough money to build a "fine," expensive church.
Given the large numbers of African Americans in the area, these
attempts at independence would have been viewed as a threat by
area whites. And, as Freedmen's Bureau Agent Edward W. Gantt
had predicted the previous December, in the face of such a threat
and the fear of insurrection, the wrath of local whites "would be
poured upon the heads of the helpless ones once their slaves."[21]

Reports and rumors of insurrections continued during the
spring of 1866, when there were scattered rebellions in Cuba and
an uprising in Panama was put down by force. The situation in
Cuba merited a brief front-page report in the *Arkansas Gazette*.[22]
In early May, there were two days of conflict between blacks
and whites in Memphis, Tennessee.[23] Five days after this initial
report, Ohio's *Wyandott Pioneer* reported on the "most horrible
butcheries and barbarities [that were] inflicted on the negroes" of
Memphis. The *Pioneer* attributed the situation to "hatred to freedom and the negro…which inspirited brutish men in their deeds
of murder, robbery and shame."[24]

There was further trouble in Memphis in late May, when a
white man reportedly attempted to organize a strike among black
steamboat hands. The strikers were rebuffed at first, but eventually a group of 200 men began to march toward the river. A "party
of regulars" met them, and the African Americans, along with the
white organizer, were arrested. According to the *Arkansas Gazette*, "it is to be hoped that any one [*sic*] who incites insurrection,

---

[21] Quoted in Grif Stockley, *Ruled by Race: Black/White Relations in Arkansas from Slavery to the Present* (Fayetteville: University of Arkansas Press,
2008), 66.
[22] *Arkansas Gazette*, April 11, 1866, p. 1.
[23] "The Memphis Riots," *Daily Union and American* (Nashville, TN), May
5, 1866, p. 2.
[24] "Terrible Riot at Memphis," *Wyandott Pioneer* (Upper Sandusky, OH),
May 10, 1866, p. 2. For more on the Memphis incident, see Stephen V. Ash,
*A Massacre in Memphis: The Race Riot That Shook the Nation One Year
after the Civil War* (New York: Hill & Wang, 2013).

no matter from what quarter, will receive the extreme length of the law."[25]

There were some cooler heads in the South, however. On September 14, 1866, the *Arkansas Gazette* published an interesting editorial titled "Our Duty to the Negro." The editorial described African Americans' "brutish instincts," which, when they were slaves, had been controlled by their masters. The newly freed slave, however, as the editorial argued, "has opportunities of organizing, and has been thoroughly corrupted by unscrupulous emissaries. The same inducements are held out to him as formerly—a gratification of his lust, the possession of our wealth, and the elevation to power of his race." The writer saw two possible outcomes of this situation: that whites would become the victims of the freedman's "unbridled ferocity," or that white anger would result in the "wholesale slaughter of [the entire black] race among us." His conclusion was that Arkansans needed to exercise humanity, promote religion, and educate black citizens so that the freedman would understand society and the "relations which exist between him and his fellow-man [and] the duties and obligations that religion, and humanity impose upon him."[26]

When Congressional Reconstruction took effect in 1867, African Americans gained important rights, including due process, the right to vote, and equal protection under the law. The South was divided into military districts, and the only way to escape military supervision was for a state to pass the Fourteenth Amendment and to write a new constitution ensuring that African American men could vote.[27] Almost 700 blacks registered to vote in Arkansas that year, and the Republican Party established the Union League to help them in their efforts.[28]

In June 1867, the *New York Herald* published an extensive re-

---

[25] "The Negro Troubles on Tuesday," *Arkansas Gazette*, June 1, 1866, p. 1.
[26] "Our Duty to the Negro." *Arkansas Gazette*, September 14, 1866, p. 2.
[27] Stockley, *Ruled by Race*, 71.
[28] Stockley, *Ruled by Race*, 72–81.

port on the situation in Arkansas, apparently penned by a correspondent from Little Rock. He noted that the African American was now politically equal to the white man, a "full-fledged American citizen" who had "become a vast and indisputable power in the land." He asserted that the government had "called up a mighty genii," and wondered if "the spirit we have summoned [would] turn upon us and in turn rule us…or have we the power either to exorcise it or make it tamely submissive to our behests?" He concluded on an optimistic note, with the hope that "the white people, as a class, are beginning to lose the prejudices they were disposed at first to entertain against freedmen, and show an increased disposition to do them justice." This is reminiscent of the editorial published in the *Arkansas Gazette* nine months earlier.[29]

His optimism, however, was misplaced. Anxious whites were fearful of African Americans speaking in whispers, gathering together for whatever purpose. As historian Mark Summers noted, "Every small action of the freedpeople came freighted with meaning…small incidents became signs of larger purposes, and isolated events linked into patterns."[30] This constant fear of black insurrection, inflamed by the press, was used to justify the white man's violence against his African American neighbors.

After the Civil War, the contractual relationships being entered into by white landowners and freedmen closely resembled the relationship between masters and slaves. A Freedmen's Bureau agent wrote that former slaves were likely to be "starved, murdered, or forced into a condition more horrible than the worst stage of slavery." Freedmen were frequently murdered, and attempts were made to intimidate Freedmen's Bureau agents and other well-disposed whites.[31] In May 1867, there were reports that two Union sympathizers were hanged in Chicot County by

[29] "Arkansas. Special Correspondence of the Herald," *New York Herald*, June 10, 1867, 6.
[30] Mark Wahlgren Summers, *The Ordeal of the Reunion: A New History of Reconstruction* (Chapel Hill: University of North Carolina Press, 2014), 56.
[31] Stockley, *Ruled by Race*, 65–66.

"rebel desperadoes." The assailants then hanged an old man and a boy who witnessed this lynching. Two soldiers on their way from Little Rock to Arkadelphia were killed, their bodies left in the woods. And several agents of the Freedmen's Bureau were shot at, including Lieutenant Ira McLean Barton in Pine Bluff.[32]

Many of those in charge of military districts across the South voiced their concern about black insurrections and took steps against them. In Florida in 1867, African Americans were supposedly holding night meetings and arming themselves. As a result, General John K. Pope forbade meetings held after dark. In Mississippi, General O. C. Ord feared a Christmas race war in which cotton gins would be burned and bands of plundering African Americans would roam the countryside. He asked for troops to protect people in the counties along the Mississippi River, but his superiors did not accede to his request.[33]

The following year, there was more bad news for whites who feared black control. When the Arkansas constitutional convention convened in January 1868, two-thirds of the delegates were Republican, and the resulting constitution gave African Americans the right to hold office, serve on juries, and serve in the militia. Whites were determined to stop blacks from voting, and as a consequence, Governor Powell Clayton established a state militia in July—and all eligible voters were qualified to join. The day after the election that year, Clayton declared martial law in ten counties, an order that was later amended to include four more counties.[34]

In August 1868, there were problems between African American Republicans and Democrats near Lewisburg, a river town in Conway County. A group of radical blacks attempted to attack a black Democrat in his home, and when the attackers were finally brought to trial in Lewisburg, the two factions of African Amer-

---

[32] "Outrages on Union Men in Arkansas," *New York Herald*, May 31, 1867.
[33] Mark Wahlgren Summers, *The Ordeal of Reunion*, 109–110.
[34] Stockley, *Ruled by Race*, 72–81.

icans refused to serve on a jury together. Weapons were drawn, and court was adjourned. A number of the area's prominent citizens disarmed the blacks, telling them that their arms would be restored if they returned home quietly. The African Americans re-armed and gathered east of Lewisburg. In the meantime, several hundred men gathered to defend Lewisburg if necessary. Several skirmishes resulted, and one white man was seriously wounded. The *Arkansas Gazette* attributed the events to "the threatening attitude assumed by the radical negroes of that section, incited by the white scoundrels, who seem careless of life or the peace of the community."[35]

On September 28, 1868, former Confederate general Thomas C. Hindman was shot by an assassin through the window of his home in Helena. Although no one was ever arrested for the murder, in March 1869 the *New York Times* reported that his death was the result of a purported black conspiracy and named Charles Porter as the killer. According to this account, the conspiracy included plans to burn Helena and kill several other white men, but the conspirators who were assigned to do so lost courage and did not fulfill their assignment.[36]

In late November 1868, the Ku Klux Klan in Crittenden County reportedly committed "many horrible deeds of murder and outrages…upon loyal men and negroes."[37] In early December, there was more trouble in Arkansas when a group of men in Conway County raided the house of two African Americans who were living with white women. One of the black men was killed, and the other escaped. In retaliation, Captain John L. Matthews brought his company of black militia into the neighborhood and killed three white men. Governor Clayton declared martial law.[38] In Lewisburg later that month, several militias, one of them African

[35] "Riot in Conway County," *Arkansas Gazette*, August 28, 1868, p. 3.
[36] "General Hindman," *New York Times*, March 27, 1869, p. 11.
[37] "Tragedy," *Evening Telegraph* (Philadelphia, PA), December 2, 1868.
[38] "Outrages in Arkansas," *New Orleans Crescent*, December 17, 1868, p. 2.

52

American, entered town and set fire to a number of stores. According to a correspondent for the *Gazette*, the militias then began to patrol the streets, allowing no one to leave their homes without a pass. He concluded by declaring, "These outrages must cease, or every mountain pass in the state will be made a Thermopolae, and 300,000 white people be terribly avenged."[39]

In his message to the legislature in November 1868, Governor Powell Clayton spoke of the widespread "spirit of lawlessness and opposition to civil authorities" in Arkansas. He attributed the situation to a conspiracy to overthrow lawful government by a "treasonable organization," a reference to the Ku Klux Klan. He said that, across the state, African Americans, county officeholders, and Union men were being murdered or driven out of their communities. He listed events in many Arkansas counties, including "armed forces (ku-klux) riding through" Columbia County, and Klan killings in Crittenden County, where "the bullet and assassins hold the county in terror."[40]

In the early 1870s, there were two incidents in Arkansas, described as race wars or insurrections, that, notably, did not result in lynchings. The first occurred in Chicot County in 1871, when hundreds of African Americans, under the leadership of state legislator and county judge James W. Mason, took over the area in response to the murder of an African American lawyer. Many white residents fled the area in fear.[41] The following year, a similar uprising called the Black Hawk War erupted in Mississippi County when Charles Fitzpatrick gathered a group of 200 African Americans to protect him while he was under suspicion of murder. One newspaper referred to the incident as "a foray of infuriated blacks armed to the teeth, and led on by a scoundrel carpet-bagger upon a town, with avowed intent to slay the men

[39] "Another Fire at Lewisburg," *Arkansas Gazette*, December 20, 1868, p. 2.
[40] "Governor's Message," *Arkansas Gazette*, November 26, 1868, p. 1.
[41] "The Arkansas Troubles," *New York Times*, December. 29, 1871, p. 2; "Bloody Chicot," *Arkansas Gazette*, February 10, 1872, p. 1.

and violate the women thereof."[42] Reports of insurrection in the South continued throughout the 1870s. The so-called Tunica Race War in Mississippi in 1874 received front-page coverage in the *Arkansas Gazette*.[43] The *Gazette* also reported on events in Vicksburg in December of that year that resulted in fifty to one hundred African American deaths and a number of arrests.[44]

Although Reconstruction did not end across most of the South until 1876, it ended in Arkansas in 1874. By this time, Arkansans were more resigned to African Americans voting and holding public office. Democrat Augustus Garland, elected governor in 1874, proved to be a moderate on racial issues, and William R. Miller, elected in 1877, promised to guarantee the rights of the state's black citizens. In 1878, the Democratic platform actually invited African American cooperation. This resulted in the creation of fusion governments, where blacks were guaranteed certain posts, and made Arkansas attractive enough to draw the African American labor that it so desperately needed. But most of these new arrivals, having been promised better prospects in the state, were sorely disappointed, and ended up in poverty.[45]

According to the *Arkansas Gazette*, around Christmas of 1882, there were rumors about planned African American insurrections near Hope and Prescott in southwestern Arkansas. Black people in these areas were supposedly going to "rise in their might…to pillage and burn and murder and rob and run the country." The *Gazette*'s correspondent maintained that these threats were probably "hatched in the fertile brain of a white man…for what pur-

---

[42] *Biographical and Historical Memoirs of Eastern Arkansas* (Chicago: Goodspeed Publishers, 1890), online at http://files.usgwarchives.net/ar/mississippi/history/goodspd.txt (accessed June 8, 2017); Ruth C. Hale, "Black Hawk War of 1872," *Encyclopedia of Arkansas History & Culture*, http://www.encyclopediaofarkansas.net/encyclopedia/entry-detail.aspx?entry-ID=5282 (accessed January 20, 2017.)
[43] "The Mississippi Muss," *Arkansas Gazette*, August 12, 1874, p. 1.
[44] "A Later Dispatch," *Arkansas Gazette*, December 8, 1874, p. 1; "Vicksburg," *Arkansas Gazette*, December 13, 1874, p. 1.
[45] Stockley, *Ruled by Race*, 86–100.

poses can only be divined at present." He went on to say that there was no need for such an uprising because the area's "colored people…are prosperous and contented, living at perfect peace with the white race, and, be it said to their credit, they are law-abiding and give comparatively little trouble." Indeed, according to the report, "most of the older and more influential people in the area find the rumors laughable."[46]

This deep-seated fear of black rebellion continued to occupy Arkansans throughout the late nineteenth and early twentieth centuries, culminating in the Elaine Massacre, the worst such incident in Arkansas's history. While the events in Elaine were purportedly sparked by the fact that African American farmers were organizing in order to get better wages, they were really rooted in whites' fear of potential insurrection by the county's majority black population. Similar fears produced incidents in Howard County (1883), Lee County (1891), Calhoun County (1892), Little River County (1899), and Arkansas County (1904). Exploring the circumstances surrounding these earlier mass lynchings will serve to illuminate further the events in Elaine in 1919.

Howard County Race Riot of 1883

Despite claims about "prosperous and contented" African Americans in the area, living "at perfect peace with the white race," there was to be trouble in Hempstead County and neighboring Howard County just eight months after those claims were voiced. And the relative prosperity of blacks in the region may have been a factor in the situation. Since the murder that was the impetus for the events occurred in Howard County, and the arrests and trial took place in that county, most historians refer to this as the Howard County Race Riot. However, since many of the participants came from Hempstead County, numerous reports at the time, including some in the *Arkansas Gazette*, described

[46] "Prescott Paragraphs," *Arkansas Gazette*, January 4, 1883, p. 2.

it as "The Hempstead War." As Sheriff Robert G. Shaver (a former Confederate general) told the *Gazette* on August 12, 1883, "Hempstead furnished the mob, Howard provided the victim."[47]

In late July or early August 1883, a white sharecropper named Tom Wyatt and a surveyor identified only as Montgomery had a disagreement with two elderly African American brothers named Prince and James Marshall over a boundary line in Hempstead County. Shaver reported that when the Marshalls began to argue with Montgomery, described as a one-armed school teacher, Wyatt came to his defense and "knocked one of them down with a fence-rail." A few days later, James Marshall's daughter was found unconscious in a field. Her story was that Wyatt had come into the field and knocked her over the head with a club, although there were some doubts about this account.[48]

According to some reports, local African Americans, who considered Wyatt a "violent white man" with a "dangerous character," consulted lawyers, who suggested they go to a justice of the peace and swear out a warrant. When the justice of the peace refused, about twenty African Americans gathered in a church on July 30, intent on performing a citizens' arrest on Wyatt the following day. Shaver's account is somewhat different, indicating that the armed blacks consisted of a group of seventy-two, "officered in military style," and having in mind a list of white people that they wanted to kill. They found Wyatt in a field on the Howard County/ Hempstead County line and surrounded him. Wyatt managed to kill Joe Booker, one of the African Americans, before two other blacks shot and killed him. His body happened to fall in Howard County.[49]

[47] "The Uprising of the Negroes in Hempstead County," *Arkansas Gazette*, August 12, 1883, p. 5.
[48] "The Uprising of the Negroes in Hempstead County," *Arkansas Gazette*, August 12, 1883, p. 5.
[49] "Oppression in Arkansas—The Howard County Cases—Facts Developed at the Last Trial," *Arkansas Gazette*, June 6, 1884, p. 2; "The Uprising of the Negroes in Hempstead County," *Arkansas Gazette*, August 12, 1883, p. 5; Peggy S. Lloyd, "The Howard County Race Riot of 1883," *Encyclopedia*

White men from Howard and Hempstead counties immediately formed posses to pursue the alleged perpetrators. One posse encountered some African Americans who were building a coffin in which to bury Joe Booker. They promptly shot the two unresisting men and a twelve-year-old boy.[50] The three were identified as Eli Gamble, Alonzo Flowers, and Abraham Booker. Shaver reported that the whites camped overnight near Cross Roads Church in Hempstead County and resumed their search the following day. A posse led by Deputy Sheriff Oscar Pope of Howard County chased a group of African Americans to a house, where he demanded that they surrender. The blacks fired, wounding James D. Shafer, and the posse fired back, "killing two negroes and capturing several, one of whom was wounded." A second posse then proceeded to the home of an African American named Sam Johnson, described by Shaver as "their leader and instigator of the entire affair," where a number of African Americans had gathered. They surrounded the house, and there was a standoff.[51] James F. Smith, a prosperous white Howard County merchant, was wounded but managed to defuse the situation.[52]

By Wednesday night, twenty-four African Americans were in custody. Deputy Sheriff Pope then asked Shaver to aid him in capturing the rest of the suspects. Shaver called up the militia and captured twenty more blacks. Those captured were placed under strong guard at Center Point.[53] According to historian Peggy Lloyd, there were forty-three men in custody at Center Point, charged with murder, and an additional group of men was

of *Arkansas History & Culture*, http://www.encyclopediaofarkansas.net/encyclopedia/entry-detail.aspx?entryID=3663 (accessed March 19, 2017).
[50] "Oppression in Arkansas—The Howard County Cases—Facts Developed at the Last Trial," *Arkansas Gazette*, June 6, 1884, p. 2.
[51] "The Uprising of the Negroes in Hempstead County," *Arkansas Gazette*, August 12, 1883, p. 5.
[52] Lloyd, "The Howard County Race Riot of 1883."
[53] "The Uprising of the Negroes in Hempstead County," *Arkansas Gazette*, August 12, 1883, p. 5.

held at Washington, charged with rioting.[54]

The trials of Wyatt's alleged murderers began on November 12, 1883. Ten men were acquitted. Charles Wright, Henry Carr, and Elijah Thompson were convicted of murder and sentenced to death. Julius Y. Johnson was sentenced to eighteen years for second-degree murder. Ten men were sentenced to fifteen years, nine others to ten years, and an additional ten sentenced to five years. Charles Wright was hanged at Center Point on April 25, 1884. Carr and Thompson appealed their convictions, and their sentences were ultimately reduced to eighteen years. In October 1884, those accused of rioting appeared in court in Hempstead County. Four men were released when they were able to prove that they did not participate in the rioting. Three men were acquitted. Eight men were found guilty, but their $10 fine was eventually reduced to $1.[55]

In an interview published in the *Arkansas Gazette* on August 12, 1883, Shaver cited the killing of Wyatt as the root cause of the events in Howard County.[56] However, his story was quite different in an interview published two days later. By then, Shaver was describing the events as the result of a well-planned plot that went awry. According to this account, the area's African Americans, including some from Little River and Sevier County who had been gathering in the Saline River bottoms, had been organizing. Had they not "been too hasty and had waited only two weeks longer," they would have had a force of 1,000 men, armed with a "long list of some of the best names in our country, whom they had sworn to kill."[57]

[54] Lloyd, "The Howard County Race Riot of 1883."
[55] Lloyd, "The Howard County Race Riot of 1883"; "A Wholesale Conviction of Negroes Engaged in the Howard County Murder," *Arkansas Gazette*, November 25, 1883, p. 1; "Oppression in Arkansas—The Howard County Cases—Facts Developed at the Last Trial," *Arkansas Gazette*, June 6, 1884, p. 2.
[56] "The Uprising of the Negroes in Hempstead County," *Arkansas Gazette*, August 12, 1883, p. 5.
[57] "Nipped in the Bud," *Arkansas Gazette*, August 14, 1883, p. 5.

According to Lloyd, there may have been more than just a threat of violent insurrection involved here. Referring to an article in the *Arkansas Mansion* by someone identified only as "W. C. J.," Lloyd noted that the events in Howard County may have been part of a plot by the area's white landowners to frighten off prosperous African American farmers and seize their farms. There were apparently between fifty and sixty black farmers in the area who had good land and were able to live without owing anything to anyone. Prince Marshall of Hempstead County, for instance, owned much more personal property than Thomas Wyatt did. Sam Johnson of Howard County was even more prosperous, owning 400 acres of land and almost $800 in personal property—sizeable wealth for anyone, black or white, in the area.[58] Thus, by disturbing the system of white control that was at the heart of the postwar Southern farming system, at least some of the area's African Americans may have posed an economic, as well as a physical, threat to the area's white population.

Whatever the causes of the events in Howard County, the results were familiar. As stated in one African American's response to the situation: "The excitement was beyond all reason. The prosecutions became a cruel proscription, and have disgraced the state. Just think! Four colored men murdered, three sentenced to be hanged, thirty-one in the penitentiary and not one white man was indicted or even arrested!"[59]

As the 1880s progressed, there were continued rumors of black insurrection. In August 1887, there was trouble in Lonoke County when a white man refused to pay an African American fairly for work he had done.[60] During this same period, both black and white

---

[58] *Arkansas Weekly Mansion*, September 1, September 8, 1883; Quoted by Peggy S. Lloyd, "The Howard County Race Riot of 1883," *Arkansas Historical Quarterly* 59 (Winter 2000): 358.

[59] "Oppression in Arkansas—The Howard County Cases—Facts Developed at the Last Trial," *Arkansas Gazette*, June 6, 1884, 2.

[60] "Another Negro Scare," *New York Times*, August 27, 1887, p. 5; "A Negro Scare Ended," *New York Times*, August 28, 1887, p. 9.

farmers were beginning to organize. Blacks in the Arkansas Delta organized the Sons of the Agricultural Star, and membership grew so much by 1886 that the formerly all-white Agricultural Wheel opened its membership to African Americans. In 1888, there were twelve black Wheels in Arkansas, representing thirteen counties. But when the Agricultural Wheel merged with the Farmers' Alliance, it once again limited its membership to whites.[61] Consequently, blacks organized chapters of the Colored Farmers' Alliance, founded by a white man, R. M. Humphrey, in 1888.

These organizations, intended to improve the lot of tenant farmers and sharecroppers, were a threat to the economic and political dominance of the area's white farmers. In addition, white residents feared that their meetings would provide fertile ground for black insurrection. As J. L. Moore, superintendent of the Putnam County (Florida) Colored Farmers' Alliance, said about reporting in a white newspaper in 1891, "In all the discussions of the whites in all the various meetings they attend and the different resolutions, remarks, and speeches they make against the Negro, I never hear you, Mr. Editor, nor any of the other leading journals, once criticize their action or say they are antagonizing the races, neither do you ever call a halt. But let the Negro speak once, and what do you hear? Antagonizing races, Negro uprising, Negro domination, etc. Anything to keep the reading public hostile toward the Negro."[62]

White Democrats reacted to this threat to white hegemony by trying to get blacks out of politics, and to keep them from voting. An 1888 incident in Crittenden County typifies this. Since 1874, when the Democratic Party returned to power in Arkansas, Crittenden County had been operating under a fusion government. Things did not go smoothly, however. Benjamin Westmoreland,

[61] Stockley, *Ruled by Race*, 112.
[62] J. L. Moore, "The Florida Colored Farmers' Alliance 1891," *National Economist* (Washington DC), March 7, 1891, online at http://www.historyisaweapon.com/defcon1/moorecoloredfarmersalliance.html (accessed February 21, 2017).

an African American who was elected county treasurer in 1874, was killed by a white man before his term expired. In 1878, voter fraud and destruction of ballots resulted in the election of an all-white slate of Democratic officials in a county where African Americans made up eighty percent of the population. In addition, economic hardship led farmers to form third-party alliances like the Union Labor Party.

White Democrats, sick of fusion governments and threatened by this third-party movement, met in Memphis to decide how to rid Crittenden County of its black officials. During the first week of July, rumors spread that African Americans were determined to either drive whites out of the county or kill them. Whites armed themselves, supposedly for self-protection. At the same time, two African American officials, county judge D. W. Lewis and county clerk David Ferguson, were indicted for public drunkenness. On July 12, several prominent citizens who attended the meeting in Memphis claimed that they had received anonymous letters asking them to leave the county. Whites responded by surrounding the courthouse and ordering Lewis, Ferguson, and Ferguson's deputy (and editor of the *Marion Headlight*, a black Republican newspaper) to leave the county. Additional whites rounded up a number of the county's other prominent black citizens. Eventually eleven African Americans were forced to go to Memphis. A second round of expulsions focused on other prominent black citizens and landowners, among them some members of the Agricultural Wheel. African Americans appealed to Governor Simon Hughes, but he refused to help, ultimately filling all of the vacant county offices with white Democrats. In the end, no whites were prosecuted, but nineteen African Americans were indicted for producing and disseminating the anonymous letters.[63]

There were continuing attempts to disenfranchise African

[63] Nancy Snell Griffith, "Crittenden County Expulsion of 1888," *Encyclopedia of Arkansas History & Culture*, http://www.encyclopediaofarkansas.net/encyclopedia/entry-detail.aspx?entryID=6962 (accessed March 21, 2017).

Americans. During the fall of 1888, John M. Clayton, former Arkansas governor Powell Clayton's brother, was the Republican candidate for the Second Congressional District of the U.S. House of Representatives. On election day, white Democrats in Plumerville challenged two black Republican election judges. These judges were eventually replaced by two white Democrats, and the balloting proceeded. Clayton's opponent, Clifton R. Breckinridge, was declared the winner by a close margin. The ballot box in Plumerville, however, which reportedly contained 572 votes for Clayton, was stolen by four masked men. Clayton challenged the election and was assassinated in January 1889. His murderer was never found, but several prominent men were arrested and tried for tampering with the ballot box. Judge George Cunningham's charge to the grand jury in the case was scathing: "There is no man with three ideas above an oyster who does not know that murder and assassination are the results and continue to be the results of the political methods that have been employed in this county to carry the last election....The organic law and life of this great nation says the colored people have a right to vote, and if they have no right to vote, where did you get your right?... Politicians try to scare you with the myth and buga-boo of negeo [*sic*] domination. Where have they dominated? No, sir; it is merely an excuse for committing outrages on their rights, which no sensible man should consider."[64] The state legislature, however, further discouraged blacks from voting in 1891 by mandating that ballots be cast in secret, thereby denying illiterate voters help with completing their ballots; the following year, a poll tax was also instituted.

Lee County Incidents, 1891

In late September 1891, there were a number of incidents in

---

[64] "C. C. Reid Found Guilty," *Memphis Appeal*, April 28, 1889, p. 5; "Terrorism in the South," *Indianapolis Journal*, February 5, 1889, p. 1; Untitled, *The Appeal* (St. Paul, MN), March 16, 1889, p. 2.

Lee County, Arkansas, that were eerily similar to the events surrounding the Elaine Massacre twenty-eight years later. African
Americans made up seventy-five percent of the county's population, and most of them were poor tenants or sharecroppers, dependent on white planters for their livelihood. The so-called uprising,
sometimes referred to as the Cotton Pickers Strike of 1891, was
rooted in a labor dispute. Resulting in the murders of at least fifteen African American laborers, it is evidence of the lengths to
which prominent whites would go to preserve their domination
and prevent area blacks from improving their lot.

By 1891, R. M. Humphrey's Colored Farmers' Alliance boasted over a million members. In the fall of that year, Humphrey advocated a strike by the nation's black cotton pickers in an effort to
increase their wages. The strike was scheduled for September 12,
during harvest time, to give the workers increased leverage. In the
end, it was unsuccessful, with only a handful of workers participating.[65] Ten days later, however, events in Lee County provided
the impetus for an actual strike there.

According to accounts, the problems in Lee County began
when J. F. Frank, a wealthy Memphis merchant with large land-
holdings in the county, visited his plantation there and decided
that his cotton crop was not being picked quickly enough. The
contract that most local landowners had agreed to was fifty cents
per hundred pounds picked. Frank's manager, Tom Miller, said he
could not arrange for the crop to be picked faster with the workers
he had and offered to pay more than the going rate. In front of
about 100 black workers, Frank offered to spend up to $1.00 per
100 pounds.[66] This encouraged other African American workers
in the county to strike in hopes of getting better wages.

According to the *Gazette*, on September 24, some 100 armed

[65] Guy Lancaster, "Cotton Pickers Strike of 1891," *Encyclopedia of Arkansas History & Culture*, http://www.encyclopediaofarkansas.net/encyclope-
dia/entry-detail.aspx?entryID=4267 (accessed April 19, 2017).
[66] "Peace Prevails," *Arkansas Gazette*, October 3, 1891, p. 1.

and mounted black strikers posted themselves along the road leading to Frank's plantation. Encountering Miller, they shot him and then "proceeded on their way, cursing and abusing every white man they met and threatening all their property with destruction." They also burned a gin house. Several county citizens appealed to Governor James Eagle for help, but he refused to offer a reward without further information. The armed strikers then began going from farm to farm, trying to drive other pickers from the fields until wages were increased. Among these were Joe Peyton, Met and Early Jones, and Ben Patterson, described by the *Arkansas Gazette* as coming from "the crap dens of Memphis and other cities." Newspapers described the strikers as a mob "bent on death and devastation," which was terrorizing the county.[67] Many pickers stopped working and tried to force others to join them. In the process, two pickers, who perhaps refused to join the strike, were shot and killed.

There were newspaper reports that, by this time, the rioting African Americans had "almost taken possession of Lee County," and that the local people were "terror-stricken."[68] Enraged white planters, fearing ruin at the hands of the mob, responded with force. In the face of white outrage, the strikers fled, and by September 29 many of them were hiding on Cat Island, situated on the Mississippi River in Crittenden County. Sheriff W. T. Derrick organized a posse to pursue them and stormed the island, killing two strikers and capturing nine. Two others, one of whom was Ben Patterson, escaped. When the sheriff and his men attempted to take the prisoners to jail in Marianna, a mob of 300 men waylaid them and demanded the prisoners. Being outnumbered, the sheriff's posse

---

[67] "Negroes in Arms," *Arkansas Gazette*, September 29, 1891, p. 1; "Peace Prevails," *Arkansas Gazette*, October 3, 1891, p. 1; "Nine Negroes Lynched," *Arkansas Gazette*, October 2, 1891, p. 1.

[68] "Race War in Arkansas," *Los Angeles Herald*, September 29, 1891, p. 1; "Rioting Negroes," *Big Stone Post* (Big Stone Gap, VA), October 2, 1891, p. 1.

64

surrendered them, and they were taken to a thicket and hanged.[69]

Patterson, badly wounded, managed to hide in the swamp and later boarded the steamer *James Lee*. There, he was questioned and allegedly confessed that he was involved in Miller's murder. A mob, probably the same one involved in the events near Cat Island, removed him from the boat. They were "cool, orderly, and heavily armed" and forced the boat's officers and passengers to stand by as they carried Patterson onto the bank. There, according to the *Arkansas Gazette*, "a number of shots were heard, and the presumption is that he was killed."[70] By the time the situation ended, fifteen of the nineteen black laborers involved in the strike and subsequent violence had been killed, and three of the remaining four were in jail in Marianna and Forrest City. This situation, supposedly rooted in a dispute over wages, culminated in a hunt for the ringleaders and the deaths of fifteen men. The attempts that black workers made to organize not only threatened the labor system and the wealth of the planters but even the lives of the county's citizens, both black and white.

The 1891 election laws took effect in 1892, and as a result many African Americans did not vote that year. There was a sharp increase in lynchings during this period. Indeed, racial unrest was widespread in Arkansas in the 1890s, especially across the southern counties. According to the *Chicago Tribune*'s annual tabulation of lynchings across the United States, twenty-five people were lynched in Arkansas in 1892, a number that placed the state third in the nation behind Louisiana and Tennessee. Sociologist Mattias Smångs has observed that there does, in fact, exist a positive correlation between disfranchisement efforts and increased racial violence, despite the claim advanced at the time that the removal of African Americans from the political sphere would help to prevent violence, for these practices "complemented each other

<hr>

[69] "Peace Prevails," *Arkansas Gazette*, October 3, 1891, p. 1; "Wiping Out the Negroes," *Indianapolis Journal*, October 2, 1891, p. 1.
[70] "Nine Negroes Lynched," *Arkansas Gazette*, October 2, 1891, p. 1.

in promoting and enacting white group unity and power."[71] Arkansas pastor E. Malcolm Argyle of the African Methodist Episcopal Zion Church spoke of this trend in March 1892, noting that "there is much uneasiness and unrest all over this State among our people, owing to the fact that the people (our race variety)... are being lynched upon the slightest provocation....In the last 30 days there have been not less than eight colored persons lynched in this State....It is evident that the white people of the South have no further use for the Negro."[72] According to historian Vincent Vinikas, "With each unpunished killing, with every unprosecuted outrage, whites learned that, as citizens, blacks could be treated with complete contempt."[73]

Hampton Race War of 1892

The Hampton Race War (also referred to as the Calhoun County Race War) occurred in September 1892 and entailed incidents of racial violence all across the southern part of the county. While many sources have attributed the events in Calhoun County to Arkansas's passage of the Election Law of 1891, which effectively disfranchised African Americans in the state and legally suppressed Republican and third-party political opposition to Democratic rule, it seems that the trouble in the county started the following year, prior to the early September election.

Contemporary accounts of the incident indicate that racial conflict erupted at least as early as March 1892, when whitecappers whipped a black man for insulting a white woman.[74] Whitecap-

[71] Mattias Smångs, *Doing Violence, Making Race: Lynching and White Racial Group Formation in the U.S. South, 1882–1930* (New York: Routledge, 2017), 103.
[72] E. Malcolm Argyle, "Report from Arkansas," *Christian Recorder*, March 24, 1892.
[73] Vincent Vinikas, "Specters in the Past: The St. Charles, Arkansas, Lynching of 1904 and the Limits of Historical Inquiry," *Journal of Southern History* 55 (August 1999): 553.
[74] "Race War in Arkansas," *Sacramento Daily Union*, September 21, 1892, p. 1.

ping (or nightriding) was a form of vigilantism practiced mostly by poor white farmers and farm laborers during the late nineteenth and early twentieth centuries. Disguised men, often members of a secret society, would employ both physical attacks and threats to intimidate their victims. In some instances, like the whipping of the black man mentioned above, this practice was used to enforce community mores; in other cases, the causes were economic. Such incidents in Calhoun County apparently inflamed black citizens, and they reportedly vowed to kill whitecappers. According to several contemporary sources, a white man named Unsill, described variously as a "Peoples-party man" or a Republican, as well as an ex-convict, encouraged this retaliation. Tensions in the county increased at the time of the September 5 election when, according to some newspaper reports, Unsill led forty-two armed blacks to the polls, where they demanded to vote.[75]

Jim Dunn, the *Arkansas Gazette*'s informant on the events, indicated that on the evening of the election, an African American man named Jim Harrison met with a group of other blacks at a church. Harrison, described as a "desperate negro" who bore "a mean reputation among negroes and whites," disturbed the service by calling for the arrest of another African American, who had supposedly given away their plans for retaliation. Guns were fired, and the crowd rushed the preacher, who escaped through a window with the accused. Both went to hide with friends. The preacher swore out a warrant against Harrison for disturbing public worship, and when Harrison learned of it, he "at once proceeded to arouse the younger negroes to riot, hoping thereby to escape." The more conservative in the African American community refused to participate, as they were already tired of Harrison's activities. While an additional report from the town of Thornton, published alongside Dunn's account, said that the trouble was mainly political in origin, Dunn disputed this fact,

---

[75] "Jim Harrison: He's the 'Coon' That Started All That Trouble in Calhoun County," *Arkansas Gazette*, September 21, 1892, pp. 1, 2.

maintaining that "it was only a case of bad niggers."[76]

According to the *New York Sun*, additional incidents of white-capping followed. Several more African Americans were removed from their cabins by vigilantes and "severely flogged." In addition, a man named Charley Jones was whipped for deserting his wife, "a punishment which all the negroes endorsed." The *Sun*, like many other newspapers, greatly exaggerated the number of African Americans in the county. They noted that blacks outnumbered whites in the county by a margin of six to one, when in fact only 37.4 percent of Calhoun County citizens in 1890 were black. The *Sun* reported that black residents had begun to roam the county in large bands, threatening any whites they saw.[77]

On September 17, news came to Hampton that armed African Americans in Champagnolle Township "were fortified at Bob Davis' house and defied the white people to approach them and also said that none of them could be taken." Other area blacks told authorities that the group holed up in Davis's house intended to kill Sheriff W. A. Tomlinson, Clerk T. N. Means, and several other prominent citizens. The organization allegedly extended "all over the county," and other African Americans were reportedly "still in hiding, making threats to kill every white man, woman and child in the county before they stop."[78]

A posse of twenty white men set off for Davis's house, armed with warrants for five of the African Americans. The black men had posted guards around the house, and as posse members started to climb the fence, one of these men stood up. When told to put his hands up, he fired, and the posse shot and killed him. Several other guards appeared, and they were also shot. According to Dunn's account, among the dead were Matthew Farris and Abe Cook. Turner Goodwin, shot seven times, was mortally wounded,

[76] "Jim Harrison: He's the 'Coon' That Started All That Trouble in Calhoun County," *Arkansas Gazette*, September 21, 1892, pp. 1, 2.
[77] "Urged on by White Men," *New York Sun*, September 21, 1892, p. 1.
[78] "Jim Harrison: He's the 'Coon' That Started All That Trouble in Calhoun County," *Arkansas Gazette*, September 21, 1892, pp. 1, 2.

as was Sidney Huffman. Both were expected to die. Several other African Americans were arrested.[79]

According to the *Sun*, the posse was ambushed on its way back to Hampton. The posse returned fire, and their attackers fled, with no casualties on either side. On September 18, a posse met 150 mounted African Americans, only half of whom were armed. The blacks fired on the deputies for several minutes to no effect, after which the deputies charged, killing one unidentified African American and wounding seven.[80] Newspaper accounts differ as to those who escaped the posse. Jim Dunn reported that Jim Harrison, Phelix Perdue, Bob Davis, Alex Lawson, and Ad Tate escaped. Other newspapers reported that the ringleader, Jim Harrison, had been lynched.[81]

There was further violence that same week when, according to the *New York Times* and several other newspapers, a "well-respected negro" who was gathering corn with two white men, was killed by two other whites. This was probably a murder of convenience, as the alleged murderers were on trial for hog-stealing, and the black man was the main witness against them.[82] Around this same time, rumors began to swirl that enraged black residents were going to storm the jail at Malvern in Hot Spring County, where many African Americans from Calhoun County had been imprisoned. Several hundred white men stood guard at the jail one night, but the imagined raid never materialized.[83]

While these events were attributed to whitecapping or politics, it is clear that white residents of Calhoun County responded to

[79] "Jim Harrison: He's the 'Coon' That Started All That Trouble in Calhoun County," *Arkansas Gazette*, September 21, 1892, pp. 1, 2.
[80] "Urged on by White Men," *New York Sun*, September 21, 1892, p. 1.
[81] "Jim Harrison: He's the 'Coon' That Started All That Trouble in Calhoun County," *Arkansas Gazette*, September 21, 1892, pp. 1, 2; "Race War in Arkansas," *Sacramento Daily Union*, September 21, 1892, p. 1; "Whites and Blacks," *Anaconda Standard* (Anaconda, MT), September 21, 1892, p. 7.
[82] "Another Assassination in Arkansas," *New York Times*, September 25, 1892, p. 8.
[83] "Race War Still On," *Daily Globe* (St. Paul, MN), September 25, 1892, p. 1.

fears that angry African Americans would rise up, attacking not only prominent residents, but any white person they encountered. The *Evening Star* reported that normally quiet Calhoun County had been "transformed into a region of anarchy and death." Outrage over these incidents reportedly caused African Americans to begin roaming the area, threatening and insulting any white person they encountered. The situation became unbearable to the area's whites, who embarked on an effort to kill the troublemakers.[84] Once again, the deep-seated fear of insurrection had reared its ugly head.

In 1894, blacks were further discouraged from voting by the newly instituted poll tax. That year, 65,000 fewer people voted in Arkansas than had voted in 1890. For the first time since Reconstruction, there were no African Americans elected to either branch of the Arkansas legislature.[85] Blacks were also beginning to leave the state. Pastor Malcolm Argyle noted this trend in his 1892 article, and it continued. In 1893, a group of African Americans in Cleveland County declared: "We is tired of having the white folks rule us and we are gwine where the nigger has some say."[86] Blacks were also being driven away from job sites. There were numerous incidents of white workers forcing African Americans, who typically worked for lower wages, to leave their jobs. In 1896 alone, there were at least three incidents: in Canfield in Lafayette County, among railroad workers in Polk and Ouachita Counties, and at a sawmill in McNeil in Columbia County.

Little River County Race War of 1899

In the spring of 1899, there was a "race war" in Little River County that was clearly based on rumors of insurrection, supposedly fomented by an African American man named General

---

[84] "Race War in Arkansas," *Evening Star* (Washington DC), September 20, 1892, p. 3.
[85] Stockley, *Ruled by Race*, 125.
[86] Stockley, *Ruled by Race*, 128.

Duckett.[87] Newspaper reports indicate that the county was experiencing a period of lawlessness, which residents attributed to the actions of the black population. Murders, thefts, and fights were rampant. Several months earlier, there had been a clash between whites and blacks at a sawmill in Alleene, and a small riot ensued. According to the *Nebraska State Journal*, "One or two negroes have previously been severely dealt with when people found it necessary to take the law into their own hands."[88]

The situation worsened when county planter James Stockton was told by some of his "trusted" black workers that General Duckett was inciting blacks into insurrection. On March 18, 1899, Stockton asked Duckett to cease his activities or be taken before the local grand jury. Duckett left, but allegedly returned with a rifle later that night and killed Stockton. He then escaped. He reportedly informed other blacks whom he passed along his way that he had killed one white man, and with their help, he would kill more. This brought the simmering trouble in the county to a boil.[89]

On March 21, Duckett surrendered after hiding for several days in the Red River bottoms. The county sheriff took him to the crime scene near Rocky Comfort and then began to escort him to Richmond, then the county seat. According to the *Journal*, "It seemed as if every man in the ten miles knew of the capture and before the officer and prisoner could get fairly started the whole

---

[87] While local newspapers like the *Arkansas Gazette* did report unrest in Little River County in March 1899, it is possible that the events surrounding this "race war" and the number of casualties were greatly inflated by the national press, part of a pattern of demonizing the South. See Randy Finley, "A Lynching State: Arkansas in the 1890s," in *Bullets and Fire: Lynching and Authority in Arkansas, 1840–1950*, edited by Guy Lancaster (Fayetteville: University of Arkansas Press, 2018).

[88] "Race War Is On: Whites of Arkansas Killing off the Colored Men," *Nebraska State Journal*, March 24, 1899, online at http://yesteryearsnews. wordpress.com/2009/01/19/little-river-county-arkansas-lynchings-1899/ (accessed June 8, 2017).

[89] "Tried to Stir Up Trouble: Duckett Wanted a General Assassination of Whites," *Houston Daily Post*, March 23, 1899, p. 6.

country was aroused." At the George plantation, a few miles into the trip, a mob of 200 men overtook them, took Duckett from the sheriff, and hanged him. Duckett reportedly confessed to the crime before he was killed.[90]

The *Arkansas Gazette* claimed that the area's African Americans were planning a race war but changed their minds when they recognized how angry white citizens were about Stockton's murder, and small groups of whites began roaming local roads in search of additional conspirators. Again, they were apparently helped by friendly local blacks, who gave them the names of twenty-three men who were supposedly involved. By March 23, at least six additional African Americans had been killed, and the *Gazette* reported that "news of a severe race war is looked for hourly."[91] Although the *New York Times* noted that "very little authentic information [could] be gathered" about the situation, newspapers do indicate the names and purported crimes of these victims, six of whom were identified. Moses Jones, who was either hanged or shot, was killed because his wife prepared food for Duckett while he was in hiding. Ed Godwin was killed because he delivered the food to Duckett. Joe King was apparently first beaten and then no doubt killed after he refused to surrender his gun, commenting that Stockton "ought to have been killed sooner, and…that others would be killed before the matter was settled." John Johnson was also whipped and was then reportedly hanged. Joseph Jones and Benjamin Jones were killed for unspecified reasons. One victim, who tried to escape, was shot and thrown into the Red River. Another unnamed victim was found naked in the river bottoms between Rocky Comfort and New Boston, Texas. According to several newspapers, a justice of the peace held an

---

[90] "Murderer Is Mob's Victim," *Atlanta Constitution*, March 22, 1899, p. 2; "Race War Is On: Whites of Arkansas Killing off the Colored Men," *Nebraska State Journal*, March 24, 1899; "Body Filled with Bullets," *Arkansas Gazette*, March 22, 1899, p. 1.

[91] "Race War Planned," *Arkansas Gazette*, March 23, 1899, p. 1; "Seven Negro Men Lynched," *Arkansas Gazette*, March 24, 1899, p. 1.

inquest to look into these deaths and proclaimed that the victims died "by natural causes or were frozen to death. The verdict is regarded as a gruesome joke."[92]

On March 26, the *New York Times* reported that all was quiet and that there were no further signs of trouble. According to the *Times*, "It is impossible to learn how many negroes have really been lynched as nearly all the colored population has fled. The few remaining negroes are still in a state of great excitement. They assert positively that a dozen or more men have been killed in the Red River bottoms, mentioning names of negroes who have disappeared since the lynching of Duckett to substantiate their assertions." The *Mena Star* speculated that most likely "the entire number [23] have been strung up in the thickets."[93]

Although the *Star* asserted that the events in Little River County arose "directly from the assassination of the planter James A. Stockton," it is clear in most accounts that the real fear was black insurrection—a fear reflected in contemporaneous newspaper reports. The *New York Times* called Duckett "a power among the negroes," who had attracted many followers. The *Houston Daily Post* called him "an intelligent negro" with a "strong force of character," which he used energetically to foment racial troubles and organize the area's blacks against the whites. The *Sacramento Record Union* referred to the blacks' careful planning, intended to incite a race war in which "many white men had been marked for victims."[94]

Several weeks after the events in Little River County, the *New York Sun* published an article indicating that there were ten victims. The report ruefully asserted, however, that "not one of those

[92] "Lynchings in Arkansas," *New York Times*, March 25, 1899, p. 4; *Arkansas Gazette*, March 25, 1899, p. 1.

[93] "Lynchings in Arkansas," *New York Times*, March 25, 1899, p. 4; "A Wholesale Lynching," *Mena Star*, March 24, 1899, p. 2.

[94] "Lynchings in Arkansas," *New York Times*, March 25, 1899, p. 4; "Tried to Stir up Trouble: Duckett Wanted a General Assassination of Whites," *Houston Daily Post*, March 23, 1899, p. 6; "A War of Races Rages in Arkansas," *Sacramento Record-Union*, March 24, 1899, p. 1.

reported to be organizing to kill off the whites did anything in the way of defending himself. Hence it is clearly evident that the white men of the section were murdering many defenceless [*sic*] negroes to avenge the death of one white man."[95]

In 1901, Jeff Davis, an avowed racist, became Arkansas's new governor, and violent suppression of blacks gained even greater official sanction. At a rally during his campaign for reelection in 1904, he famously stated that "'nigger' dominion will never prevail in this beautiful Southland of ours, as long as shotguns and rifles lie around loose, and we are able to pull the trigger."[96] Davis was opposed to the enfranchisement of blacks, noting that the black voter was an "ever present eating, cantankerous sore" on American democracy.[97] According to historian Grif Stockley, "Davis was merely the messenger of a racism and white supremacist doctrine that already had become deeply ingrained in the psyche of white Arkansans."[98]

During Davis's tenure as governor, the legislature passed several more laws affecting the rights of African Americans. A 1903 law that relegated black riders to the back of streetcars caused boycotts in Hot Springs, Pine Bluff, and Little Rock. Shortly thereafter, legislators approved a law requiring total segregation of the races in state prisons, even down to their furniture and bedding. It was against this background that another massacre of blacks took place in Arkansas County.

St. Charles Lynching of 1904

In late March 1904, there was another mass lynching, this time near St. Charles in Arkansas County. The violence left thirteen African Americans dead. According to numerous newspaper accounts, there had been trouble near St. Charles for several years.

[95] "Is the South Becoming Barbarous?" *New York Sun*, May 15, 1899, p. 6.
[96] Quoted in Grif Stockley, *Blood in their Eyes: The Elaine Race Massacre of 1919* (Fayetteville: University of Arkansas Press, 2001), 6.
[97] Quoted in Stockley, *Ruled by Race*, 135.
[98] Stockley, *Ruled by Race*, 134.

While African Americans made up only twenty-eight percent of the county's population in 1900, the *New York Times* reported that there were between 200 and 300 whites living in St. Charles at the time of the incident, outnumbered by 500 blacks "scattered about the outskirts of the town and in the timber along the [White] river."[99] Several newspapers, including the *Atlanta Constitution*, reported that there was a history of trouble in the area, with local blacks becoming increasingly "insolent and belligerent."[100] In his memoir, J. M. Henderson Jr. of nearby DeWitt attributed the incident in part to a tough "class of white men" who would drink and gamble with the area's African Americans and then, "when trouble arose...were the first to want to excite prejudice and hard action against the negroes." In addition, starting with the election of 1896, Republicans increased their efforts to control the African American vote. These tactics continued through 1900, and "there a developed a very discourteous attitude on the part of some negroes toward the white people."[101]

The event that touched off the eventual murder of thirteen African Americans was what numerous newspaper reports referred to as "a trivial matter," a "simple brawl," or "a matter of no consequence."[102] Despite the apparently inconsequential roots of the incident, however, the events in St. Charles were later described by newspapers as "wholesale butchery...the greatest in the South" and the "Most Dangerous Riots in [the] State's History."[103]

[99] "War on Negroes for Simple Brawl: Arkansas Whites Begin Slaughter," *New York Times*, April 3, 1904, p. 1.
[100] "Griffin Boys Make Thirteen," *Atlanta Constitution*, March 28, 1904, p. 3.
[101] J. M. Henderson Jr., *Brief Stories of St. Charles in Romance and Tragedy*, quoted in Vinikas, "Specters in the Past," 550.
[102] "In Arkansas a Mob Kills Five Negroes," *Lancaster Ledger* (South Carolina), March 30, 1904, p. 1; "Five Blacks Shot to Death in Arkansas," *Atlanta Constitution*, March 26, 1904, p. 1; "Five Negroes Shot to Death by Mob," *Arkansas Gazette*, March 26, 1904, p. 1; "War on Negroes for Simple Brawl: Arkansas Whites Begin Slaughter," *New York Times*, April 3, 1904, p. 1; "Nine Negroes Shot to Death," *Arkansas Democrat*, March 27, 1904, p. 1.
[103] "Arkansas Race Riot," *Evening Star* (Washington DC), April 4, 1904, p.

The "simple brawl" that supposedly set off the incident occurred in mid-March when a white man named James Searcy and two African American brothers named Henry and Walker Griffin began to argue while drinking and gambling, and the Griffins threatened to hit Searcy over the head with a beer bottle. According to the *Arkansas Gazette*, nothing came of it at the time, but on March 21 the Griffins met Searcy and his brother at Woolfork & Norsworthy's store in St. Charles. Tempers flared again, and one of the Griffin brothers hit the Searcys over the head, knocking both unconscious and leaving one near death. When Deputy Sheriff James Kirkpatrick tried to arrest the Griffins, they knocked him down and escaped in the confusion.[104] According to the *Gazette*, "Further trouble might have been avoided if the negroes had not banded together and defied the authorities, giving as their ultimatum that no white man could arrest them. In fact, the threatening attitude of the negroes was such that the citizens were alarmed." Authorities sent to DeWitt for aid, and additional help began to stream in from a number of towns in the eastern part of Arkansas County.[105]

A reporter from the *Chicago Tribune*, who later visited the scene and whose report was reprinted in the *New York Times*, gave this account:

> As soon as the alarm was sounded, some older African Americans who were on friendly terms with the town's whites came into St. Charles to turn themselves in. Before they were sent back home, they reported that the Griffins were organizing younger African Americans for an insurrection. The reporter asserted, however, that this tale was "an unconscious invention of the frightened and superstitious old negroes," or

9; "Victims of Race War in Arkansas Number Thirteen," *St. Louis Republic*, March 28, 1904, p. 1.
[104] "Five Negroes Shot to Death by Mob," *Arkansas Gazette*, March 26, 1904, p. 1.
[105] "Eleven Negroes Victim of Mob," *Arkansas Gazette*, March 27, 1904, p. 1.

76

at worst only a recounting of "the boasting of a drunken and vicious young black."[106]

Whatever the case, the white citizens of St. Charles were extremely anxious—sure, according to Henderson in his memoir, that the blacks were planning an uprising. In order to protect themselves and their families, they stationed guards around the town and on the roads leading into it. In an effort to apprehend the Griffins, white posses spread out across the area. On Wednesday morning, a posse encountered Randall Flood, Will Baldwin, and Will Madison, and demanded to know where the Griffins were hiding. According to reports, the three refused to tell them anything, drew their pistols, and were promptly shot by posse members. At some point during the search, a posse encountered an elderly African American named Aaron Hinton. He reportedly shot at them from ambush, and he, too, was killed.[107]

These posses began to gather up blacks whom they encountered along the roads and take them back to St. Charles, where they were imprisoned in a black-owned store. Eventually, there were between sixty and seventy African Americans in custody. On Thursday night, a mob surrounded the store, ready, according to Henderson, to "exterminate the negro race." Some shouted for the store to be burned, but cooler heads eventually prevailed. The mob dispersed at midnight, only to gather again at 3:00 a.m. on Friday. They dragged six prisoners from the store, took them to the DeWitt–St. Charles highway, and shot them.[108] Jim Smith, Charley Smith, Mack Baldwin, Abe Bailey, and Garrett Flood (brother of Randall Flood) died instantly.[109] A sixth man, Per-

[106] "War on Negroes for Simple Brawl: Arkansas Whites Begin Slaughter," *New York Times*, April 3, 1904, p. 1.
[107] "Five Negroes Shot to Death by Mob," *Arkansas Gazette*, March 26, 1904, p. 1.
[108] Vinikas, "Specters in the Past," 561.
[109] "Five Negroes Shot to Death by Mob," *Arkansas Gazette*, March 26, 1904, p. 1.

ry Carter, was shot in the leg but played dead and later crawled away. He was found and killed the next morning.[110] According to the *Tribune*'s reporter, these men were chosen because they were "notorious as dissolute and drunken young blacks, who had been leaders in stirring up their fellows through threats of violence."[111] Kellis Johnson, described by the *Gazette* as "the last of the gang of negroes that caused the trouble," was later shot in the northeastern part of the county, bringing the death toll to eleven.[112] At some point, Henry and Walker Griffin were also apprehended and killed, bringing the total of African American victims to thirteen.

Newspaper accounts leave little doubt that these thirteen murders were not the result of a trivial dispute but an attempt to purge the community of African Americans who were viewed as defiant and possibly insurrectionary. The victims were referred to in many newspapers as belligerent, unruly, objectionable, and dangerous. According to the *Gazette*, race war was inevitable when African Americans resisted arrest, believing that their superior numbers gave them "the right or the power to do as they please."[113] As in so many other reputed "uprisings," the result was that there were no white deaths, the only injury occurring when one white picket was slightly wounded by one of his comrades. The supposed rebels, however, sustained heavy casualties at the hands of the whites. In the end, with the most "dangerous" African Americans having been killed, many newspapers, including the *St. Paul Globe*, reported that "the negroes are quiet and attending strictly to their work."[114] Hardly surprising, considering the murderous events of the previous week.

---

[110] "Eleven Negroes Victim of Mob," *Arkansas Gazette*, March 27, 1904, p. 1.

[111] "War on Negroes for Simple Brawl: Arkansas Whites Begin Slaughter," *New York Times*, April 3, 1904, p. 1.

[112] "Eleven Negroes Victim of Mob," *Arkansas Gazette*, March 27, 1904, p. 1.

[113] "In Arkansas County," *Arkansas Gazette*, March 29, 1904, p. 4.

[114] "Race War Still On," *St. Paul Globe*, March 28, 1904, p. 1.

The Stage Set for the Elaine Massacre

This study makes it clear that following the Civil War, Southern whites often killed African Americans whom they believed, at least upon reflection, to be involved in race riots or planning insurrection. The result was almost always that no whites were killed, no white property was destroyed, and numerous African Americans were killed or incarcerated. Scholars have given many reasons for this phenomenon.

Historians George C. Rable and Ryan Poe, for example, attribute some such incidents to whites' attempts to prevent blacks from voting. Rable asserts that anxious whites interpreted black political meetings as precursors to race wars, causing imaginary reports of black insurrection to sweep the South during Reconstruction-era elections.[115] Poe maintains that mob action against blacks between Reconstruction and the passing of Jim Crow legislation was partly a result of increased African American political participation. Whites attempted not only to stop African Americans from voting, but to remove black officials from office once they were elected.[116] Some newspaper reports indicated that this was the case, for example, when Robert Unsill took a group of armed African Americans to vote in Hampton in 1892.

Other scholars have noted the importance of economic factors. Some mass lynchings occurred in places where blacks were fairly prosperous and posed a threat to white landowners. This may have been the case in Howard County in 1883.[117] Others were apparently rooted in labor disputes, like the incident in Lee County in 1891.

---

[115] George C. Rable, *But There Was No Peace: The Role of Violence in the Politics of Reconstruction* (Athens: University of Georgia Press, 2007), 71.
[116] Ryan Poe, "Race Riots," *Encyclopedia of Arkansas History & Culture*, http://www.encyclopediaofarkansas.net/encyclopedia/entry-detail.aspx?entryID=5170 (accessed May 3, 2017).
[117] Peggy S. Lloyd, "The Howard County Race Riot of 1883," *Encyclopedia of Arkansas History & Culture*, http://www.encyclopediaofarkansas.net/encyclopedia/entry-detail.aspx?entryID=3663 (accessed March 19, 2017).

Newspaper accounts of some incidents attribute the events to violence perpetrated by African Americans against whites. The violence in Howard County, for example, purportedly arose directly from the murder of Thomas Wyatt. In Lee County, one reason cited was the murder of Tom Miller. In Little River County, the cause was reportedly the murder of James Stockton by General Duckett. In St. Charles, the cause most often cited was a brawl between a white man named Searcy and two African Americans, Henry and Walker Griffin.

These observations, however, apply only to precipitating events and not to deeper causes. As Frederick Douglass asserted in 1895, Southern lynchings were frequently due to fears of black insurrection and attempts to "secure the absolute rule of the Anglo-Saxon race."[118] Ida B. Wells-Barnett made similar claims: "The first excuse given to the civilized world for the murder of unoffending Negroes was the necessity of the white man to repress and stamp out alleged 'race riots.' For years immediately succeeding the war there was an appalling slaughter of colored people, and the wires usually conveyed to northern people and the world the intelligence, first, that an insurrection was being planned by Negroes which, a few hours later, would prove to have been vigorously resisted by white men, and controlled with a resulting loss of several killed and wounded."[119]

While Douglass and Wells-Barnett were speaking about the Reconstruction era, their assumptions apply to later mass lynchings as well, including the Elaine Massacre. According to historian Mark Summers, "A war of the races was seen as always imminent....And that fear remained a persistent part of the white psyche for long after Reconstruction was under way." In fact, these insurrections, supposedly so carefully planned, never came

---

[118] Frederick Douglass, "Why is the Negro Lynched?," 12–13.
[119] Ida B. Wells-Barnett, *The Red Record Tabulated Statistics and Alleged Causes of Lynching in the United States* (Hamburg, Germany: Tredition, 2012).

to fruition. The specter of them, however, gave whites an excuse for widespread violence.[120]

An examination of these mass lynchings, which spanned over twenty years, supports these claims, revealing that whatever the putative reason, the underlying cause was almost always the fear of black insurrection. While Robert Shaver's initial report on the 1883 lynchings in Howard County indicated that the "whole thing hinged upon the killing of Wyatt," his second report attributed the rampage to a "deep-seated" African American plot that, had it not erupted prematurely, would have resulted in "nothing less than an insurrection." According to his account, area blacks had an almost military organization and were armed with a list of white targets.[121]

In the 1891 incident in Lee County, newspaper reports often attributed the events to a dispute over wages, resulting in the murder of Tom Miller. But they soon turned to the theme of insurrection. On September 29, the *Arkansas Gazette* reported that a mob of blacks was "carrying terror" across the county.[122] By October 3, the *Gazette* was asserting that the massacre occurred because "the blood of the white planters, whom ruin stared in the face, whose homes and vital interests were at the mercy of the brutal mob, began running, hissing hot, through their veins."[123]

One pretext given for the Hampton Race War in 1892 was the fact that Robert Unsill had taken a group of armed African Americans to the polls and demanded they be allowed to vote. Contemporary accounts indicate, however, that the underlying fear was one of a black uprising in response to numerous incidents of whitecapping in the county. On September 21, the *Arkansas*

[120] Mark Wahlgren Summers, *The Ordeal of the Reunion: A New History of Reconstruction* (Chapel: University of North Carolina Press, 2014), 66.
[121] "The Uprising of the Negroes in Hempstead County," *Arkansas Gazette*, August 12, 1883, p. 5; "Nipped in the Bud," *Arkansas Gazette*, August 14, 1883, p. 5.
[122] "Negroes in Arms," *Arkansas Gazette*, September 29, 1891, p. 1.
[123] "Force against Force," *Arkansas Gazette*, October 3, 1891, p. 4.

Gazette attributed the incident to the fact that Jim Harrison was organizing a group of "bad niggers" who were threatening to "kill every white man, woman and child in the county." According to the *Evening Star*, the county had been turned into a "region of anarchy and death," with roving blacks "armed to the teeth and muttering threats of the most incendiary nature."[124]

The events in Little River County in 1899 were purportedly precipitated by the murder of James Stockton by General Duckett. However, there had been an increase in murders, thefts, and fights in the county, and most whites blamed the African American population for this. Some blacks had been "severely dealt with" by vigilantes who chose to take the law into their own hands.[125] Against this background, several of Stockton's "trusted" black workers told him that another of his workers, General Duckett, was plotting insurrection. Stockton threatened Duckett with arrest, which resulted in Stockton's murder. Newspapers quickly reported that Duckett was urging other African Americans to join him in a "general assassination of whites." Even though Duckett's supposed followers had disbanded after the murder, small groups of whites continued to roam the roads searching for his supposed co-conspirators.

A conflict between James Searcy and brothers Henry and Walker Griffin supposedly sparked events near St. Charles in 1904. But many newspapers asserted that blacks in the area had been increasingly belligerent during recent years, and that the Griffins "had organized the younger negroes, who are mostly members of a secret society....into an army of invasion."[126] On March 27, the *Arkansas Gazette* reported calm in the area, the "most dan-

---

[124] "Race War in Arkansas," *Evening Star* (Washington DC), September 20, 1892, p. 3.
[125] "Race War Is On: Whites of Arkansas Killing off the Colored Men," *Nebraska State Journal*, March 24, 1899.
[126] "War on Negroes for Simple Brawl: Arkansas Whites Begin Slaughter," *New York Times*, April 3, 1904, p. 1.

gerous negroes" having been slain.[127] Two days later, the *Gazette* offered the following justification for the events in St. Charles: "Wherever the negroes take the position that they won't submit to arrest, that their weight of numbers gives them the right or the power to do as they please, a conflict between the two races is inevitable."[128]

In her memoir about life in the Arkansas Delta, historian Margaret Jones Bolsterli expressed what may be the cause of the prevailing fear of black insurrection across Arkansas and the South:

> I wonder if the traditional southern white fear of violence at the hands of blacks is at bottom really a belief that the whites deserve it, that one night the blacks will have taken all the abuse they can stand and will simply rise as one and murder the whites in their beds. On the face of it, this is a fairly logical explanation, since the whites routinely have committed more violence on blacks than the reverse. The entire social structure from the time of slavery on has been organized for an easy assault on black people.[129]

Writing in 1920, journalist Herbert Jacob Seligmann expressed a similar sentiment, noting that the "dread of Negro insurrection…[had] at one time or another darkened every hearthstone in the South." He added: "Uneasy lies the Southerner's head whose ascendancy, like the king's, depends upon repression."[130]

As a writer for *Cayton's Weekly* declared following the Elaine Massacre, readers of national newspapers would conclude that Southern whites were correct in being constantly on the alert and using "whatever force that seemed necessary to prevent the al-

[127] "Eleven Negroes Victim of Mob," *Arkansas Gazette*, March 27, 1904, p. 1.
[128] "In Arkansas County," *Arkansas Gazette*, March 29, 1904, p. 4.
[129] Margaret Jones Bolsterli, *Born in the Delta: Reflections on the Making of a Southern White Sensibility*; quoted in Grif Stockley, *Ruled by Race*, 62–63.
[130] Herbert Jacob Seligmann, *The Negro Faces America* (New York: Harper and Brothers, 1920), 69.

most barbaric Negro from becoming a public menace to society in most of the states of our own sunny South." The author went on to note that only one side of events, the white man's side, was reported in the press, and "if at any time colored men defend themselves when attacked by mobs, the daily press pronounces it a 'negro uprising.'" The reality, however, was quite different. These supposed uprisings were "no uprising[s] at all, but only a couple or more of the Negroes refusing to be bulldozed to death; and after having killed the 'smart neggers' and severely whipped a score or more of those who refused to help them kill or punish their brethren, the whites would return to their homes and praise the Lord with one accord."[131]

An examination of the historical record of late nineteenth- and early twentieth-century Arkansas makes it clear that whites harbored an entrenched fear of black rebellion and, interpreting every conflict through the lens of this fear, responded to their feelings with widespread violence against African Americans. The mass killings in Howard County, Lee County, Calhoun County, Little River County, and Arkansas County represent the logical outcome of the simmering fear and anger that were prevalent across the state, and across the South as a whole. The violence would reach its peak in 1919, with the murders of over 200 African Americans at Elaine in Phillips County.

---

[131] "Fake Negro Uprising," *Cayton's Weekly* (Seattle, WA), October 11, 1919, p. 1.

Chapter 3

With Intent to Destroy: What Labels Can Reveal about the Elaine Event

Guy Lancaster and Richard Buckelew

What happened at Elaine? This question has two different, but interrelated, meanings. First, there is the question of the order of events, cause and effect, exactly who did exactly what and why—everything the historian hopes to uncover. However, this question can also relate to how this particular occurrence of racial violence should be classified as a social event. Reporting at the time tended to use the term "riot" or "race riot" to describe what happened at Elaine, and some of the earliest historical analyses followed suit, as with Bessie Ferguson's 1927 master's thesis, titled simply "The Elaine Race Riot."[1] Such descriptions were employed by newspapers to signify ostensible revolts against white authority—suspected "insurrections" or "uprisings"—but scholarship has long rejected such one-sided views while retaining the terminology as a useful shorthand for such large-scale violence. Historian Grif Stockley, in 2001, employed the term "massacre" to describe what happened at Elaine, and this term has since caught on, especially among those who wish to emphasize the one-sided nature of the violence—by whites, against African Americans.[2] In 2015, the Equal Justice Initiative released a report, *Lynching in America: Confronting the Legacy of Racial Terror*, that counted the dead at Elaine as victims of lynching, thus drawing parallels to a phenomenon—and a word—

---

[1] Bessie Ferguson, "The Elaine Race Riot" (Master's thesis, George Peabody College for Teachers, now Peabody College of Education and Human Development at Vanderbilt University, 1927).

[2] Grif Stockley, *Blood in Their Eyes: The Elaine Race Massacres of 1919* (Fayetteville: University of Arkansas Press, 2001).

that has significant evocative power, given that the term "lynch-ing" has been employed not only as a category of violence but also as a term of moral opprobrium.[3]

So what happened at Elaine? Was it a race riot, a massacre, a lynching, or something else? Actually, none of these terms are mutually exclusive—there is plenty of overlap between them, and it is not the aim of this chapter to make the case for one over an-other. Instead, we intend to examine what these and other labels can reveal about the nature of the violence that occurred in south-ern Phillips County in 1919 and, thereby, also reveal the continu-ities between that event and others across the nation and world.

Lynching

What exactly constitutes a lynching? The origins of this term date back to the American Revolution, if not earlier, yet there is little consensus on a precise definition. In 1905, James Cutler published the first book-length study of lynching, in which he de-fines lynching as "an illegal and summary execution at the hands of a mob, or a number of persons, who have in some degree the public opinion of the community behind them."[4] Writing as a wit-ness to the lynching period, Cutler stated that "popular justifica-tion is the *sine qua non* of lynching."[5] It should be no surprise that two of his contemporaries—Jessie Daniel Ames, founder of the Association of Southern Women for the Prevention of Lynching (ASWPL), and anti-lynching activist Ida B. Wells-Barnett—share a similar definition of lynching, arguing that eliminating commu-nity support was key to preventing lynchings.[6] Such community

---

[3] Equal Justice Initiative, *Lynching in America: Confronting the Legacy of Racial Terror*, 3rd edition, https://lynchinginamerica.eji.org/report/ (accessed January 9, 2018).
[4] James Elbert Cutler, *Lynch Law: An Investigation into the History of Lynching in the United States* (New York: Longmans, Green, & Co.), 276.
[5] Cutler, *Lynch Law*, 276.
[6] Christopher Waldrep, "War of Words: The Controversy over the Definition of Lynching, 1899–1940," *Journal of Southern History* 66 (February 2000): 77, 76.

support for the violence was certainly on display when it comes to the Elaine event; not only did local elites approve of the mob action, but the governor himself led troops to the site and formally signed off on the local response. Swedish social economist Gunnar Myrdal, too, sees community approval as a key characteristic but also advances "white guilt" over the rape of slave women, along with boredom, as contributing to lynching.[7]

A number of lynching scholars cite a definition that is often improperly credited to the National Association for the Advancement of Colored People (NAACP) based on a conference at Tuskegee in 1940 attended by representatives from the NAACP, the ASWPL, and the International Labor Defense (ILD). During the conference, the group managed to agree tentatively on a definition consisting of the following four primary conditions:

- there must be evidence that a person was killed;
- the person must have met his death illegally;
- three or more persons must have participated in the killing;
- the group must have acted under the pretext of service to justice or tradition.[8]

The NAACP was particularly active in the anti-lynching movement and routinely published lynching statistics, and what this definition provides is specificity based on years of research. In 1992, sociologists Stewart Tolnay and E. M. Beck published *A Festival of Violence: An Analysis of Southern Lynchings, 1882–1930*, a detailed statistical study of lynching in the South, based upon this definition of lynching. Their findings, along with the data that it was based upon, contributed to the increase in

[7] Gunnar Myrdal, *An American Dilemma: The Negro Problem and Modern Democracy* (New York: Harper & Brothers Publishers), 562, 563.
[8] Christopher Waldrep, *The Many Faces of Judge Lynch: Extralegal Violence and Punishment in America* (New York: Palgrave Macmillan, 2002), 2. After the conference, each of these rival organizations abandoned the definition because they found it incongruent with their organizational goals.

lynching-related studies.[9] Most current scholarship on lynching is based to some degree on this definition of lynching, even as scholars recognize the shortcomings of such a definition. Consider historian Christopher Waldrep's 2002 book, *The Many Faces of Judge Lynch: Extralegal Violence and Punishment in America*, in which he contends that the evolution of the word "lynching" has rendered it undefinable: "There is no single behavior that can be called 'lynching.' Any attempt to impose a definition on such a diverse, subtle, and complex reality will inevitably miss the point."[10]

Scholars have long interrogated the relationship between lynchings and so-called race riots. In *An American Dilemma*, Myrdal rejects the use of "riot" to describe incidents involving "the killing and beating of a large number of Negroes." He considers such events, instead, as "magnified, or mass, lynchings," arguing that "its effects are those of a lynching."[11] Historians Gilles Vandal, Robert Zangrando, and Manfred Berg advance more expansive definitions of lynchings to include non-lethal acts of violence that were often characteristic of race riots. Vandal, for instance, includes non-lethal punishments, such as whippings, as a way to account for Reconstruction-era violence committed by vigilance committees in post–Civil War Louisiana.[12] For Zangrando and Berg, the reference to non-lethal lynching is the acknowledgement that the term "lynching" was also used to describe non-lethal punishments during the late eighteenth and early nineteenth centuries. Of particular relevance to Elaine is how both authors interpret the term "riot" and its relationship to the phenomenon of lynching. Berg regards riots as "large scale collective violence in

[9] Stewart E. Tolnay and E. M. Beck, *A Festival of Violence: An Analysis of Southern Lynchings, 1882–1930* (Urbana: University of Illinois Press, 1992), 260.
[10] Waldrep, *The Many Faces of Judge Lynch*, 182.
[11] Myrdal, *An American Dilemma*, 566.
[12] Gilles Vandal, *Rethinking Southern Violence: Homicides in Post–Civil War Louisiana, 1866–1844* (Columbus: Ohio State University Press, 2000).

which the participants make no claims to be agents of justice."[13] In the Elaine incident, however, both sides claimed to pursue justice. African Americans were seeking economic justice through the legal system, and the initial posse, white vigilante groups, and the U.S. troops all claimed to seek justice by eliminating, through force, the so-called "insurrection."[14] Zangrando, in contrast to Berg, finds "striking similarities" between lynchings and riots: "Like lynchings, riots often originated in rumors and false accusations against members of the black community." In addition, outside authorities called in to restore order would often "harass and punish blacks" or side with whites and fight against blacks.[15] More recently, Ashraf Rushdy, a professor of English, has advocated the adoption of a two separate definitions of lynching—one "specific" and one "capacious" definition.[16] He reasons that the specific definition would allow scholars to account for variations between cases, while the capacious definition would more fully encompass the "continuity" between cases over time. Rushdy argues that the existing definitions of lynching are inherently flawed because the meaning of the term varies so considerably over time. He views most race riots as "massacres" and finds that they "differ from lynchings only in that they have multiple victims and occur in more widespread terrain."[17]

Lynching was a characteristic feature of race relations in Arkansas dating back to 1836 and lasting until 1936. During that period, a recorded 276 black Arkansans died as a result of lynching.[18] Some of the circumstances of those lynchings differed very

---

[13] Manfred Berg, *Popular Justice: A History of Lynching in America* (Chicago: Ivan R. Dee), ix.

[14] "General Uprising Had Been Planned Says Correspondent," *Arkansas Democrat*, October 3, 1919, p. 1.

[15] Robert L. Zangrando, *The NAACP Crusade Against Lynching, 1909–1950* (Philadelphia: Temple University Press, 1980), 8.

[16] Ashraf Rushdy, *American Lynching* (New Haven: Yale University Press, 2012), 18.

[17] Rushdy, *American Lynching*, 21.

[18] Brent E. Riffel, "Lynching," *Encyclopedia of Arkansas History & Culture*, http://www.encyclopediaofarkansas.net/encyclopedia/entry-detail.aspx?en-

little with what happened at Elaine in 1919. Consider the Cotton Pickers Strike of 1891 in Lee County. On September 20, black cotton pickers organized by Ben Patterson of Memphis, Tennessee, demanded a wage increase from their employer, Colonel H. P. Rogers, after they learned that another local landowner, J. F. Frank, claimed that he would be willing to pay as much as a dollar per hundred pounds of cotton if necessary to secure the labor he needed. This was double the standard rate of fifty cents per hundred pounds. When Rogers refused, the pickers went on strike. On September 25, two cotton pickers were killed during a violent conflict between strikers and those who had remained on the job. This prompted the sheriff to form a posse to apprehend Patterson and the striking workers. On September 28, the violence continued when two strikers killed Tom Miller, plantation manager for J. F. Frank, and other strikers burned down a cotton gin. The strikers attempted to flee the area, but the posse cornered most of them on Cat Island, managing to capture nine and kill two. A mob, described only as masked men, took the nine captured strikers and hanged them. Ben Patterson was recognized attempting to escape onboard a steamboat and was killed. By the time the strike ended, a total of fifteen African Americans lay dead and six had been jailed. While the numbers involved in this case are much smaller, the actions undertaken by these black workers—and the violent response on the part of white authorities—were similar to what happened at Elaine.[19] This event meets the definitions of lynching outlined above, but it also exhibits the characteristics of a race riot, a phenomenon discussed in further detail below.

In 1899, another hybrid lynching/riot took place in Little River County in which the local white population claimed that local blacks were plotting a "race war."[20] The incident began on March

tryID=346 (accessed January 25, 2018).

[19] William F. Holmes, "The Arkansas Cotton Pickers Strike of 1891 and the Demise of the Colored Farmers' Alliance," *Arkansas Historical Quarterly* 32 (Summer 1973): 107–113.

[20] Randy Finley, "A Lynching State: Arkansas in the 1890s," in *Bullets and*

18, when planter James Stockton threatened one of his African American workers, General Duckett, with violence if he refused to pay his debt. It was rumored that Duckett had a history of organizing his fellow workers, and this may have been an underlying impetus for Stockton's violent threats. Duckett went home to retrieve his shotgun, and then returned and killed Stockton before going into hiding. Local whites immediately claimed that this was the beginning of an "insurrection" organized by Duckett, and his thirty-three co-conspirators.[21] Bands of local whites scoured the countryside searching for the conspirators, killing them wherever they found them. On March 21, Duckett surrendered, and the sheriff returned him to the scene of the crime before heading toward the jail, when a large mob took Duckett and lynched him, leaving his bullet-riddled body hanging from a tree. By March 24, the *Arkansas Gazette* reported that seven African Americans had been lynched, though some of these took place in Texas. While the exact details of the case vary, local whites again used the claim of an insurrection or race war as an excuse to lynch blacks attempting to organize. With the rumors of organizing, followed by a demonstration of mass lynching by local whites, this case also exhibits characteristics of both a lynching and a riot.

In 1904 an even more deadly example of a lynching/riot occurred in St. Charles, Arkansas. On March 21, a white man named James Searcy was gambling with an African American named Griffin when a disagreement led to Griffin assaulting Searcy. A policeman responded and arrested Griffin for assault, but Griffin became frightened, hitting the officer before grabbing his gun and fleeing the scene.[22] Although the details of the case are un-

Fire: Lynching and Authority in Arkansas, 1840–1950, edited by Guy Lancaster (Fayetteville: University of Arkansas Press, 2018), 82.
[21] "Seven Negro Men Lynched," *Arkansas Gazette,* March 24, 1899, p. 1; Finley, "A Lynching State," 83; Nancy Snell Griffith, "Little River County Race War of 1899," *Encyclopedia of Arkansas History & Culture,* http://www.encyclopediaofarkansas.net/encyclopedia/entry-detail.aspx?-search=1&entryID=7062 (accessed January 7, 2018).
[22] "Eleven Negroes Victims of Mob," *Arkansas Gazette,* March 27, 1904, p.

clear, with accounts varying considerably, what seemed like a fairly simple assault quickly turned into a mass lynching as local African Americans banded together and refused to help the white posses find Griffin. Local whites, combined with posses from surrounding towns, interpreted the solidarity of local African Americans as a sign of a possible uprising, which they used as an excuse to kill a number of African Americans and drive many more out of town. This case reveals striking similarities to the Elaine incident. Characterized by newspapers as a "race war," the alignment of African Americans against the white community was deemed an unacceptable threat that justified mass lynching and terrorization.[23]

Pogrom / Race Riot

As author Robert Whitaker notes, some black newspapers described what happened at Elaine as a "pogrom," a word typically associated with anti-Jewish massacres, especially in Russia.[24] However, the category of "pogrom" has not been subjected to much critical inquiry outside that narrow sphere. Indeed, Donald L. Horowitz, a specialist on ethnic conflict, asserts that the category can easily be subsumed by that of the deadly ethnic riot (discussed below): "If *pogrom* is taken to mean a massacre of helpless people, then it obviously connotes something about the situation of the targets and the outcome of the violence. Since my definition of ethnic riot does not turn on the outcome or retaliatory capacity of the target group, what others may call a pogrom I shall call a riot if the other definitional properties are present."[25]

1.

[23] "13 Negroes Were Slain: Wholesale Killing Occurred in Arkansas Co. Race War Last Week," *Arkansas Democrat*, March 29, 1904, p. 5; Vincent Vinikas, "Thirteen Dead at Saint Charles: Arkansas's Most Lethal Lynching and the Abrogation of Equal Protection," in Lancaster, ed., *Bullets and Fire*, 103–129; *Chicago Tribune*, April 3, 1904, pp., 1, 2.

[24] Robert Whitaker, *On the Laps of Gods: The Red Summer of 1919 and the Struggle for Justice That Remade a Nation* (New York: Crown, 2008), 157.

[25] Donald L. Horowitz, *The Deadly Ethnic Riot* (Berkeley: University of

Moreover, the idea that the victims in the Elaine Massacre were entirely helpless, which is built into the definition of "pogrom," has been challenged by a number of scholars. As Jeannie Whayne, in a review essay on Whitaker's book, asserts, "The positioning of black union men as *merely* the objects of white violence can seem to minimize the challenge they offered." She adds: "The fact is that the black union organizers were men, *southern* men. They were angry over their treatment, they understood the seriousness of the actions they were taking, they were familiar with guns, and they were ready to use them."[26] Historian David F. Krugler puts the armed black response to planter aggression in the context of other instances of collective anti-black violence that occurred in 1919, during which black World War I veterans used their skills and training to mobilize for armed self-defense, noting that share-cropper Frank Moore, despite a lack of military experience, "was emulating the black men who had used their army training to fend off white mobs in Bisbee, Washington, Chicago, and Knoxville."[27]

One scholar who has used the term "pogrom" is historian Charles L. Lumpkins, author of the 2008 book *American Pogrom: The East St. Louis Race Riot and Black Politics*. He describes that July 1917 event as "an American pogrom, or ethnic cleansing, in which officials directed the organized, physical destruction of a racially defined community."[28] However, applying the term in such a way to the events that occurred in Phillips County in 1919 would be misguided, for it was control, not cleansing, that the white population sought; indeed, driving away the black labor force at the very time cotton was to be harvested would have been disastrous. Numerous cases of violence aimed at extirpating a black popula-

California Press, 2001), 20.

[26] Jeannie Whayne, "Black Farmers in the Red Autumn: A Review Essay," *Arkansas Historical Quarterly* 68 (Autumn 2009): 331.

[27] David F. Krugler, *1919, the Year of Racial Violence: How African Americans Fought Back* (New York: Cambridge University Press, 2015), 172.

[28] Charles L. Lumpkins, *American Pogrom: The East St. Louis Race Riot and Black Politics* (Athens: Ohio University Press, 2008), 8.

tion did occur in Arkansas, but this was not one of them.[29]

The term "race riot" is typically employed to describe occurrences in the United States that fall under the umbrella of what Horowitz dubs the "deadly ethnic riot," defined as "an intense, sudden, though not wholly unplanned, lethal attack by civilian members of one ethnic group on civilian members of another ethnic group, the victims chosen because of their group membership."[30] In the specifically American context, race riots are, according to political scientist Ann V. Collins, "rational, extralegal, relatively short eruptions of white-on-black violence aimed at influencing social change."[31] This term, however, is not without controversy. Although Krugler employs it for reasons of style, he prefers to describe such phenomena as "antiblack collective violence" on the grounds that the term "race riot implies that rioters of all races were equally responsible for the violence." In addition, he argues, "the word *riot* also suggests spontaneity" rather than the "deliberate, methodical, and purposeful" nature of the incidents in his study.[32] Collins, despite her own use of the term, emphasizes that race riots should not be viewed as completely spontaneous acts "because white individuals mired in a culture committed to hate, destruction, and the annihilation of the African American race carried them out so deliberately."[33] Indeed, she emphasizes in her study the macro-level conditions that facilitate the turn toward violence at the local level, stating that three conditions must exist for a riot to occur: "certain *structural factors*—primarily demographic, economic, labor, political, legal, social, and institutional features; *cultural framing*, or actions and discourse by both whites and blacks to further their own causes; and a *precipitating event*,

[29] For a study of such violence, see Guy Lancaster, *Racial Cleansing in Arkansas, 1883–1924: Politics, Land, Labor, and Criminality* (Lanham, MD: Lexington Books, 2014).
[30] Horowitz, *The Deadly Ethnic Riot*, 1.
[31] Ann V. Collins, *All Hell Broke Loose: American Race Riots from the Progressive Era through World War II* (Santa Barbara, CA: Praeger, 2012), xvi.
[32] Krugler, *1919, the Year of Racial Violence*, 11.
[33] Collins, *All Hell Broke Loose*, xvi.

the immediate spark that ignites the violence."[34]

According to Horowitz, the riot episode consists of four components. First is rumor, specifically "rumors of aggression inflicted *by* the target group," which are typically employed "in setting a crowd on a course of mass violence *against* the target group."[35] Such rumors help to justify the violence that is about to occur. Next, there is the stage of the lull, a brief interval of time that "occurs mainly in cases where the last precipitant comes on suddenly and the question is what to make of it," although if the precipitating event is sufficiently grave and sudden, the lull will be comparatively short.[36] Third comes the period of time when the would-be rioters arm and prepare themselves for violence, followed, finally, by the atrocity killing, when loosened restrains combine with group identification to lower the inhibitions and increase the likelihood of brutality.[37] Of course, these stages also mirror the general evolution of a lynching event; as author Jan Voogd writes, "Both lynching mobs and rioting mobs used precipitating events as excuses to try to justify their violence, and in both cases these excuses were usually an alleged crime of social trespass of some sort of black individual." Too, both events identified as lynchings and those dubbed riots were inflamed by rumor and sensational newspaper coverage that occurred between the precipitating event and the violent end. However, as Voogd writes, "The direct target of a lynching was the individual(s), and the community was targeted indirectly. By contrast, a riot targeted the community directly."[38]

What happened at Elaine easily meets either Horowitz's or Collins's definitions of a deadly ethnic riot/race riot: the structural factors of Jim Crow Arkansas that make the position of black

[34] Collins, *All Hell Broke Loose*, 5.
[35] Horowitz, *The Deadly Ethnic Riot*, 79.
[36] Horowitz, *The Deadly Ethnic Riot*, 89.
[37] Horowitz, *The Deadly Ethnic Riot*, 116–117.
[38] Jan Voogd, *Race Riots and Resistance: The Red Summer of 1919* (New York: Peter Lang, 2008), 19.

sharecroppers particularly weak vis-à-vis that of white landowners and authorities; a cultural framing that includes not only racist
beliefs about the nature and intentions of African Americans but
also a large dose of anti-communist paranoia that casts a particularly sinister shadow over the rumors surrounding black mobilization; and the precipitating event that was the shootout at Hoop
Spur. However, the Elaine event could also be described as a massacre, a phenomenon explored next.

Massacre

Historians Philip G. Dwyer and Lyndall Ryan have worked to
provide some sound conceptual basis for the study of massacres
as independent from the broader phenomenon of genocide, giv-
en that while the latter cannot feasibly occur without the former,
massacres can indeed take place outside the context of genocide.
Noting the lack of a widely accepted legal definition, along with
the lack of consensus on what constitutes a massacre (the number of victims necessary to qualify, the role of the state, the time
period over which something can constitute one such act of violence), Dwyer and Ryan advance the following description of a
massacre:

> The killing by one group of people by another group of peo-
> ple, regardless of whether the victims are helpless or not,
> regardless of age or sex, race, religion and language, and re-
> gardless of political, cultural, racial, religious or economic
> motives for the killing. The killing can be either driven by
> official state policy or can occur as a result of the state's lack
> of control over those groups or collectives on the ground.
> Massacres, in other words, can occur with or without official
> state sanctions although the state, especially in the colonial
> context, often turns a blind eye to the killing of indigenous
> peoples by groups of settler-colonizers that are geographical-
> ly removed from the centre of power and over which it has
> little or no control. The massacre is limited in time, that is, it

takes place over hours or days, not months and years, and is generally confined in one geographical place.[39]

Massacres share a number of common features. For starters, they "are, fundamentally, a masculine enterprise. They are often a brutal but short event, aimed at intimidating the survivors."[40] As separate from a case of genocidal violence, a massacre does not aim for the extermination of an entire population but rather a number of people in a geographically limited space, primarily for the purposes of sowing terror among the population at large. Too, the act of killing involves "the direct physical intervention of the perpetrator."[41] Massive aerial bombardment, for example, would be excluded from this definition. Finally, while massacres are often premised upon specific local grievances, "they invariably require a higher authority to either approve or to turn a blind eye to the killings."[42] This can often result in a cover-up from those in positions of power, as well as the failure to punish the perpetrators of such massacres, even when their violence runs directly counter to the law, for example.

Military operations could easily produce massacres. For example, during the April 18, 1864, Engagement at Poison Spring in southwestern Arkansas, Confederate forces murdered black Union troops, who were members of the First Kansas Colored Infantry, after their capture. As one Confederate soldier wrote shortly afterward, "I have seen enough myself to know it is correct our men [are determined] not to take negro prisoners, and if all of the negroes could have seen what occured [sic] that day, they would stay at home."[43] Historian Gregory J. W. Urwin has

---

[39] Philip G. Dwyer and Lyndall Ryan, "The Massacre and History," in *Theatres of Violence: Massacre, Mass Killing and Atrocity throughout History*, edited by Philip G. Dwyer and Lyndall Ryan (New York: Berghahn Books, 2012), xv.

[40] Dwyer and Ryan, "The Massacre and History," xv.

[41] Dwyer and Ryan, "The Massacre and History," xvi.

[42] Dwyer and Ryan, "The Massacre and History," xvii.

[43] Quoted in Mark K. Christ, "Who Wrote the Poison Spring Letter?" in

described the "Poison Spring Massacre" as "the worst war crime ever committed on Arkansas soil."[44] Dwyer and Ryan's groundbreaking 2012 edited volume devoted to the subject of massacre, *Theatres of Violence: Massacre, Mass Killing and Atrocity throughout History*, surveys a number of events that occurred in a military context such as the Peloponnesian War or anti-communist violence in 1960s Indonesia. Some of these massacres were directed at enemy soldiers no longer in a position to fight, such as the Katyn Forest Massacre of 1940, in which Soviet forces killed Polish prisoners of war, while others were perpetrated by soldiers against civilian populations, such as the 1870 Blackfeet Massacre, in which soldiers of the U.S. Army killed 173 men, women, and children of the Pikuni (Blackfeet) band.

Just as the events at Elaine meet the definition of a riot, so, too, do they meet this definition of massacre. The action took place over a limited time span of just a few days within the geographically limited area of southern Phillips County, and the reports of killing emphasize direct physical intervention, acts perpetrated exclusively by men. While resulting from specific local grievances, the violence was essentially permitted by higher authorities, as local and state officials worked to cover up the nature of the atrocities that occurred; indeed, if Stockley is correct in his view that Camp Pike soldiers participated in the massacre, then there is also a federal component to the cover-up.[45] As Alex J. Bellamy, a professor of peace and conflict studies, notes, massacres are violations of the norm of civil immunity, the "moral belief, shared by most of the world's major ethical traditions and embedded in different parts of international law, that it is wrong to intentionally

"All Cut to Pieces and Gone to Hell": The Civil War, Race Relations, and the Battle of Poison Spring, edited by Mark K. Christ (Little Rock: August House, 2003), 100.
[44] Gregory J. W. Urwin, "Poison Spring and Jenkins' Ferry: Racial Atrocities during the Camden Expedition," in Christ, ed., *"All Cut to Pieces and Gone to Hell"*, 125.
[45] Stockley, *Blood in Their Eyes*, 34–60.

kill people who are neither members of the armed forces nor criminals legitimately convicted of crimes that carry the death penalty."[46] Of course, the norm of civilian immunity does not always inhibit atrocity because, as Bellamy argues, "perpetrators might calculate that the risk of potential punishment is outweighed by the utility of mass killing. This, in turn, suggests that they believe they can secure *sufficient legitimacy* and avoid punishment."[47] As far as the Elaine Massacre goes, the perpetrators were, indeed, correct on this count, and the impunity with which they acted did succeed in producing an environment of terror—our next subject.

Terror / Terrorism

Perhaps no terms analyzed in this chapter seem more subjective than do "terror" and "terrorism." Indeed, the over-application of these terms for rhetorical advantage has practically drained them of meaning over the last two decades. As anthropologists Andrew Strathern and Pamela J. Stewart note, "Whereas 'terror' is a term that refers to an emotional response, even though its more specific components, manifestations, and triggers may vary culturally and historically, 'terrorism' at one evokes political rhetoric," the term being used to delegitimize certain violent actions while legitimizing the response to those actions.[48] However, not all acts of violence are equal producers of terror, as a critical component for the production of terror is the imagination and expectations about the future. Terror, in fact, is based on an interlocking feedback between memory and anticipation, the same nexus that makes possible continuity in human interaction generally. Here, however, the feedback is based on a sense of rupture.

---

[46] Alex J. Bellamy, *Massacres and Morality: Mass Atrocities in an Age of Civilian Immunity* (New York: Oxford University Press, 2012), 17.
[47] Bellamy, *Massacres and Morality*, 28.
[48] Andrew Strathern and Pamela J. Stewart, "Introduction: Terror, the Imagination, and Cosmology," in *Terror and Violence: Imagination and the Unimaginable*, edited by Andrew Strathern, Pamela J. Stewart, and Neil L. Whitehead (Ann Arbor, MI: Pluto Press, 2006), 3.

Terror consists precisely of intrusions into expectations about security, making moot the mundane processes on which social life
otherwise depends. Repeated ruptures shift people's perceptions
and render people progressively more anxious and vulnerable to
disturbance.[49]

This terror can either be produced by challengers to the state,
whose attacks upon civilian life are intended to call into question
a society's collective sense of security, or it may be produced by
the state itself through the use of special police or paramilitary
units who engage in kidnapping, torture, and extrajudicial execution. Indeed, these are often related. As Danish researcher Mikkel
Thorup writes, "State and terrorist share the same cultural, structural and legitmatory environment," meaning that "one has to
write the history of terrorism as a dialectics or 'dialogue' between
the state and its violent challengers."[50] State policies can produce
pervasive social and economic injustices, often concentrated in
particular "disturbed areas," such as slums or sites of intense
resource extraction, and resistance to elite-driven priorities that
produce such inequalities can give rise to resistance, both violent and non-violent—resistance that is often labeled "terrorism."
And as journalist Tasneem Khalil writes, "Those in the disturbed
areas who try fighting the structural violence or protest against
socio-economic injustices are the first group of targets of state
terror. These are the political opponents of the state: dissenting
intellectuals/activists and armed rebels/insurgents."[51]

The state is classically understood to possess the monopoly on
legitimate violence, and legitimate violence is primarily defensive. According to researcher Sonja Schillings: "Whoever claims
legitimate violence marks something as worthy of protection—

[49] Strathern and Stewart, "Introduction: Terror, the Imagination, and Cosmology," 7.
[50] Mikkel Thorup, *An Intellectual History of Terror: War, Violence and the
State* (New York: Routledge, 2010), 2.
[51] Tasneem Khalil, *Jallad: Death Squads and State Terror in South Asia*
(London: Pluto Press, 2016), 10.

say, a community—and simultaneously formulates the expectation that even those who are (potentially) the target of violence accept this community's basic worthiness of protection. In this sense, an act of legitimate violence does not begin but ends the conflict; it simply reacts to a violent attack that transgresses a boundary and everything 'behind' it."[52] Legitimate violence is often constructed in relation to the concept of *hostis humani generis* (the enemy of all humankind). The function of this concept, as Schillings explains, "is to describe conflict with a perpetrator whose actions against certain people or groups are thought to betray a fundamental hostility toward humankind and the laws that govern humankind," and because these people are viewed as inherently violent, and their violence inherently legitimate, "violence against such perpetrators is, in turn, inherently legitimate," serving to preserve community boundaries.[53] According to Thorup, "The other is *violence incarnate*, while I am only *violent incidental*. This leads to the utmost important conclusion: the violence of the other perpetuates and perhaps even universalizes violence, whereas my violence promises an end to violence."[54] This, from the perspective of the possessor of legitimate violence, is the difference between terrorism and state terror.

Where does American racial violence fit into this? One can certainly see lynchings as functioning to produce terror, given that the violence could break out with little warning and consume the lives of people unaffiliated with the precipitating act. However, such an acknowledgement threatens more standard definitions of terror and terrorism. After all, such lynch mobs did not technically operate with the remit of state authority—indeed, such mobs regularly targeted courthouses and jails, attacking sheriffs

---

[52] Sonja Schillings, *Enemies of All Humankind: Fictions of Legitimate Violence* (Hanover, NH: Dartmouth College Press, 2017), 2. Or as Mikkel Thorup puts it, "No major murderous enterprise anywhere is without a reference to world peace." See Thorup, *An Intellectual History of Terror*, 8.
[53] Schillings, *Enemies of All Humankind*, 4.
[54] Thorup, *An Intellectual History of Terror*, 17.

and deputies, in order to carry out ostensibly illegal executions. These activities have the superficial trappings of anti-state violence, but we should not be deceived by this; as historian Thomas C. Wright observes, "Terrorism against the state is designed to force the government to modify its policies, to overthrow the government, or even to destroy the state"—none of which was a goal, stated or implied, expressed via lynching. Furthermore, members of lynch mobs were rarely punished, and the agencies of the state often conspired in covering up the identities of those who participated in these extrajudicial killings (with coroners regularly describing a lynching as being perpetrated "by a person or persons unknown"). This is more in line with Wright's description of state terrorism: "The intent of terrorism by the state is to eliminate some or all of the people who are considered actual or potential enemies of the regime, and to marginalize those not eliminated through the fear that terrorism instills."[55] After all, such actions were regularly viewed as necessary to protect the larger white community from inherently violent people of African descent. The boundary worth protecting was a racial boundary.

Therefore, lynch mobs better fit the mold of state terror than of terrorism. In pure American style, lynch mobs function as fundamentally democratic death squads—anyone (at least, anyone white) can participate, no special skills are required, and they exist on an ad hoc basis, to be summoned as needed. At Elaine, the presence of American soldiers essentially working toward the same ends as the mob—the restoration of "order," no matter how injurious or inequitable that order was for certain people—only further confirms this event as a case of state terror.

---

[55] Thomas C. Wright, *State Terrorism in Latin America: Chile, Argentina, and International Human Rights* (Lanham, MD: Rowman and Littlefield, 2007), 10.

Genocide

Some people have even attached to the events at Elaine that label signifying the ostensible "crime of all crimes" and the ultimate representation of moral opprobrium: genocide. For example, historian Michael K. Honey describes the Elaine Massacre as "a spectacular act of genocide."[56] Even shortly after the 1948 adoption of the United Nations Convention on the Prevention and Punishment of the Crime of Genocide (United Nations Genocide Convention, UNGC for short), some groups adopted the term as best representing the collective violence experienced by black Americans. The Civil Rights Congress (1946–1956) published its petition, *We Charge Genocide*, in 1951. Subtitled *The Historic Petition to the United Nations for Relief from a Crime of the United States Government against the Negro People*, the petition asserted that the "oppressed Negro citizens of the United States… suffer from genocide as the result of the consistent, conscious, and unified policies of every branch of government."[57] By focusing upon crimes against African Americans that happened after World War II, the petitioners hoped to illustrate that genocide was not only a historical phenomenon but one that was still going on, and their list of crimes included a variety of "race murders," especially murders carried out by law enforcement, though one can rightly assume that had the authors expanded their field back through time, the Elaine Massacre and other such events would have fallen into their purview. More than physical violence was delineated, however—*We Charge Genocide* also cited the mental harm perpetrated upon African American populations due to psychological campaigns of terror carried out by the Ku Klux Klan, the economic denigration experienced by black citizens due to

[56] Michael K. Honey, "Review of *Racial Cleansing in Arkansas, 1883–1924: Politics, Land, Labor, and Criminality* by Guy Lancaster," *Arkansas Historical Quarterly* 74 (Spring 2015): 87.
[57] *We Charge Genocide: The Historic Petition to the United Nations for Relief from a Crime of the United States Government against the Negro People* (New York: Civil Rights Congress, 1951), xi.

residential segregation, and the political chicanery that stymied black political power and, thus, any form of self-determination for the population. This petition is certainly the most well-known example of such an application of genocide as a concept to the experience of the black community, but it was not the first; as historian Pera Gaglo Dagbovie points out, "Before *We Charge Genocide* was published, the black popular press was critically thinking about genocide's relationship to the black community," with discussions showing in the *Chicago Defender*, for example, as early as 1946.[58]

We Charge Genocide regularly cites the UNGC and works to draw comparisons between Nazi Germany and the United States. However, the United Nations never gave serious consideration to the petition. As genocide scholar James Waller writes, "Despite that failure, *We Charge Genocide* was well received throughout Europe, adding to an increasing global awareness about the magnitude of racial problems in the United States," even though American powerholders "dismissed the petition as mere Communist propaganda, suggesting that Americans who voiced such complaints were 'disloyal.'"[59] Few within the field of genocide studies have followed in the footsteps of the Civil Rights Congress and seriously asked the question of whether or not the black experience in the United States ranks to the level of genocide. Indeed, after many years of ever-expansive definitions of genocide designed to incorporate a broader variety of phenomena and include a greater number of groups throughout history, there has occurred in some quarters a backlash. Legal scholar Payam Akhavan, for one, laments the "unfounded efforts to appropriate genocide and the historical imagery of the Holocaust" as fostering a "banalization of suffering" or representing "a political culture of

---

[58] Pero Gaglo Dagbovie, *African American History Reconsidered* (Urbana: University of Illinois Press, 2010), 177.
[59] James Waller, *Confronting Evil: Engaging Our Responsibility to Prevent Genocide* (New York: Oxford University Press, 2016), 29.

recognition in which ownership of anguish is not merely a means of working through trauma…but also a means of achieving a form of celebrity."[60]

But could an argument be made for the Elaine Massacre ranking as an instance of genocide? That depends, in part, upon the definition applied to the case. Raphaël Lemkin, the Polish jurist who coined the term "genocide" in 1944, defines it broadly as "the destruction of a nation or of an ethnic group" but emphasized that this "does not necessarily mean the immediate destruction of a nation, except when accomplished by mass killings of all members of a nation" but "is intended rather to signify a coordinated plan of different actions aiming at the destruction of essential foundations of the life of national groups, with the aim of annihilating the groups themselves." This can include actions aimed at the destruction of a group's language, culture, religion, economic independence, and attacks upon "the personal security, liberty, health, [and] dignity," along with the destruction of the individual lives of a group. Not only does genocide consist of the "destruction of the national pattern of the oppressed group," Lemkin argues, it also entails "the imposition of the national pattern of the oppressor."[61]

Lemkin does not draw a neat line between the destruction of cultures and the destruction of the people who are the bearers of those cultures. However, the 1948 UNGC sidelined the issue of what is now generally called "cultural genocide" by defining genocide as "any of the following acts committed with intent to destroy, in whole or in part, a national, ethnical, racial or religious group, as such: (a) Killing members of the group; (b) Causing serious bodily or mental harm to members of the group; (c) Deliber-

---

[60] Payam Akhavan, *Reducing Genocide to Law: Definition, Meaning, and the Ultimate Crime* (New York: Cambridge University Press, 2012), 131, 124.
[61] Raphaël Lemkin, *Axis Rule in Occupied Europe: Laws of Occupation, Analysis of Government, Proposals for Redress* (Washington DC: Carnegie Endowment for International Peace, 1944), 79–81.

ately inflicting on the group conditions of life calculated to bring about its physical destruction in whole or in part; (d) Imposing measures intended to prevent births within the group; (e) Forcibly transferring children of the group to another group."[62] While this definition remains that typically employed by most scholars, if primarily on account of its relatively universal acceptance, legally and politically, the UNGC has come under criticism from many quarters, in part due to its narrow range of protected groups. Sociologist Helen Fein, for one, takes issue with the fact that several collectivities were ignored by the convention, including "political, sexual, and class-dominated status groups or collectivities," and has advocated for a new definition: "Genocide is sustained purposeful action by a perpetrator to physically destroy a collectivity directly or indirectly, through interdiction of the biological and social reproduction of group members, sustained regardless of the surrender or lack of threat offered by the victim."[63]

Many other scholars have advanced their own definitions of genocide or advocated for the recognition of related phenomena as a means of filling in the gaps of the UNGC (such as politicide, democide, gendercide, etc.).[64] Sifting through all of these would be far too extensive a task for our purposes here, but there exist, in our estimation, two attempts at defining genocide that highlight variations on the general theme that are applicable in this instance. First, sociologist Martin Shaw emphasizes the fact that genocide typically occurs in the context of military conflict to define genocide thusly: "A form of violent social conflict or war between armed power organizations that aim to destroy civilian

---

[62] Convention on the Prevention and Punishment of the Crime of Genocide, United Nations Treaty Collection, https://treaties.un.org/doc/publication/unts/volume%2078/volume-78-i-1021-english.pdf (accessed January 25, 2018).

[63] Helen Fein, *Genocide: A Sociological Perspective* (London: Sage, 1991), 23–25.

[64] The reader who is interested in this would do well to consult Jens Meierhenrich, ed., *Genocide: A Reader* (New York: Oxford University Press, 2014).

social groups, and those groups or actors who resist this destruction." In a genocide, he argues, "armed power organizations treat
civilian social groups as enemies and aim to destroy their real
or putative social power by means of killing, violence and coercion against individuals whom they regard as members of the
groups."[65] An important aspect of his definition is the recognition
that genocide need not always be perpetrated by the state and that,
unlike standard military conflicts, during a genocide it is civilian
populations who are violently treated as the enemy. Christopher
Powell aims for a somewhat more expansive definition, propos-
ing that "we understand genocide sociologically as directed not
just at individuals or even groups but also at social structures or
figurations and, further, that we define it critically as *a relation of
violent obliteration*, a relation that involves the production of difference through the performance of violence."[66] In other words,
genocide is not just collective violence directed at a group, but
also violence that aims to create those very group identities.[67]

Finally, some scholars have argued that the concept of genocide does not adequately encompass what is actually a much wider phenomenon. Historian Christian Gerlach, for one, makes a
compelling argument for collectively classifying the perpetrators
of mass violence, recognizing the similarities among them, rather than trying to link the acts they commit, especially given that

---

[65] Martin Shaw, *What Is Genocide?*, 2nd ed. (Malden, MA: Polity Press,
2015), 193.
[66] Christopher Powell, *Barbaric Civilization: A Critical Sociology of Genocide* (Montreal: McGill-Queen's University Press, 2011), 60.
[67] T. K. Wilson's monograph comparing violence in Ulster and Upper
Silesia is probably one of the best studies of the use of violence for either
maintaining already established boundaries or establishing new boundaries
in ambiguous social, cultural, and political settings. See T. K. Wilson, *Frontiers of Violence: Conflict and Identity in Ulster and Upper Silesia, 1918–
1922* (New York: Oxford University Press, 2010). In addition, sociologist
Mattias Smångs has explored how lynching in the South served to create
hard racial boundaries in a post-Reconstruction environment stripped of the
former markers for whiteness and citizenship; see Mattias Smångs, *Doing
Violence, Making Race: Lynching and White Racial Formation in the U.S.
South, 1882–1930* (New York: Routledge, 2017).

mass violence can take a variety of forms, from actual killings to strategic bombing, forced labor, mass rapes, and much more. Instead, he turns his analytical lens upon what he dubs "extremely violent societies," a term meaning "formations where *various population groups* become victims of massive physical violence, in which, acting together with organs of the state, *diverse social groups participate for a multitude of reasons*."[68] Such a formulation does eliminate one of the problems of looking at mass violence through the prism of the UNGC, given that the issue of "genocidal intent," or the "intent to destroy," has typically been hard to prove. After all, perpetrators of violence may hail from a variety of backgrounds and participate for a number of reasons. Too, Gerlach argues, such a perspective illuminates "the entire social process of which mass violence is only a part, the relationships between structural and physical violence, between direct violence and dynamic shifts in inequality, and between groups and state organs."[69] One important conclusion of his study, applicable here, is that "violence is rather linked to a wide range of aspects of social mobility: drastic drops in living standards, or perceived threats to the livelihood of people who may even be living a comfortable life, or opportunities for individuals to enrich themselves, tend to generate destructive action."[70]

The field of criminology has in recent years opened up some intriguing possibilities for studying the overlap between genocide and other crimes. Criminologist Nicole Rafter, for one, has presented data showing similar characteristics between the perpetrators of genocide and those who commit more ordinary violent crime, writing that "across genocides, the perpetrators are young or middle-aged men hot for a fight; they are bullies who pick on the weak." The genocidal army now sounds a lot like the

---

[68] Christian Gerlach, *Extremely Violent Societies: Mass Violence in the Twentieth-Century World* (New York: Cambridge University Press, 2010), 1.
[69] Gerlach, *Extremely Violent Societies*, 3.
[70] Gerlach, *Extremely Violent Societies*, 267.

American lynch mob. Likewise, the victims of both crimes tend to be those with inadequate means of defense. Rafter continues, "Genocide, like street crime, involves multiple types of violence, and its form and occurrence are deeply rooted in local circumstances. Indeed, both kinds of event are even similar in tending to occur in hot spots. The difference lies in genocide's magnitude and intent to destroy a group."[71] Or as Kjell Anderson writes in his own criminological account, "Non-genocidal episodes of mass killing may involve many similar social processes as legally-defined genocide, particularly at the micro level of individual perpetration."[72] But the difference in scale means that placing what happened at Elaine firmly within the context of genocide is a much trickier proposition than the other categories of violence thus far delineated in this chapter, given that genocide, by whatever definition is employed, represents not just a single outburst of violence but rather whole campaigns that, one way or another, have the elimination of a group, "in whole or in part," at their center, at least in the long term. As legal scholar Larry May points out, it is harm to the group that constitutes the unique harm of genocide, given that "some groups act as a last refuge for the minimal protection of human rights…[and] provide an important ingredient in an individual's sense of self-worth." Genocide, therefore, constitutes "a catastrophic assault on the person, both in terms of the destruction of the last bulwark protecting the rights of the individual, and also in terms of potential destruction of the self. Genocide leaves the individual group member without resources to claim his or her rights as a human, and sometimes without resources even to understand who he or she is."[73]

Genocide is more than murder multiplied; as Anderson has

---

[71] Nicole Rafter, *The Crime of All Crimes: Toward a Criminology of Genocide* (New York: New York University Press, 2016), 52–53.

[72] Larry May, *Genocide: A Normative Account* (New York: Cambridge University Press, 2010), 71.

[73] Kjell Anderson, *Perpetrating Genocide: A Criminological Account* (New York: Routledge, 2018), 4.

written, "Mere mob violence is not enough to effect total annihilation. The sustained, organized nature of genocide is one of
the characteristics that distinguishes it from other forms of mass
violence, such as pogroms."[72] Genocide never consists of only
one event, only one outburst of violence, but, instead, constitutes
an ongoing campaign lasting years or even (as with many cases
of colonial genocides) generations, often implicating more than
just the people who actually pull the trigger. Gerlach's conceptual shift from the act of genocide to the society that perpetrates
such extreme violence speaks to this reality. Therefore, if we wish
to examine what happened at Elaine in the context of genocide
or the "extremely violent societies" model, we need more than
just this one event in our data set—an entire catalogue of white-
supremacist violence must be considered. Such is beyond the
scope of this chapter, or even this book (although the previous
chapter examines other cases of large-scale anti-black violence in
Arkansas). However, though we cannot immediately rule on the
applicability of the genocide label to what happened in eastern
Arkansas in 1919, neither can we rule it out. Powell's definition
of genocide—"*a relation of violent obliteration*, a relation that
involves the production of difference through the performance
of violence"—in particular speaks to the potential for considering Elaine, and broader swaths of American history in general,
through the prism of this "crime of all crimes." After all, black
and white, laboring class and owning class, do not constitute
"natural" categories; instead, those categories have been created
and recreated through the practice of violence. What happened at
Elaine was not so unique but was, instead, yet another example of
what happened to those who dared to cross those lines.

Chapter 4

Labor Activism, Third-Party Politics, and African Americans in Arkansas, 1865–1892

Matthew Hild

T he Elaine Massacre of 1919 shocked the nation, but it would have been less shocking to those who were familiar with the history of race relations in Arkansas since the Civil War. African American farm workers who tried to engage in collective bargaining had met with violent opposition before; both the organization known as the Progressive Farmers and Household Union of America and its murderous destruction at Elaine had deep roots in the state. Black farmers and laborers in Arkansas began organizing shortly after the Civil War ended, and almost immediately these efforts provoked white oppression and resistance. Organizations such as the Union League, the Knights of Labor, the Sons of the Agricultural Star, the Agricultural Wheel, and the Colored Farmers' Alliance recruited and mobilized black Arkansans during the three decades that followed the war. Furthermore, after Democrats "redeemed" the state from Republican rule in 1874, many African Americans participated in the struggle against their dominance through third parties such as the Greenback-Labor Party (GLP), the Union Labor Party (ULP), and the People's (or Populist) Party. White men, sometimes under the aegis of organizations such as the Ku Klux Klan but usually in less formal posses or mobs, frequently resorted to violence and bloodshed to crush these efforts. As elsewhere in the South, Arkansas Democrats also implemented disfranchisement measures during the early 1890s that disqualified the vast majority of prospective black voters (as well as many whites) for decades to come. The Elaine Massacre, then, represented the apex of decades of black activism and white oppression in the state, although it marked the end of neither.

In 1860, according to the U.S. Census, slaves constituted 25.5 percent of the population of Arkansas. (The census counted 144 "free colored" persons, which amounted to 0.03 percent of the state's population.) The ratio of whites to blacks in the state remained constant over the course of the decade; in 1870, the Census Bureau reported that 74.7 percent of Arkansans were white and 25.2 percent black.[1] After the Civil War ended, most former slaves became sharecroppers, tenant farmers, or contract laborers. As historian M. Langley Biegert has noted, in parts of the Arkansas Delta, a "tremendous shortage of labor in the area" during the years immediately following the war meant that farm workers "were in a good position to negotiate."[2] The Freedmen's Bureau helped African Americans arrange contracts with planters, and the Union League, an organization started by Northern whites during the war, helped some 22,000 black men register to vote in Arkansas between May and November of 1868.[3] Black voters helped Powell Clayton become Arkansas's first elected Republican governor in 1868, and during the six years of Republican governorships that followed, the state government enacted a number of laws and measures that attempted to provide African Americans with a degree of political and social equality. Eight black men participated in the state constitutional convention of 1868, which established a free public school system that, for the first time, included African Americans. The school system became segregated in 1871, but, according to historian Fon Louise Gordon, this "segregation aided class formation among black Arkansans

---

[1] *Ninth Census of the United States. Statistics of Population* (Washington DC: Government Printing Office, 1872), 3–6.
[2] M. Langley Biegert, "Legacy of Resistance: Uncovering the History of Collective Action by Black Agricultural Workers in Central East Arkansas from the 1860s to the 1930s," *Journal of Social History* 32 (Fall 1998): 79.
[3] Jeannie M. Whayne, Thomas A. DeBlack, George Sabo III, and Morris S. Arnold, *Arkansas: A Narrative History*, 2nd ed. (Fayetteville: University of Arkansas Press, 2013), 232, 237.

by providing jobs for black teachers and a college to train them."
The state also passed a civil rights act in 1873 that mandated that
the segregated school system provide "equal and like accommodations." That act also outlawed racial discrimination in all public
accommodations.[4]

Such advances for Arkansas's African Americans did not go
uncontested, though, especially when black citizens themselves
played a proactive role in attempting to improve their social and
economic conditions. By the end of 1867, Ku Klux Klan groups
had formed in Arkansas and soon began campaigns of terror and
violence against African Americans. The Klan targeted white
Unionists and Republicans as well; in Little River County, Klans-
men killed a Freedmen's Bureau agent in 1868. About two weeks
before that year's presidential election, Republican congressman
James Hinds and another prominent white Arkansas Republican,
Joseph Brooks, were shot by local Democratic leader and Klans-
man George Clark in Monroe County while traveling to a rally
for Republican presidential candidate Ulysses S. Grant. Brooks
survived the attack, but Hinds did not. The number of Arkansans
killed by the Klan by election day reportedly exceeded 200, most
of them African Americans.[5] That Powell Clayton won the guber-

---

[4] Fon Louise Gordon, *Caste and Class: The Black Experience in Arkansas,
1880–1920* (Athens: University of Georgia Press, 1995), 9–11 (quotations
on 9); Tom Dillard, *Statesmen, Scoundrels, and Eccentrics: A Gallery of
Amazing Arkansans* (Fayetteville: University of Arkansas Press, 2010), 55.
Clayton's predecessor as the governor of Arkansas, Isaac Murphy, was a Republican, but he was not actually elected. A state constitutional convention
appointed him as provisional governor in 1864, and when that constitution
was ratified in a special election under the supervision of Union troops, in
which only 12,000 Arkansans voted, Murphy was also "elected" as governor. William L. Shea, "Isaac Murphy, 1864–1868," in *The Governors of
Arkansas: Essays in Political Biography*, edited by Timothy P. Donovan and
Willard B. Gatewood Jr. (Fayetteville: University of Arkansas Press, 1981),
39–40; Kenneth C. Barnes, *Who Killed John Clayton? Political Violence
and the Emergence of the New South, 1861–1893* (Durham, NC: Duke University Press, 1998), 21.
[5] Randy Finley, *From Slavery to Uncertain Freedom: The Freedmen's
Bureau in Arkansas, 1865–1869* (Fayetteville: University of Arkansas Press,
1996), 148–151, 159; Nancy E. Marion and Willard M. Oliver, *Killing Con-*

natorial election earlier that year despite the ruthless and vicious efforts of the Klan underscores how seriously African American men took their right to vote.

A more localized episode involving black activism and violent white repression occurred in Phillips County shortly after emancipation, when a former slave named Bryant Singfield began to organize black farm workers who were trying to negotiate new labor contracts with their former masters. Another former slave later recalled that federal military commanders stationed in the Phillips County town of Helena "encouraged and assisted" Singfield in these efforts. When one group of the former slaves organized by Singfield left the plantations and formed "an independent farm colony on an abandoned plot of land," white planters (reportedly led by future county sheriff Bart Turner) retaliated by rounding up Singfield and some of those who had left the plantations and apparently murdering them. Subsequent local legend claimed that Singfield's ghost haunted the swamp where he had been killed.[6] Although the Union League is not known to have played a role in the efforts of Singfield and his followers, the organization was very active in mobilizing African Americans in Phillips County after the Civil War. The same would be true, to a lesser extent, of the Knights of Labor beginning in 1887, decades before the activities of the Progressive Farmers and Household Union of America in the county.[7]

The Freedmen's Bureau ended its activities in Arkansas in 1870, by which time the Union League was also winding down.

gress: *Assassinations, Attempted Assassinations and Other Violence against Members of Congress* (Lanham, MD: Lexington Books, 2014), 2, 8–12.
[6] Grif Stockley, *Ruled By Race: Black/White Relations in Arkansas from Slavery to the Present* (Fayetteville: University of Arkansas Press, 2009), 49–50 (first quotation on 49); Biegert, "Legacy of Resistance," 79 (second quotation).
[7] Thomas C. Kennedy, *A History of Southland College: The Society of Friends and Black Education in Arkansas* (Fayetteville: University of Arkansas Press, 2009), 45–46; Jonathan Garlock, comp., *Guide to the Local Assemblies of the Knights of Labor* (Westport, CT: Greenwood Press, 1982), 16.

In 1872, another organization that originated outside of Arkansas entered the state: the National Grange of the Order of the Patrons of Husbandry (better known simply as the Grange). Formed in Washington DC in 1867 by former U.S. Department of Agriculture clerk Oliver H. Kelley, the Grange focused on establishing cooperative enterprises for farmers and evinced a sense of agrarian class consciousness, frequently denouncing "middlemen" and "monopolists."[8] Although the Grange was officially nonpartisan, it made political demands. For example, at its annual meeting in January 1877, the Arkansas State Grange passed a resolution urging the Arkansas General Assembly that "some just and equitable law...be passed regulating the rates of passenger and freight tariffs on lines of railroads in this State, if it be within the power of the General Assembly to enact such a law."[9] In contrast to the Union League, however, the Grange, in Arkansas and much of the rest of the South, apparently consisted solely of white men and women. In 1873, National Grange Master Dudley W. Adams stated that "the [Grange] Constitution is silent in regard to color.... If a Grange chooses to admit Negroes it may do so....The matter is purely a local one." In most of the South, however, the local decision of Grangers was to exclude African Americans. The few exceptions included Alabama, where the Grange eventually chartered some segregated black chapters, and the northern uplands of Louisiana, where some local chapters became racially integrated.[10]

By the late 1870s, the Grange had declined in numbers and

---

[8] Finley, *From Slavery to Uncertain Freedom*, 139; Michael W. Fitzgerald, "Union League of America," in *Encyclopedia of the Reconstruction Era*, edited by Richard Zuczek (Westport, CT: Greenwood Publishing Group, 2006), 2: 672; Matthew Hild, *Greenbackers, Knights of Labor, and Populists: Farmer-Labor Insurgency in the Late-Nineteenth-Century South* (Athens: University of Georgia Press, 2007), 12–17.

[9] *Proceedings of the Fifth Annual Session of the Arkansas State Grange, Patrons of Husbandry, Held at Little Rock, January 22, 23, 24, 25 and 26, 1877* (Little Rock: Webb & Burrows, 1877), 24.

[10] Hild, *Greenbackers, Knights of Labor, and Populists*, 13.

influence in Arkansas and elsewhere, but by then some Grangers had helped launch the Greenback-Labor Party (GLP) in the state. This party combined protest against the national system of money and banking with an anti-monopoly ideology that the Grange had helped to cultivate.[11] One historian who closely examined the Arkansas Greenback movement asserted that "former Grangers probably constituted much of the Greenback voting strength in the state."[12] As in some other Southern states, the Arkansas GLP also served as a vehicle of opposition to the "Redeemer" or "Bourbon" Democrats as the Republican Party declined at the end of Reconstruction. Not surprisingly, then, the GLP did not exclude African Americans as had the Grange. In fact, black members played a significant role in the Arkansas GLP, especially in Little Rock, where the party elected the former slave and Union veteran Isaac T. Gillam to the state legislature and swept the municipal elections in 1878. The biracial character of the party made it vulnerable to charges by Democrats that it threatened white supremacy and was an adjunct to the Republican Party, a tactic that Arkansas Democrats would repeat in the late nineteenth century. The GLP did not last long and never seriously threatened the Democratic Party's rule in the state, electing only seven of 124 legislators in 1878 and garnering only 27 percent of the vote for its candidate, W. P. "Buck" Parks (whom the Arkansas Republican Party endorsed) in the gubernatorial election of 1880. Nevertheless, the GLP laid an important foundation for biracial farmer-labor political insurgency in the state.[13]

[11] Hild, *Greenbackers, Knights of Labor, and Populists*, 29–31.

[12] Judith Barjenbruch, "The Greenback Political Movement: An Arkansas View," *Arkansas Historical Quarterly* 36 (Summer 1977): 109.

[13] Hild, *Greenbackers, Knights of Labor, and Populists*, 20–44; Tom W. Dillard, "Gillam, Isaac T.," in *Arkansas Biography: A Collection of Notable Lives*, edited by Nancy A. Williams (Fayetteville: University of Arkansas Press, 2000), 122–123; Barjenbruch, "The Greenback Political Movement," 114–116. The opponents of "Redeemer" Democrats used the term "Bourbon" derisively, comparing the Redeemers to the French Bourbons who, upon being restored to power in 1814, seemed to have "learned nothing and…forgotten nothing from the French Revolution." The Bourbon Dem-

As the Greenback-Labor Party disintegrated after the elections of 1882, three organizations appeared in Arkansas that would play major roles in the state's farmer and labor movements and help bring the third-party movement to its apotheosis. Two of these organizations, the Agricultural Wheel and the Brothers of Freedom, started in Arkansas. Both eventually spread into other states, and in 1885 they merged under the name of the Agricultural Wheel. Farmers constituted most of the membership of both organizations, but "mechanics" (a general term for most kinds of skilled or semi-skilled workingmen at that time) could join. Initially, neither organization admitted women or African Americans, but eventually, after the merger, those restrictions were lifted. The third organization of working-class significance to emerge in Arkansas, in 1882, was the Knights of Labor, which began as a secret order in Philadelphia, Pennsylvania, in 1869 and spread slowly across the nation. The Knights of Labor admitted men and women of virtually all occupations, and the only racial restriction was a ban against Chinese members. The first local chapter (or, officially, "local assembly") of the Knights of Labor in Arkansas, based in Hot Springs, held a preliminary meeting for the purposes of organizing on November 22, 1882, and held its official first meeting on December 30, 1882. One month later, members of this local assembly helped to organize the state's second local assembly, also in Hot Springs, consisting entirely of black men. Before the end of 1885, white women and black women also joined the ranks of the Knights of Labor in Arkansas.[14]

---

ocrats, their critics charged, reacted similarly to the Civil War. Leonard Schlup and James G. Ryan, eds., *Historical Dictionary of the Gilded Age* (Armonk, NY: M. E. Sharpe, 2003), 56.
[14] Barjenbruch, "The Greenback Political Movement," 117–118; Hild, *Greenbackers, Knights of Labor, and Populists*, 45, 48, 58–61, 88; Matthew Hild, "Labor, Third-Party Politics, and New South Democracy in Arkansas, 1884–1896," *Arkansas Historical Quarterly* 43 (Spring 2004): 27–28; Melton A. McLaurin, *The Knights of Labor in the South* (Westport, CT: Greenwood Press, 1978), 150; Joseph Gerteis, *Class and the Color Line: Interracial Class Coalition in the Knights of Labor and the Populist Movement* (Durham, NC: Duke University Press, 2007), 50; Garlock, *Guide to*

The Agricultural Wheel, the Brothers of Freedom, and the Knights of Labor shared, in many ways, what today would be called a similar worldview. Each of these organizations believed that workers, on farms or in industrial settings, were the "producers" of the world and that "middlemen" and "monopolists" were depriving the producers of the just fruits of their labor. The distinction between those who toiled on farms and in factories did not necessarily represent a chasm; not only did the Agricultural Wheel and the Brothers of Freedom admit "mechanics," but many local assemblies of the Knights of Labor in Arkansas (and elsewhere) included farmers, be they landowners or tenants/sharecroppers.[15] The similarities between the Knights of Labor and the two predominantly agricultural organizations quickly became apparent to one of the founders and leaders of the Knights in Arkansas, Dan Fraser Tomson. In September 1884, Tomson contacted Terence V. Powderly, the General Master Workman (or president) of the Knights of Labor, and informed him that "I am in correspondence with 'Hon. Isaac McCracken,' Clarksville, Ark., one of the leaders [of the] 'B. of F.' [Brothers of Freedom] and with 'A. Walter, Esq.' of the 'Ag. Wheel,' Beebe, Ark., endeavoring to turn these bodies into the K. of L." Tomson asked Powderly to contact leaders of the Brothers of Freedom and the Agricultural Wheel to encourage such a merger, and Powderly instructed one of his lieutenants to do so.[16] Although the Knights of Labor would never actually merge with any of the farmers' groups, Tomson

---

the Local Assemblies, 13, 17, 18.

[15] On the similarities between the Knights of Labor and its contemporary farmers' organizations, see Hild, *Greenbackers, Knights of Labor, and Populists*, and on the similarities between their political platforms, see Robert C. McMath Jr., *American Populism: A Social History, 1877–1898* (New York: Hill and Wang, 1993), 79. On the composition of local assemblies of the Knights of Labor, in Arkansas and elsewhere, see Garlock, *Guide to the Local Assemblies*.

[16] Dan Fraser Tomson to T. V. Powderly, September 26, 1884, Terence Vincent Powderly Papers, microfilm edition (Glen Rock, NJ: Microfilming Corporation of America, 1974), reel 8. Powderly's instructions about contacting McCracken and Walter are handwritten on this letter.

nevertheless was correct in believing that the Knights could work closely with them in the pursuit of shared goals.

The Agricultural Wheel, the Brothers of Freedom, and the Knights of Labor were supposedly non-partisan organizations, yet many of the demands they made could not be achieved without the passage of legislation.[17] Perhaps not surprisingly, then, all three of the organizations entered the political fray in Arkansas in 1884. For the Knights of Labor, with only half a dozen local assemblies in the entire state at the time, this merely meant that the rank-and-file in Hot Springs, home of the state's first white and first black locals, put forth a "Working man's ticket" headed by Tomson as a candidate for the state legislature, without success.[18] The Agricultural Wheel and the Brothers of Freedom, with far more members, fared better. Tomson reported in a letter to the national Knights of Labor newspaper that those two organizations elected fifteen of the 127 members of the state legislature in 1884, including Brothers president Isaac McCracken, a former railroad machine shop worker and trade unionist who later joined the Knights of Labor.[19]

While the Brothers of Freedom and, at that time, the Agricultural Wheel were both all-white organizations, in some counties

---

[17] N. A. Dunning, ed., *The Farmers' Alliance History and Agricultural Digest* (Washington DC: Alliance Publishing Co., 1891), 214; Berton E. Henningson Jr., "Root Hog or Die: The Brothers of Freedom and the 1884 Arkansas Election," *Arkansas Historical Quarterly* 45 (Autumn 1986): 198; Matthew Hild, "The Knights of Labor and the Third-Party Movement in Texas, 1886–1896," *Southwestern Historical Quarterly* 119 (July 2015): 28; McLaurin, *The Knights of Labor in the South*, 80–81.

[18] Jonathan Garlock, "A Structural Analysis of the Knights of Labor: A Prolegomenon to the History of the Producing Classes" (PhD diss., University of Rochester, 1974), 236; Tomson to Powderly, September 26, 1884, Powderly Papers, reel 8 (quotation).

[19] *Journal of United Labor* (Philadelphia), March 25, 1885; F. Clark Elkins, "State Politics and the Agricultural Wheel," *Arkansas Historical Quarterly* 38 (Autumn 1979): 252–253; Nashville *Weekly Toiler*, September 5, 1888; John H. Robertson to W. B. W. Heartsill, August 31, 1896, W. B. W. Heartsill Papers, 1864–1945, Center for Arkansas History and Culture, University of Arkansas at Little Rock, Box 4, File 11.

the farmers' groups engaged in fusion (or the process of jointly supporting a ticket) with the Republican Party. In Conway County, where African Americans constituted a quarter of the population in 1880, the extent of fusion between the Brothers, the Wheel, and Republicans remains unclear even after close examination by scholars, but according to historian Kenneth C. Barnes, "The farmers and Republicans defeated the Democrats for every county office, with most of the winners appearing to be Republican." Black voters played enough of a role in the defeat of the Democrats that white men who were loyal to that party waged a campaign of violence and terror in Conway County in early 1885, leading black men to form their own military company for self-defense.[20]

In October 1885, the Agricultural Wheel and the Brothers of Freedom merged, keeping the name of the former and naming Brothers president Isaac McCracken as the president of the consolidated Wheel, which now represented a membership of some 50,000. The restriction against black members remained intact at this point, but by then black farmers in the state had formed their own organization, the Sons of the Agricultural Star, headquartered in Monroe County. When the state convention of the Agricultural Wheel, after "much animated discussion" according to a contemporary account, dropped the whites-only clause from its membership requirements in 1886, the chapters of the Sons of the Agricultural Star entered the Wheel as the latter's first black locals. By 1888, black local Wheels constituted slightly more than 10 percent of the total chapters, and the seven delegates selected by the Arkansas State Wheel to attend the National Agricultural Wheel convention that year included an African American from Crittenden County.[21]

---

[20] Henningson, "Root Hog or Die," 209 including *n.*41; *Compendium of the Tenth Census (June 1, 1880)*, Part I (Washington DC: Government Printing Office, 1883), 336; Barnes, *Who Killed John Clayton?*, 52–55 (quotation on 53).

[21] F. Clark Elkins, "The Agricultural Wheel: County Politics and Consol-

The Knights of Labor, meanwhile, began to grow more rapidly in Arkansas; the number of local assemblies in the state rose from 20 in 1885 to 111 the following year, and membership rose to well over 5,000 by 1887. In 1886, the Knights waged at least two noteworthy strikes in Arkansas. The first, the "Great Southwest Railroad Strike," began in Texas and spread through several states. While whites constituted the majority of the striking workforce and provided most of the leadership, blacks participated, too, and the Knights managed a biracial alliance that, while not without limits, could nevertheless be deemed impressive for its time and place. The strike ended in failure within two months, and in Arkansas the obstacles included court injunctions, arrests, and even the mobilization of the state militia in Texarkana, sent by Democratic governor Simon P. Hughes to restore and maintain order.[22]

On the heels of the railroad strike, a more localized and undoubtedly more startling strike started in Pulaski County at the beginning of July, south of Little Rock. Some forty African American farmhands, some of whom were women, walked off the job at the Tate Plantation for higher wages and payment in cash instead of scrip. Press reports indicated that at least thirty of the strikers, who were demanding one dollar per day instead of seventy-five cents, belonged to the Knights of Labor. On the fifth day of the strike, Pulaski County sheriff Robert Worthen raided the plantation with several deputies. One of the deputies shot one of the strike leaders, Hugh Gill, with a double-barreled shotgun, wounding him in both arms. As the news spread throughout the county, approximately 250 black men, many of them armed, came to the fields surrounding the Tate Plantation. Sheriff Worthen and his

idation, 1884–1885," *Arkansas Historical Quarterly* 29 (Summer 1970): 172–173; John W. Graves, *Town and Country: Race Relations in an Urban-Rural Context, Arkansas, 1865–1905* (Fayetteville: University of Arkansas Press, 1990), 203 (first quotation); Gordon, *Caste and Class*, 15 (second quotation).
[22] Hild, "Labor, Third-Party Politics, and New South Democracy," 29–30; Theresa A. Case, *The Great Southwest Railroad Strike and Free Labor* (College Station: Texas A&M University Press, 2010).

deputies remained ensconced in Gill's house and sent out word for a posse to come to the plantation. As tensions rose, the *New York Times* reported concerns that the "county is on the verge of one of the bloodiest race conflicts that has occurred since the war." Fortunately, no further violence occurred, due in part to the arrival on the scene of Dan Fraser Tomson and a black Knights of Labor leader. The strike ended about a week after it had begun, with most of the strikers returning to work under the same terms as before the strike. Tomson subsequently wrote in the Arkansas Knights of Labor state newspaper, the *Industrial Liberator*, that Sheriff Worthen and his deputies had committed "outrages" at the plantation "in the hope that the colored people, being organized, would resist, and that this would serve as a pretext to break up organization among them."[23]

While both the railroad strike and the plantation strike ended in defeat for the Knights of Labor, the strikes spurred the Arkansas Knights toward a political coalition with the Agricultural Wheel in opposition to the state's dominant Democratic Party. On May 14, 1886, less than two weeks after the railroad strike ended, a biracial committee of Little Rock Knights attended a meeting of the Pulaski County Wheel. The Wheel appointed a committee to confer with the Knights about the possibility of nominating a county ticket. Less than one month later, on June 8, Pulaski County Wheelers and Knights met in a joint "secret session" in the hall of the Brotherhood of Locomotive Engineers in Little Rock. About 110 men attended the meeting, a number of whom were African Americans. Isom P. Langley presided; he played a major role in each organization as the chaplain of the State Wheel

[23] Matthew Hild, "Tate Plantation Strike of 1886," *Encyclopedia of Arkansas History & Culture*, http://www.encyclopediaofarkansas.net/encyclopedia/entry-detail.aspx?entryID=9243 (accessed February 23, 2018); *New York Times*, July 9, 1886, quoted in William Warren Rogers, "Negro Knights of Labor in Arkansas: A Case Study of the 'Miscellaneous' Strike," *Labor History* 10 (Summer 1969): 502; Case, *The Great Southwest Railroad Strike*, 215 (Tomson quotation).

and the editor of the *Industrial Liberator*.

Although the meeting did not put forth a county ticket, the next day the State Wheel met in Little Rock and nominated a state ticket. Some of the candidates nominated by the Wheel, including gubernatorial nominee John G. Fletcher of Little Rock, dropped off the ticket, and ultimately Charles Cunningham (also of Little Rock) ran as the Wheel's candidate for governor. A prominent Granger in the 1870s and a Greenback-Labor congressional candidate in 1882, Cunningham received just over 19,000 votes in the September 1886 election, a mere 12 percent of those cast in a three-man contest. Nevertheless, the Wheel managed to elect candidates to the state legislature in at least twenty Arkansas counties, including Carroll County where Knights and Wheelers jointly nominated a ticket. In November 1886, Wheel candidates ran in three of the state's five congressional districts. In the Fourth District, which included Pulaski County, the Republican Party tacitly endorsed Isom P. Langley's candidacy by not nominating anyone. Langley lost the race (as did the other Wheel candidates), but he carried Pulaski County, where the Knights had thirty-seven local assemblies in 1886, with 56 percent of the vote.[24]

Whereas both the Knights of Labor and, by this time, the Agricultural Wheel were facilitating black activism and biracial political insurgency, another organization entered Arkansas in late 1886 that would soon emerge as a rival to the Wheel: the Texas-based

[24] Little Rock *Arkansas Gazette*, May 16, June 9 (quotation), 1886; Elkins, "State Politics and the Agricultural Wheel," 252, 255–257; Matthew Hild, "Charles E. Cunningham (1823–1895)," *Encyclopedia of Arkansas History & Culture*, http://www.encyclopediaofarkansas.net/encyclopedia/entry-detail.aspx?entryID=6983 (accessed February 23, 2018); Barjenbruch, "The Greenback Political Movement," 121; *New York Times*, August 6, September 26, 1886; F. Clark Elkins, "The Agricultural Wheel in Arkansas, 1887," *Arkansas Historical Quarterly* 40 (Autumn 1981): 249*n*.2; Edward T. James, "American Labor and Political Action, 1865–1896: The Knights of Labor and Its Predecessors" (PhD diss., Harvard University, 1954), 315*n*.87; *Biennial Report of the Secretary of State of the State of Arkansas, 1886* (Little Rock: A. M. Woodruff, 1886), 259; Garlock, *Guide to the Local Assemblies*, 17–19.

Farmers' Alliance. Formed in Texas during the mid-to-late 1870s, the Farmers' Alliance remained confined to that state until 1886. As the Alliance began to spread, an organizer entered Arkansas in late 1886 and established chapters in Miller County. For all of its similarities to the Agricultural Wheel, however, the Farmers' Alliance differed from the Wheel in at least one significant way: the Alliance never lifted its whites-only membership restriction. Instead, the Colored Farmers' Alliance emerged in Texas in 1886 and soon followed its white counterpart across the South.[25]

During the late 1880s, however, the Agricultural Wheel remained the largest and most influential farmers' organization in Arkansas. The organization's scant success in the elections of 1886 did not discourage the faction of leaders and members known as "political Wheelers," and by 1888 Arkansas Wheelers and Knights had a new third party with which to challenge the state's dominant Democratic Party. Formed by agrarian and labor reformers at what was called an Industrial Labor Conference in Cincinnati, Ohio, in February 1887, the Union Labor Party (ULP) served in many ways as a bridge between the Greenback-Labor Party and the People's (or Populist) Party that emerged in the early 1890s.[26] In Arkansas, however, the ULP would actually represent the height of the third-party challenge of the Gilded Age.

In 1887, Arkansas leaders and members of the Agricultural Wheel and the Knights of Labor took further steps toward collaboration. In the black-majority county of Woodruff, located just within the Arkansas Delta where tenant-operated farms slightly outnumbered owner-operated farms, Knights and Wheelers jointly petitioned landowners for a 25 percent reduction in land rent

[25] Robert C. McMath Jr., *Populist Vanguard: A History of the Southern Farmers' Alliance* (Chapel Hill: University of North Carolina Press, 1975), 4, 33–34, 44–45.
[26] Hild, *Greenbackers, Knights of Labor, and Populists*, 105–106. On "political Wheelers," see Elkins, "State Politics and the Agricultural Wheel"; Clifton Paisley, "The Political Wheelers and Arkansas's Election of 1888," *Arkansas Historical Quarterly* 25 (Spring 1966): 3–21.

in the autumn of that year. Both organizations made more efforts to include African Americans as well, as the Knights organized more all-black local assemblies in the state, and delegates at the State Wheel convention in July voted to seat a delegation of "colored Wheelers" from St. Francis County.[27]

In the spring of 1888, press reports began to appear in Arkansas foretelling joint Knights of Labor–Agricultural Wheel political efforts. In April, the *Marianna Index* reported that "a kind of joint convention of Wheelers and Knights of Labor" had made either "the nomination or recommendation" of State Wheel president L. P. Featherston as a candidate for Congress in the First District of eastern Arkansas.[28] On April 30, the first state convention of the Union Labor Party convened in Little Rock. "The Arkansas party's ranks," writes historian Clifton Paisley, "were so filled with 'political Wheelers' that the leadership was scarcely distinguishable from that of the Agricultural Wheel of Arkansas." Arkansas Knights of Labor leaders, including several African Americans, attended the convention as well. The ULP endorsed the platforms of the Knights, the Wheel, and the Farmers' Alliance. Specific party demands taken from those platforms included governmental ownership of the means of communication and transportation, the free coinage of silver, a graduated income tax, and—of particular importance to African Americans—the abolition of the convict lease system. African Americans constituted "the greatest majority" of convicts in this "system [that] gained a reputation for imposing 'slavery by another name.'" The Arkansas ULP platform

[27] Elkins, "The Agricultural Wheel in Arkansas, 1887," 253–254; *Compendium of the Eleventh Census: 1890* (Washington DC: Government Printing Office, 1892), Part I, 477; John S. Otto, *The Final Frontiers, 1880–1930: Settling the Southern Bottomlands* (Westport, CT: Greenwood Press, 1999), 16, 117; *Journal of United Labor* (Philadelphia), December 3, 1887; Garlock, *Guide to the Local Assemblies*, 11–21.
[28] *Marianna* (Ark.) *Index*, n.d., quoted in the Little Rock *Arkansas Gazette*, April 11, 1888; W. Scott Morgan, *History of the Wheel and Alliance, and the Impending Revolution*, 3rd. ed. (Hardy, AR: s.p., 1891; reprint, New York: Burt Franklin, 1968), 319.

also included a demand for laws regulating mining and ensuring proper ventilation in the mines, probably at the behest of Knights of Labor coal miners in the western part of the state, who would wage a strike at Coal Hill later in the year.[29]

The Union Labor convention nominated Charles M. Norwood, a former Confederate and state senator, for governor of Arkansas. The *St. Louis Post-Dispatch* reported that the candidate was "regarded as a strong man," while the bitterly partisan *Arkansas Gazette* characterized him as "probably the most ignorant man who ever aspired to high position in Arkansas." Democrats' contempt turned to alarm, however, when the state Republican Party, still led by former governor Powell Clayton, endorsed Norwood. The six delegates selected by the Arkansas ULP convention to attend the national party convention in Cincinnati in May included an African American delegate, P. M. E. Thompson, and the man who had run as the Agricultural Wheel candidate for governor in 1886, Charles E. Cunningham, who became the party's vice-presidential candidate.[30]

Knights of Labor General Master Workman Terence V. Powderly refused to endorse the ULP, insisting in the summer of 1888

---

[29] Little Rock *Arkansas Gazette*, May 1, 1888; Paisley, "Political Wheelers," 4 (first quotation); Whayne et al., *Arkansas*, 299 (second and third quotations); *Journal of United Labor* (Philadelphia), June 30, September 6, 1888. For the platform of the Knights of Labor, see Norman J. Ware, *The Labor Movement in the United States, 1860–1895: A Study in Democracy* (New York: D. Appleton and Co., 1929), 377–380. For the demands made by the National Agricultural Wheel at McKenzie, Tenn., in November 1887, see the Moulton *Alabama State Wheel*, January 11, 1888. For the demands made by the National Farmers' Alliance and Cooperative Union at Shreveport, La., in October 1887, see Morgan, *History of the Wheel and Alliance*, 141–144.

[30] *St. Louis Post-Dispatch*, May 1, 1888; Little Rock *Arkansas Gazette*, August 14, 1888, quoted in Paisley, "Political Wheelers," 4; Little Rock *Arkansas Gazette*, May 1, 1888; Mark Wahlgren Summers, *Party Games: Getting, Keeping, and Using Power in Gilded Age Politics* (Chapel Hill: University of North Carolina Press, 2004), 118; *Biographical and Historical Memoirs of Pulaski, Jefferson, Lonoke, Faulkner, Grant, Saline, Perry, Garland, and Hot Spring Counties, Arkansas* (Chicago: Goodspeed Publishing Co., 1889; reprint, Easley, SC: Southern Historical Press, 1978), 439.

that "there is no Knight[s] of Labor ticket in the field anywhere in the United States," and neither the Arkansas State Wheel nor Knights of Labor State Assembly endorsed Norwood.[31] Both organizations, however, clearly supported the Arkansas ULP. As the *Marianna Index* had reported in April, Lewis P. Featherston did indeed run for Congress, as a ULP candidate, while the Knights of Labor set about organizing new district assemblies (which represented groups of local assemblies) in the First District where the State Wheel president was running and in the Third District where another ULP candidate was running.[32]

The Arkansas state election of 1888, held on September 3, set a record for the largest number of votes ever recorded in a statewide election in Arkansas to that point, but it would also go down in infamy as one of the most fraudulent elections in the annals of U.S. history. The official tally went in favor of Democrat James P. Eagle with 99,214 votes to Norwood's 84,213. Reuben CarlLee, a Union Laborite and ardent "political Wheeler," expressed the sentiment of many of Norwood's supporters when he asserted, "We undoubtedly carried the state and have been counted out." CarlLee charged that Democrats had stolen ballot boxes in townships that the ULP had carried, prohibited Union Labor supporters from voting in other communities, and used violence and intimidation against Union Labor men and African American men in particular. In Union County, he claimed, Democrats had "whipped over twenty colored men, some of them so badly that they had to keep [to] their beds" on the night before the election, which they followed on election day by fatally shooting seven "Union Labor men" and wounding over twenty more. While CarlLee cannot be considered a non-partisan source, historians have since provided support for his account. One modern study

[31] *Journal of United Labor* (Philadelphia), August 16, 1888 (quotation); Garland E. Bayliss, "Public Affairs in Arkansas, 1874–1896" (PhD diss., University of Texas at Austin, 1972), 301. The Arkansas State Wheel did pass a resolution thanking the ULP for adopting its demands.
[32] Hild, "Labor, Third-Party Politics, and New South Democracy," 33, 35.

suggests that Norwood "would probably have won the governor's office had not election fraud prevented him."[33]

The events in Crittenden County during the summer of 1888 also give credence to the general tenor of CarlLee's claims: armed white Democrats literally ran black Republican officeholders (among them some members of the Knights of Labor) out of town on a railway bound for Memphis, and when the black men appealed to Democratic governor Hughes for assistance and justice, he refused to help. The county was then "returned to white control" on election day, with no black candidates being elected even though blacks constituted over 85 percent of the county's population. Despite the rampant violence and fraud, eight African Americans won election to the Arkansas state legislature in 1888, twice as many as in 1886.[34]

Arkansas Democrats used the same tactics in the congressional elections in November to defeat Featherston in the First District and the Wheel-supported Republican candidate John M. Clayton (brother of former governor Powell Clayton) in the Second. Since these were federal elections, both candidates could and did contest the results in the U.S. House of Representatives. That body ultimately declared both contestants to have won their elections, but only Featherston took office. Clayton was assassinated in Conway County while gathering evidence, apparently as the result of a scheme planned and carried out by prominent local Democrats, although the crime officially remained an unsolved "mystery." Democratic candidates carried the state's other three

---

[33] Paisley, "Political Wheelers," 17–18; Summers, *Party Games*, 12–13, 117–121; Little Rock *Arkansas Gazette*, September 22, 1888 (all CarlLee quotations); Barnes, *Who Killed John Clayton?*, 96 (last quotation).
[34] Whayne et al., *Arkansas*, 279 (quotation); Krista M. Jones, "'It Was Awful, But It Was Politics': Crittenden County and the Demise of African American Political Participation" (MA thesis, University of Arkansas, 2012), 62–83; Story L. Matkin-Rawn, "'We Fight for the Rights of Our Race': Black Arkansans in the Era of Jim Crow" (PhD diss., University of Wisconsin–Madison, 2009), 45, 47–48.

congressional districts by comfortable margins.[35]

Despite all the violence and fraud that Arkansas Democrats brought to bear against Union Laborites and Republicans in 1888, the coalition persisted into 1890. The ULP nominated Napoleon Bonaparte Fizer, a Methodist minister, to run for governor against Eagle, and once again the state Republican Party endorsed the ULP candidate. Voter turnout set a record again, and Eagle won by a slightly larger margin this time as, according to historian Carl H. Moneyhon, "once again violence and intimidation were used to ensure a Democratic victory."[36] The number of African Americans elected to the state legislature actually increased, however, to twelve, including one state senator.[37] In the congressional elections, Featherston narrowly lost his bid for reelection in the First District. ULP candidate (and veteran Wheeler and Knight of Labor) Isom P. Langley also lost narrowly. This time, however, the declared losers did not contest the results, discouraged if not by Clayton's fate then by the fact that control of the U.S. House of Representatives had now passed to the Democratic Party.[38]

The following year proved to be, in some ways, a crushing one for black political and labor activism in Arkansas. The Democratic-controlled state legislature passed the Election Law of 1891, which created a centralized election bureaucracy that took control of the election machinery away from local authorities and gave it to state authorities (meaning, at this time and for decades to come, Democrats). The law also essentially disfranchised illiterate voters, which included at least 13 percent of white men of voting

---

[35] Graves, *Town and Country*, 142–143; Barnes, *Who Killed John Clayton?*, 65, 75–81; Michael J. Dubin, comp., *United States Congressional Elections, 1788–1997: The Official Results of the Elections of the 1st through 105th Congresses* (Jefferson, NC: McFarland & Co., 1998), 279, 286 notes 2 and 3.

[36] Little Rock *Arkansas Democrat*, June 11, 1890; Graves, *Town and Country*, 141; Carl H. Moneyhon, *Arkansas and the New South, 1874–1929* (Fayetteville: University of Arkansas Press, 1997), 89.

[37] Gordon, *Caste and Class*, 19.

[38] Hild, "Labor, Third-Party Politics, and New South Democracy," 37.

age in the state and 56 percent of black men.[39] Meanwhile, the National Agricultural Wheel and the southern Farmers' Alliance had merged; the Wheel's name disappeared—the new organization ultimately adopted the name National Farmers' Alliance and Industrial Union of America—and African American Wheelers were suddenly excluded once again. Wheelers and Alliancemen approved the merger at a joint meeting in Meridian, Mississippi, in December 1888, but the organization's state chapters would have to approve it. In Arkansas, the merger faced opposition from Wheelers and was further complicated by the existence of two competing state Alliance organizations, but it finally won approval in 1891.[40]

By then, the Colored Farmers' Alliance had already made significant inroads into Arkansas. In December 1890, Richard M. Humphrey, the white "general superintendent" of the Colored Alliance, claimed the organization had 20,000 members in the state.[41] The Colored Farmers' Alliance sometimes worked in cooperation with the National Farmers' Alliance and Industrial Union, but tensions existed between the two organizations, especially since many members of the former worked as farmhands for members of the latter. This conflict of economic interests came to a brutal head in September 1891. During that month, Humphrey issued a call for a strike of African American cotton pickers after planters in some parts of the South—including Memphis and Charleston, South Carolina—held conventions at which they decided to pay pickers no more than fifty cents per hundred pounds. When Humphrey encountered significant opposition to this proposal within the ranks of the Colored Alliance, largely on the well-founded grounds that such a strike would be dangerous, he formed a splinter group called the Cotton Pickers League to

[39] Moneyhon, *Arkansas and the New South*, 90.
[40] Hild, *Greenbackers, Knights of Labor, and Populists*, 122; McMath, *Populist Vanguard*, 46, 58–60, 87; Graves, *Town and Country*, 204–205.
[41] Omar H. Ali, *In the Lion's Mouth: Black Populism in the New South, 1886–1900* (Jackson: University Press of Mississippi, 2010), 49.

facilitate the strike. He then declared that more than one million pickers would go on strike on September 12. Historian William F. Holmes suggests, however, that in all likelihood "the majority of cotton pickers—most of whom were illiterate—never knew of the proposed strike."[42]

In most parts of the South, the strike never materialized, but in a few isolated instances it did, most notably (and tragically) in Lee County, Arkansas. The Knights of Labor had been active in Lee County from 1885 until at least as late as 1890, and while no evidence establishes that organization's involvement in the strike, it may have laid a foundation for black labor protest. An African American labor organizer from Memphis named Ben Patterson apparently started organizing efforts in Lee County in early September 1891, but local blacks soon assumed control of the movement. The results, however, proved disastrous. The Lee County strike began on September 20, and five days later strikers killed two pickers on a plantation where the pickers refused to join the strike. Three days later, strikers killed a white plantation manager. By this point, the county sheriff already had formed a posse and launched a manhunt for Patterson and other strike leaders. By the beginning of October, the strike came to a dismal conclusion, after the posse had killed fourteen strikers and Patterson. The strike also essentially destroyed the Colored Alliance, which fell into a rapid and irreversible decline.[43]

[42] William F. Holmes, "The Arkansas Cotton Pickers Strike of 1891 and the Demise of the Colored Farmers' Alliance," *Arkansas Historical Quarterly* 32 (Summer 1973): 107–119 (quotation on 113).

[43] Holmes, "The Arkansas Cotton Pickers Strike of 1891," 113–119; Gerald H. Gaither, *Blacks and the Populist Movement: Ballots and Bigotry in the New South*, rev. ed. (Tuscaloosa: University of Alabama Press, 2005), 27–30; Garlock, *Guide to the Local Assemblies*, 15; Biegert, "Legacy of Resistance," 81–83; William F. Holmes, "The Demise of the Colored Farmers' Alliance," *Journal of Southern History* 41 (May 1975): 200. Garlock does not specify that any of the Knights of Labor local assemblies in Lee County included African Americans, but as he notes, the data available "reveals relatively little about the actual racial, sex, or ethnic composition of the Knights of Labor....Such information about the members of specific LAs [local assemblies] is limited to 5 percent of all assemblies" (*Guide to the*

The combination of the Arkansas Election Law of 1891 and the disastrous cotton pickers strike halted and even reversed the momentum that the state's black political and labor activists had built during the preceding years. The white agrarian and labor protest movements were also entering a period of decline. After two spirited campaigns that were defeated by the usurpation of democracy itself by Arkansas Democrats, the Arkansas Union Labor Party gave way to the People's (or Populist) Party.[44] The Arkansas Populists continued the efforts of the Knights of Labor, Agricultural Wheel, and ULP at interracial cooperation; historian Lawrence Goodwyn contends that "Arkansas Populists, both politically and personally, demonstrated the clearest record of racial liberalism of any of the southern third parties."[45] Arkansas's Populist Party distinguished itself from its counterparts in many other states in 1892 by appointing a black delegate to the national party's Omaha, Nebraska, convention.[46]

But even as the third-party movement grew in other Southern states under the Populist banner, in Arkansas the moment had passed. Arkansas Republicans decided to nominate their own state ticket in 1892, prompting the pro-Populist *Faulkner County Wheel* to remark laconically that "the [state] Democratic committee will doubtlessly pay them well for the privilege of using their names as Republican candidates," predicting that "when [President Benjamin] Harrison is reelected he will appoint these martyrs to fill the post offices in this state."[47] Furthermore, with the Election Law of 1891 in effect, nearly 36,000 fewer voters

---

Local Assemblies, xxi–xxii).

[44] The continuity among the leadership of the Arkansas Union Labor and Populist parties can be readily discerned by examining the lists of delegates at state conventions of the two parties. See the Little Rock *Arkansas Gazette*, May 1, 1888, June 11, 1890, June 22, 1892.

[45] Lawrence Goodwyn, *Democratic Promise: The Populist Moment in America* (New York: Oxford University Press, 1976), 298.

[46] Hild, *Greenbackers, Knights of Labor, and Populists*, 147, 266n.90.

[47] Conway (Ark.) *Faulkner County Wheel*, n.d., quoted in the Atlanta *People's Party Paper*, August 5, 1892. On Populist gains in other Southern states after 1892, see McMath, *American Populism*, 195–198.

cast ballots in the state elections of 1892 than two years earlier. When some armed black men in Calhoun County who could not vote under the new law attempted to do so anyway, officials responded with force, killing at least four black men. The Populist state ticket finished third, while the Democratic ticket received a higher percentage of the vote than in any of the three previous contests.[48] In the congressional elections, the Arkansas Populist and Republican parties agreed not to compete with each other, but no Populist candidate received more than 40 percent of the vote.[49]

Men who were able to participate in the state election of 1892 were voting not only on candidates but also on a poll tax passed by the state legislature. According to the official results, 75,847 Arkansans voted to approve the poll tax, while 56,589 voted against it.[50] The next state election, two years later, tallied the lowest voter turnout in fourteen years. By the end of the century, the People's Party, the Farmers' Alliance, and the Knights of Labor were essentially finished in Arkansas, as was the case just about everywhere else as well.[51]

Nevertheless, the efforts of African Americans in Arkansas to assert their rights as workers and citizens during Reconstruction and the two decades that followed should not be considered to have been fruitless or in vein. With the perspective of hindsight, the efforts of Bryant Singfield to organize newly emancipated black farmhands in Phillips County, of the Knights of Labor in Pulaski County and elsewhere in the state among black farmhands and laborers, and of the Cotton Pickers League in Lee County all paved the way for later black labor activism in the state. Similarly, that the efforts of the Progressive Farmers and Household Union

---

[48] Moneyhon, *Arkansas and the New South*, 90–91; John L. Moore, Jon P. Preimesbeger, and David R. Tarr, eds., *Congressional Quarterly's Guide to U.S. Elections*, 4th ed. (Washington DC: CQ Press, 2001), 2: 1419.
[49] Dubin, *United States Congressional Elections*, 295.
[50] Graves, *Town and Country*, 185–194.
[51] Hild, *Greenbackers, Knights of Labor, and Populists*, 177–178, 201–204; Hild, "Labor, Third-Party Politics, and New South Democracy," 41–42.

of America, which continued the legacy of these earlier protest movements, met with violent repression in Phillips County in 1919 should not cast the pall of abject failure on those efforts, for they helped pave the way for the formation of the Southern Tenant Farmers' Union (STFU) in Poinsett County fifteen years later. Isaac Shaw embodied this connection; the black sharecropper had belonged to the Progressive Farmers and Household Union and became one of the founding members of the STFU. Not only did the STFU revive the Greenback-to-Populist-era efforts at interracial activism in Arkansas and elsewhere—although it too met with violent repression—but in some significant ways it provided a useful legacy for the civil rights movement that followed some two decades later, even to the extent that "many younger members of the STFU went on to become leaders in the local civil rights movement in Arkansas."[52] Thus the participation of African Americans in the labor and third-party movements in Arkansas during the period from Reconstruction until the 1890s should be seen as having laid the foundations for the more significant movements of the twentieth century.

---

[52] Biegert, "Legacy of Resistance," 73–99 (quotation on 88); F. Ray Marshall, *Labor in the South* (Cambridge, MA: Harvard University Press, 1967), 158–165; William H. Cobb, "Southern Tenant Farmers' Union," *Encyclopedia of Arkansas History & Culture*, http://www.encyclopediaofarkansas.net/encyclopedia/entry-detail.aspx?entryID=35 (accessed February 23, 2018).

134

Civilians welcoming military troops to Elaine; October 1, 1919.
Photo courtesy of Pat Rowe

Soldiers at bivouac awaiting inspection at Elaine.
Photo courtesy of Pat Rowe

Soldiers placing machine guns on rooftop at Elaine; October 1919.
Photo courtesy of Pat Rowe

Schoolhouse used as a temporary stockade for African-American detainees at Elaine; October 1919.
Photo courtesy of Pat Rowe

American Red Cross canteen at Elaine.; October 1919.
Photo courtesy of Pat Rowe

Machine gun company awaiting inspection at Elaine; October 1919.
Photo courtesy of Pat Rowe

Motor Transport Corps of the U.S. troops at Elaine; October 1919.
Photo courtesy of Pat Rowe

The twelve Elaine Massacre defendants.
Courtesy of the Butler Center for Arkansas Studies, Central Arkansas
Library System

Elaine Massacre defendants Ed Hicks, Frank Hicks, Frank Moore,
J. E. Knox, Ed Coleman, and Paul Hall. Scipio A. Jones, the group's
counsel, stands to the left.
Courtesy of the Butler Center for Arkansas Studies, Central Arkansas
Library System

Chapter 5

Black Organizing through Fraternal Orders: Black Mobilization and White Backlash

Adrienne A. Jones

Africa American fraternal associations have historically served black communities as a way by which members could organize, network, socialize, self-govern, and engage in politics. These associations provided a means for self-help and mutual aid to their members and their local communities—and, at times, helped the race as a whole through mutual uplift. In the years following Reconstruction, black citizens were largely restricted from exercising their newly gained civil rights. Many channels toward bettering the quality of life were blocked, such as procuring voting rights, owning real estate, and pursuing economic independence. They were also restricted from access to various forms of insurance and free assembly with one another outside of church gatherings. Fraternal associations provided solutions to this oppression in offering members a sense of community, access to services denied to them due to their race, and channels through which to exercise their rights and express their patriotism as American citizens.

Prince Hall Freemasonry is the first and oldest black fraternal order in the United States, but many fraternal organizations came to be established throughout the country, notably from the post–Civil War and Reconstruction eras through to the Great Depression, most with the shared goal of bettering their members' place in society. These fraternal orders and benevolent societies often shared one another's influences in rituals, symbolism, and providing aid to their members. By the 1900s, fraternal organizations were the highest-populated bodies of association among African Americans, second only to the black church. Black organizing through fraternal associations was personally beneficial to members, as it helped them gain access to necessities such as health, life, death, and burial insurance. But these organizations served black communities in other, intangible ways, and, as stated by scholars Ariane Liazos and Marshall Ganz, "Most of their own members and the whites who opposed them understood that they played a much more important role."[1]

Some black fraternal organizations were formed parallel to already established white orders who denied memberships to blacks, but there were also black fraternal organizations that originated from black founders without white counterparts. Both types operated autonomously from white fraternal organizations. Even though the parallel black fraternal organizations received their charters from white lodges, it appears that many did not get these charters from American white lodges but instead received their charters from the same grand lodges of European origin. Despite this, black fraternal organizations tended to be civicly centered and highly patriotic. Some were religious; others were not. A common theme that can be found in all black fraternal organizations was the underlying objective to uplift their black members and foster a sense of community.

These fraternal organizations were beneficial to thousands of African Americans and their communities. In these groups, members built up black self-worth, found pride in blackness, aided black communities, and provided channels of networking across state lines. Black fraternal organizations served as support systems to their black members at a time when overt racism and oppression were omnipresent. Despite the fact that the Reconstruction era saw a soaring number of black men in political offices

---

[1] Ariane Liazos and Marshall Ganz, "Duty to the Race: African American Fraternal Orders and the Legal Defense of the Right to Organize," *Social Science History* 28 (Fall 2004): 487.

across the country, and especially in the South, African Americans simultaneously found themselves fighting against restrictive access to engage in newly established constitutional liberties and newfound civil rights. The Jim Crow system of racial segregation effectively stripped the aforementioned liberties and civil rights to meaningless shells, thereby reestablishing legal white oppression against blacks. Black organizing of this nature, even in light of black fraternal orders promoting patriotism and solid citizenship, came to be viewed as a threat.

This chapter will focus on the earliest black fraternal organizing in this country, beginning with Prince Hall Freemasonry and its early leaders in the Arkansas lodge. Next will be an overview of the most successful and well-known black-founded fraternal organization, the Mosaic Templars of America. Finally, this chapter closes with an overview of the Progressive Farmers and Household Union of America, the fraternal farmers' union that was demonized and whose members were blamed for the horrific events of the 1919 Elaine Massacre.

Prince Hall Freemasonry

Though shrouded in secrecy and legend, Freemasonry at its most basic can be viewed as encompassing organized associations of fraternal orders that share some common aim or goal in self-improvement, morality, philosophical naturalism, and social advancement. There is no clear way in which to trace the history of Freemasonry. The origin of this network of fraternities is associated with the ancient craft guild, or the Craft, of stonemasons. This association with stonework is visible in the usage of stonemasons' tools as fraternal symbols. Fraternal symbolism is also found in various rituals and Masonic allegories. Old Masonic documents, known as Old Charges or Ancient Regulations, detail a Mason's various obligations, duties, and Masonic grades or degrees. These documents also detail elaborate, mythological lineages connecting the Craft back to ancient figures and/or biblical times.

142

The Regius poem, also known as the Halliwell Manuscript, circa 1390, is considered the oldest Masonic document. This poem describes the history of Masonry as having come out of Egypt with the Greek mathematician Euclid, who "counterfeited geometry and gave it the name of Masonry."[2] This poem, along with other Masonic manuscripts, was in use by scattered fraternal associations, but it was not until the eighteenth century when the first Masonic body was organized in London. In June 1717, the Grand Lodge of England was formed from four London lodges and established a governing law and jurisdiction over the numerous lodges as the world's first Grand Lodge.[3] Six years later, the Grand Lodge of England published *The Book of Constitutions of Masonry*, the first official rule book of the worldwide fraternal order. In 1725, the Grand Lodge of Ireland, the second Grand Lodge in the world, was established, and together the two senior lodges spread the Masonic rites, rituals, and teachings across Western Europe. By 1736, these "Home Grand Lodges" had spread Freemasonry overseas throughout the British Empire.[4] Established in 1733, the Grand Lodge of Massachusetts was the first Grand Lodge founded in the United States. Black Freemasonry would emerge from this lodge and take hold across black communities in America.

Black Freemasonry began in the tumultuous climate of the American Revolution—a time when enlightened political and philosophical ideas about liberty, freedom, individual sovereignty, and republicanism were espoused among the colonists in America. These were ideals long held as fundamental truths in Freemasonry. Therefore, it may be no coincidence that Prince Hall and at least some of the fourteen other free black men who

[2] "The Regius Poem," *PS Review of Freemasonry*, http://www.Freemasons-freeMasonry.com/regius.html (accessed August 12, 2017).
[3] "History of Freemasonry," United Grand Lodge of England, http://ugle.org.uk/about-freemasonry/history-of-freemasonry (accessed August 12, 2017).
[4] "History of Freemasonry," United Grand Lodge of England.

founded the first black Masonic lodge potentially had ties to the American Revolution.[5]

Not much is known about Prince Hall's early life prior to 1775, when he and fourteen other free black men set out to join a Masonic lodge in Boston, Massachusetts. From the early 1900s onward, historians had agreed upon Hall's place of birth, whether he was born into slavery or born free, and the ethnicity of his parents, but recent scholarship has called these details into question. What is now generally agreed upon is that there were six free black men in the Revolutionary War military records named Prince Hall living in Massachusetts and that the founder of black Masonry was probably one of these men.

The history of Prince Hall, as told by the various state lodges of the fraternal order, state that the legendary founder was born around 1735, varying regarding whether his birth was free in Barbados or enslaved in Boston. Most agree that Hall later worked in a leather workshop as a free man in America. This history goes on to say that Hall was an early champion of equal rights as a staunch patriot and abolitionist who worked toward realizing the American ideal of liberty and freedom in his service in the American Revolution and as an abolitionist.[6] As such, this history paints Hall as understanding the full meaning behind the era's revolutionary rhetoric of all men being created equal. This makes Hall a seminal figure in some of the earliest fights for black equality.

Prince Hall's legendary early life and motivation remain unclear, but the details surrounding this figure become more firmly established when he becomes initiated into Freemasonry in 1775 along with fourteen other free black men by members of

---

[5] At least six free black men in Massachusetts named Prince Hall have Revolutionary War era military records. It is theorized that the founding father of African American Freemasonry was possibly one of these soldiers. See Sidney Kaplan and Emma Nogrady Kaplan, *The Black Presence in the Era of the American Revolution*, rev. edition (Amherst: University of Massachusetts Press, 1989).

[6] Most Worshipful Prince Hall Grand Lodge Jurisdiction of Arkansas, F.&A.M., http://arkphagrandlodge.net/index.html (accessed July 15, 2017).

the Lodge of Ireland No. 441, which was one of many foreign fraternal lodges present during the American Revolutionary War. Hall and the fourteen others had already been turned away from joining Masonic lodges established in the colonies and therefore sought initiation by foreign Masons who were present among foreign military stations. The newly initiated Masons of color almost immediately found that they were not accepted by America's white Masons, nor were they considered a legitimate Masonic body by fellow white Freemasons. From 1775 to 1784, the black Masonic body established by Hall consisted of only the initial fifteen black men and, according to historian Maurice Wallace, "remained provisional...restricted to just a few of the privileges regularly exercised by permanent lodges."[7]

These black Masons were limited to performing burial rites and participating in Masonic parades but were unable either to create a charter or to initiate other black Masons (they were repeatedly discouraged from doing so by the white Masonic lodges). Recognizing the lack of fraternal equality and the need for legitimacy from a home lodge, Prince Hall petitioned the Grand Lodge of England for a charter in 1784. The originating Grand Lodge issued this charter that same year, and it was delivered in 1787 by Captain James Scott, brother-in-law of John Hancock, a signer of the Declaration of Independence.[8] After twelve years, Prince Hall and the other black Masons were finally able to establish African Lodge No. 459 in Boston with Prince Hall as the Grand Master. In 1797, Hall established two other such lodges in Pennsylvania and Rhode Island. These so-called African lodges, along with the one in Boston, would form the African Grand Lodge of North America. Hall died in 1807, and the following year the African

---

[7] Maurice Wallace, "'Are We Men?': Prince Hall, Martin Delany, and the Masculine Ideal in Black Freemasonry, 1775–1865," *American Literary History* 9 (Autumn 1997): 397, 419.

[8] Bro. George Draffen, Deputy Master, Grand Lodge of Scotland, "Prince Hall Freemasonry," http://fosterglenn.tripod.com/prince_hall_freemasonry.htm (accessed July 18, 2017).

Grand Lodge of North American changed its name to the Prince Hall Grand Lodge of Massachusetts.

Prince Hall lodges, which operated with the same autonomy as other Masonic lodges, helped fraternal orders become accessible in black communities across America. In the centuries to come, fraternal organizations served as the most popular form of association and membership in black communities, second only to black churches, which in many ways became interwoven with black fraternal organizing. Both the black church and the black fraternity sought to serve the oppressed, excluded, and socially stigmatized black community. Black access to political positions after the Civil War added a third element to an interwoven relationship between the black church and fraternal organizing, evidenced in Prince Hall Freemasonry's establishment in Arkansas.

Prince Hall Freemasonry in Arkansas

Black Freemasonry was brought to Arkansas in 1869 when the Prince Hall Grand Lodge of Missouri's Grand Lecturer, the Reverend Moses A. Dickinson, arrived in Helena, Arkansas. The Grand Lodge of Arkansas's history states that, upon arriving to Arkansas, Rev. Dickinson's first contact was influential black minister and politician William Henry Grey.[9] Soon thereafter, three Masonic lodges were established in Arkansas: J. M. Alexander Lodge in Helena, Widow's Son Lodge in Fort Smith, and Jeptha Lodge in Little Rock. In 1873, these lodges combined to form the Most Worshipful Grand Lodge (Colored) of Free and Accepted Masons (Most Worshipful Grand Lodge of F.A.A.M.) in Arkansas, with William H. Grey elected as the first Grand Master.[10] From here,

---

[9] "History of Freemasonry in Arkansas," Most Worshipful Prince Hall Grand Lodge Jurisdiction of Arkansas, F.&A.M., http://arkphagrandlodge. net/history-of-freemasonry-in-Arkansas.html (accessed July 15, 2017).
[10] "History of Freemasonry in Arkansas," Most Worshipful Prince Hall Grand Lodge Jurisdiction of Arkansas. The Grand Lodge is currently known as The Most Worshipful Prince Hall Grand Lodge Jurisdiction of Arkansas, F.&A.M.

Freemasonry continued to spread and grow across the state with highly regarded, distinguished members and Grand Masters.

Grey was elected to the Arkansas General Assembly, one of its first eight black members, in 1868. That same year, he served as the Republican delegate for the Republican National Convention. In 1872, Grey was again elected as a delegate for the GOP convention, where he delivered a speech backing Ulysses S. Grant for president. This was the first address delivered by a black person to a major political party's presidential convention.[11] Grey was elected as the Commissioner of Immigration and State Lands in 1872. In 1875, he was elected to the Arkansas Senate. During his political career, Grey spoke out against anti-miscegenation laws and was an advocate for black suffrage. His last position of public service was as Phillips County clerk before he became paralyzed from an indeterminate illness in 1878. He died in 1888.

The second Grand Master of the Most Worshipful Grand Lodge (Colored) of F.A.A.M. in Arkansas was John H. Johnson. Born in Ohio around 1840, Johnson was an attorney who moved to Arkansas at the close of the Civil War in 1865 after his service as a Union army soldier.[12] Like many other politically active blacks during the Reconstruction era, Johnson worked in the Republican Party, and he was elected to the Arkansas House of Representatives in 1873.[13] In 1884, Johnson was elected temporary chairman of the Republican National Convention, where he gave a speech, according to the *Arkansas Democrat*, calling for the party to "act in harmonious concert and work together as one man to defeat the enemy. [Johnson] believed that if the Republican Party was defeated in the coming campaign the interest and privileges of hundreds of thousands of people of the South would be imped-

---

[11] Tom Dillard, "Three Important Black Leaders in Phillips County History," *Phillips County Historical Quarterly* 19 (December 1980–March 1981): 10–21.
[12] "John H. Johnson," Arkansas Black Lawyers, http://arkansasblacklawyers.uark.edu/lawyers/jhjohnson.html (accessed August 5, 2017).
[13] "Proclamation by the Governor," *The Weekly New Era*, October 1, 1873.

ed."[14] Namely, the rights and privileges of blacks in the South would be further impeded by the Democratic Party and the rise of Jim Crow segregation laws. John H. Johnson died in Little Rock on July 12, 1884.[15]

The third Grand Master was educator Joseph C. Corbin, founder and first principal of Branch Normal College, the first black higher education institution in the state; it is now the University of Arkansas at Pine Bluff. Corbin was born in Ohio in 1833 and graduated from Ohio University. By 1871, Corbin was living in Little Rock, Arkansas, and working as a reporter.[16] From July 6, 1873, to December 18, 1875, Corbin served as Arkansas's second superintendent of public instruction.[17] In 1875, he was hired as the principal of Branch Normal College. At its first annual convention in 1887, Corbin was serving as president of the Colored Teachers' State Association of Arkansas. This teachers' association would eventually become the Arkansas Teachers Association and later the integrated Arkansas Education Association, still in operation today.[18] Corbin remained principal over Branch Normal College until 1902. Within his fraternity, Corbin was recognized as "one of the most prominent colored Masons in Arkansas."[19] In 1897 the Worshipful Grand Lodge of F.A.A.M. awarded him for his service of twenty-six consecutive years as Grand Secretary. He died in 1911.

Grey, Johnson, and Corbin exemplify many black leaders fol-

---

[14] "Republican State Convention," *Arkansas Democrat*, April 8, 1884.

[15] *Daily Arkansas Gazette*, July 14, 1885.

[16] Little Rock City Directory, 1871, 51.

[17] "J.C. Corbin Died Today; Negro Educator Who Was Once Superintendent of Public Instruction," *Arkansas Democrat*, January 9, 1911; "Educator's Pictures; Supt. George B. Cook Will Secure Picture of Each Past Superintendent," *Arkansas Democrat*, January 10, 1911.

[18] "The Colored Teachers' State Association of Arkansas," *Daily Arkansas Gazette*, June 2, 1887; "The Colored Teachers' Association of Arkansas," *Arkansas Democrat*, June 15, 1887.

[19] "The Colored Grand Lodge, Its Labors Completed Friday Night after a Three Days Session; Many Prominent Masons Were in Attendance—The Installation Exercises," *Pine Bluff Daily Graphic*, August 15, 1897.

lowing the close of the Civil War. Most who were politically active aligned themselves with the Republican Party, viewing this as the political vessel through which they could work toward ensuring that newly freed blacks and black communities had the legal protection and citizenship rights promised to them through the Reconstruction amendments. It is no surprise that many of these same individuals were interested in fraternal organizations, whose own objectives were geared toward equal treatment and civil rights. These organizations also provided beneficial services that were often denied by white providers, such as burial insurance, death policies, and sick funds. Black fraternities folded hundreds of thousands of African Americans into varied, and sometimes multiple, associations' memberships that offered networking channels for black communities to engage with one another, locally and nationally. Prince Hall Freemasonry was the first to embody this network of black connectivity, self-determination, and sense of community, providing a model for other black fraternal organizations that had white counterparts in their same struggle for autonomy after being denied access to white orders. But there are other fraternal associations with singularly black origins. One of the most visible and successful fraternal organizations whose origins are uniquely black is the Mosaic Templars of America.

Mosaic Templars of America

The Mosaic Templars of America (MTA) was a fraternal society that provided its members with insurance benefits. Taking its name from the biblical figure of Moses, who led the Israelites out from bondage in Egypt, the MTA sought to provide leadership and protection to its members, who continued to suffer from oppression as people newly freed from bondage themselves. Burial insurance and life insurance, as well as a fund to aid members who became sick, were the main focus. Blacks typically had limited access to these services from white providers. Co-founders John E. Bush and Chester W. Keatts, former slaves who became noted black leaders in business and politics, founded the MTA in 1882 and incorporated it the following year in Arkansas's capital city of Little Rock. According to its founders, the MTA was created in response to three distinct causes: "First, a white man's scorn; second, a Negro woman's poverty; third a Negro's shame."[20] Having experienced the bondage of slavery and the hardship of life as newly free blacks firsthand, Bush and Keatts sought to organize blacks and establish a means for mutual aid.

John Edward Bush was born in Tennessee in 1856. Bush came to Little Rock with his mother in 1862 but was soon orphaned by her death. He survived by the aid of strangers, sleeping where he could in the open and in abandoned structures. Born around 1854 near Little Rock, Chester W. Keatts began life in slavery and was forced to care for himself throughout much of his childhood.[21] Both Bush and Keatts were drawn to school and driven to succeed in their education. By the 1870s, both men gained respectable employment as clerks within the United States Railway Mail Service, with Bush later becoming the first black person promoted to chief clerk and Keatts serving a total of nineteen years.[22] Having worked to better their own quality of life, Bush and Keatts wanted to form a beneficial fraternity to help the local black community.

According to the fraternal order's history, the need for blacks to have a means to bury their dead and have a safety net when people became ill was a driving factor for Bush and Keatts in establishing the MTA so that black people would no longer have to engage in "public solicitation of funds."[23] These services were central to the order from the start. The insurance policies and sick fund are listed in the MTA's constitution along with MTA mem-

[20] A. E. Bush and P. L. Dorman, *History of the Mosaic Templars of America—Its Founders and Officials* (Fayetteville: University of Arkansas Press, 2008), 81.
[21] Bush and Dorman, *History of the Mosaic Templars of America*, 13.
[22] Bush and Dorman, *History of the Mosaic Templars of America*, 25; "Colored Mail Clerk Dead," *Arkansas Democrat*, January 17, 1908.
[23] Bush and Dorman, *History of the Mosaic Templars of America*, 132.

bers' objective "to unite fraternally all good, healthy and acceptable persons of good moral character of every profession, business and occupation."[24] Given the high need for these services in
Little Rock's black community, the MTA was successful in this
endeavor from its founding. In 1883, the year the MTA incorporated, John E. Bush (now Grand Scribe) reported that the order
was "spreading very fast," as seen in a festival the order held that
year with a turnout of 200 to 300 that raised about fifty dollars, the
equivalent of a little over $1,100 today.[25] This was just the start of
the order's growth.

Nearly ten years after the MTA's founding, the order's 1891
annual session was described in the *Arkansas Democrat* as "the
largest colored secret organization of the world, and has a membership of 12,000," with over 300 representatives of MTA lodges
from eight states outside of Arkansas: Alabama, Kansas, Kentucky, Louisiana, Missouri, Mississippi, Tennessee, and Texas.[26]
In 1910, the MTA's branches outside of Arkansas had grown to
over 1,000 branches across twelve states.[27] By the order's 1925
Founders' Day celebration, the MTA described itself as "the largest fraternal insurance organization among Negroes in the world,"
having begun with fifteen members but growing to over 100,000
members in twenty-six states, as well as the West Indies, Central
America, and Africa; the organization also held assets of one million dollars.[28] The MTA's success over the course of forty plus
years was impressive, but the foundation of the fraternal order's
origins was not unique. Thousands of benevolent societies, black

[24] Bush and Dorman, *History of the Mosaic Templars of America*, 141.
[25] "Local News: Mosaic Templars," *Arkansas Weekly Mansion*, October 27,
1883.
[26] "Mosaic Templars: Largest Colored Secret Order in the World in Session Here; Organization Formed Nine Years Ago and Has a Membership
of 12,000—Nine States Represented," *Arkansas Democrat*, September 9,
1891.
[27] "Mosaic Templars Here; National Committee of Management Has Many
Questions to Decide," *Arkansas Democrat*, August 31, 1910.
[28] "History of the Order," Records of Mosaic Templars of America: History
of the Mosaic Templars and Souvenir Programs 1925 and 1930.

and white, arose in the same period, offering members varied insurance benefits. The MTA stands out as being a distinctively black order that originated in the South in a former slave state before rapidly expanding across America and internationally.

Central to the MTA's appeal was the fraternal structure and the essential benefits through its insurance policies and sick fund. But another factor behind its amazing growth emerged—its effort to instill black pride. Listed in the MTA's 1925 Souvenir Program are ten reasons to join the order, the first being that the order was "the result of Negro Brain and effort."[29] Removing the shame of slavery and fighting against continued discrimination were central for establishing black pride. Bush and Keatts determined that this pride would come through education, thriftiness, and industrious work, equipping blacks to withstand and rise above poverty and racial oppression. The MTA and other fraternal and benevolent societies' success in black organizing and uplift had made great strides for numerous black communities after the Civil War, but when Reconstruction came to an end in 1874, ideologies of black positivity became even more important. Post–Civil War racial prejudice and de facto segregation were not new forms of discrimination. In Arkansas, some legislative measures establishing legal segregation within public facilities had already been enacted following the close of the Civil War, such as a statute passed in 1868 for segregated schools.[30] Actions like these, however, did not hinder black leaders and fraternal orders like the MTA from promoting black pride and speaking out against the regressive racial tensions that were on the rise.

In Arkansas, once the separate coach law passed in 1891 legally separated black passengers from all other passengers, MTA

[29] "Ten Reasons Why You Should Be a Mosaic," Records of Mosaic Templars of America: History of the Mosaic Templars and Souvenir Programs 1925 and 1930.
[30] John William Graves, "Jim Crow in Arkansas: A Reconsideration of Urban Race Relations in the Post-Reconstruction South," *Journal of Southern History* 55 (August 1989): 422–423.

Grand Master Keatts delivered a speech on how the laws were changing to turn back the rights given to blacks during the Reconstruction era. Keatts and others felt "the iron heel of oppression on the necks of colored people throughout the known world," and he questioned "[h]ow long will these things exist," making note that "the exercise of the ballot is a sacred constitutional right, and that any man who is denied the only legal protection he possesses, and the person or persons thus abridging the rights of any citizen is a violator of the law, and ought to be punished."[31] Keatts went on to say that blacks have always fought for this country as "honest, faithful and earnest soldier[s]" and are "therefore entitled to the protection of the same. A government too weak to protect her citizens is unworthy the name."[32] Black suffrage was held dear by many, as seen in Keatts's statement, but during this period it was beginning to be stripped away from blacks in large numbers. The black vote in Arkansas dropped from 71 percent in 1891 to 38 percent in 1893 with such measures as the passage of voter literacy tests and the enactment of a poll tax. It appears that Keatts, like other blacks at the end of the century, saw that the writing was on the wall—with equality, liberty, and freedom retreating on a regressive tide.

In his address to the 1903 annual Grand Lodge meeting, Keatts spoke on the "race problem" as seen at that time, stating that blacks had "made considerable progress," but "the race problem has continuously been the uppermost thought of the American people, both white and black," particularly in the South, "where master and slave were compelled to confront, face to face, the problem of a new relationship which neither was prepared to solve."[33] The solution Keatts offered aligned to the MTA's principles of black education, hard work, and thriftiness, which, in

[31] "Mosaic Templars: Resolutions Adopted by That Order Yesterday," *Arkansas Democrat*, September 12, 1891.
[32] "Mosaic Templars: Resolutions Adopted by That Order Yesterday," *Arkansas Democrat*, September 12, 1891.
[33] "Race Problem up to Negro," *Arkansas Democrat*, July 21, 1903.

turn, would continue to lift up the blacks of this country through economic independence. However, the improved quality of life of members of the black community did not change white perception, nor did it curb racial prejudice. New legislation systematically disenfranchised blacks across all facets of society as part of a white backlash that rose in direct relationship to the patriotic citizenship, political activism, civic mindedness, and economic success of African Americans.

Both highly regarded founders of the MTA had been honored upon their deaths. Chester W. Keatts died on January 17, 1908, and John E. Bush died on December 11, 1916. Both men are buried in the Oakland and Fraternal Historic Cemetery in Little Rock.

The MTA survived through the early phases of Jim Crow, but the order could not withstand the Depression and folded in the early 1930s. The MTA helped hundreds of thousands of blacks with insurance benefits, and before the fraternal order went under, it had begun providing the option of gravestones, as well as a local hospital with plans for a national hospital, though such plans were never realized.[34] Many of Arkansas's black leaders and community organizers were members or affiliated with the MTA, including but not limited to renowned attorney Scipio A. Jones, educator Joseph C. Corbin, and Judge Mifflin W. Gibbs. The MTA also attracted national black figures like Booker T. Washington, whose own principles of racial uplift aligned with the organization's.

As Keatts did in 1891, Booker T. Washington questioned in 1912—in his essay "Is the Negro Having a Fair Chance?"—whether the black community would ever be given the opportunity to succeed. Both men answered in the negative. Not only was Jim Crow the law of the land in many American states, but the administration of President Woodrow Wilson targeted access to

[34] Bryan McDade, "In Pursuit of a Better Life in the Vapor City: Understanding the Contributions of the Mosaic Templars of America in Hot Springs, Arkansas," *The Record* (Garland County Historical Society) 54 (2013): 6.1–6.24.

voting at the national level. In 1915, the reemergence of the Ku Klux Klan brought an onslaught of organized violence and terror to black communities, furthering the divide in the question of the "race problem" Keatts had tried to address. This is the climate within which the Progressive Farmers and Household Union of America emerged—and was destroyed during the 1919 massacre in Phillips County, Arkansas.

Progressive Farmers and Household Union of America

The Progressive Farmers and Household Union of America (PFHUA) was established in Winchester, a small community located in Drew County, Arkansas, by local resident Robert L. Hill in 1918. Robert Lee Hill was born June 8, 1892 (or 1898) in Dermott, located in nearby Chicot County.[35] Little is known of his early life, but Hill did not come from the same background as the other aforementioned black fraternal founders and leaders: he did not serve in politics, was not an educator, did not preside over a religious body, and was not a prominent businessman. However, Hill was enthusiastic in his leadership in the PFHUA as councilor, and members commented on his engaging oratorical skills.

The PFHUA was modeled after other black fraternal and social organizations, as seen with their use of prayer in meetings, handshakes, passwords, membership fees, elected officers, claimed secrets, and the idea that the order's members would find strength in coming together and organizing for the benefit of all of its black members. The PFHUA stated that its overall objective was "to advance the interests of the Negro, morally and intellectually, and to make him a better citizen and a better farmer."[36] Another interesting aspect found in the union's literature is the association it

[35] Official records had both 1892 and 1898 as Hill's birth year; the exact year has not been determined.
[36] *The United States Constitution and By-Laws of the Progressive Farmers and Household Union*. Investigative Case Files of the Bureau of Investigation, 1908–1922, National Archives and Records Administration, publication number M1085, case number 373159, roll 820: 11.

claims to governmental bodies. According to the PFHUA's constitution and bylaws, this union was formed from an 1865 Act of Congress and first organized by R. J. Lee in 1897.[37] The union's history goes on to state that the PFHUA was revised by Hill and incorporated through the Arkansas Supreme Court in Little Rock, Arkansas. This may have been an attempt to make the union appear more legitimate.[38] As far as it can be determined, this fraternal farmers' union was originally formed and organized by Hill—and therefore distinctly black.

The union's total membership is not specifically known. The PFHUA had both male and female members, issued membership cards, received membership fees, and had lodges in Hoop Spur, Elaine, and Ratio—all small communities within Phillips County. The union's membership certificate filled out by members and signed by Hill had citizenship-affirming and patriotic language. Aside from general information of name, age, and place of birth, the certificate asks such questions as: "Do you give due respect to all humankind?", "Do you obey the law at all times?", "Do you believe in court?", and "Will you defend the Government and her Constitution at all times?" Finally, the certificate states at the bottom: "God grant that all men be equal in Thy sight and the sight of men. Examined by me and found fit to sit in the first Congress called by the Progressive Famers & Household Union of America, which Congress will be held in August at Winchester, Arkansas. Employed in the United States Service."[39] The patriotic language used notes that members were law-abiding citizens in-

---

[37] *The United States Constitution and By-Laws of the Progressive Farmers and Household Union*, roll 820: 12.

[38] Walter F. White of the NAACP claimed that the PFHUA was incorporated by the firm of Williamson and Williamson, former slave owners. Walter F. White, "'Massacring Whites' in Arkansas," *The Nation*, December 6, 1919, p. 715. Prince Hall Freemasonry, the oldest and largest black fraternal organization in country, has its foundation in first being giving certain masonic rites by European white masons in 1776, and later receiving its charter from the Grand Lodge of England in 1784.

[39] *The United States Constitution and By-Laws of the Progressive Farmers and Household Union*, roll 820: 5.

vested in the well-being of the country in the same vein as other fraternal organizations' promotion of civic duty and patriotism.

The union's bylaws laid out stipulations on how members who failed to pay membership dues should be handled, how to elect members and the corresponding duties expected of those elected, and punishments dealt to those caught stealing or revealing the order's secrets.[40] With the history laid out, the rules detailed, and the fees established, the articles of the PFHUA's constitution and by-laws brought its members together in a fraternal-like order with a mission to mobilize their community into action. This organization took up the cause of bettering the lives of its members, namely black farmers and their families, by seeking fair treatment, equal rights, and access to economic independence. The foundational mission was traditionally aligned with many black fraternal and benevolent orders, but the PFHUA's focus was on fair wages and treatment within agrarian-based work and correcting the cyclical poverty of the sharecropping system. The black laborers and tenant farmers in Phillips County were in the process of being able to change their socioeconomic status and leave behind the sharecropping system many had labored under. The rising price of cotton and the black laborers' demand for more-equitable settlements for their crops brought tensions to a head.

In his article "'We Have Just Begun': Black Organizing and White Response in the Arkansas Delta, 1919," author Kieran Taylor points toward cotton's market prices and exhibits how both the black laborers and the white elites reacted toward shifting economic expectations. The price of cotton, like many goods during wartime, had risen during World War I, from one pound of cotton selling at eleven cents in 1915 to more than doubling the following year, with one pound selling at twenty-three cents. The price per pound rose again in 1917 to twenty-eight cents, and by 1919 it

---

[40] *The United States Constitution and By-Laws of the Progressive Farmers and Household Union,* roll 820: 8.

was forty cents.[41] This market price growth allowed black laborers to buy their own farms and led to black landownership increasing by 40 percent between 1910 and 1920. This major growth in black farm ownership partially removed the control of white planters over this emerging independent black farmer class. But despite the economic growth for blacks in the county, the white elite class still controlled much of the market into which the black farmer sold, as well as many of the other goods and services needed.

White landowners, even before rising cotton prices allowed black labor to begin buying itself out of the sharecropping system, viewed as a threat to their position anything that might diminish their control over the laboring population—and economically independent African Americans were not the only targets of their ire. Wartime need for labor resulted in many black workers being transported from the county to work at military installations, in response to which a group of white professionals and farmers formed the Business Men's League (BML) in 1916. By the following year, the BML was making waves in the press with complaints against orders for wartime laborers being removed from Helena. The BML claimed that removing black labor from the area harmed their own business interests, and therefore a special committee was formed with the goal of making sure outsiders would be "persuaded to keep their hands off the labor situation."[42] Legal action was taken by BML against the Railroad Commission in federal court in order to keep the black laborers from leaving the county. The press described the use of the area's black laborers with a contemptuous tone, stating that black laborers "were carried away...supposedly to work for a silver smelting company at that point. They were employed by an agent from out of the

[41] Kieran Taylor, "'We Have Just Begun': Black Organizing and White Response in the Arkansas Delta, 1919," *Arkansas Historical Quarterly* 58 (Autumn 1999): 269.
[42] "Army Posts Will Use No More Negro Labor," *Helena World*, August 10, 1917.

158

city."[43] That same year, the BML was also protesting the "Department of Labor in Washington against the importation from Helena of Negro labor necessary in maintaining the agricultural timber and public industries of the community."[44] It was reported from the *Helena World* newspaper that a government agent had come to the area to round up hundreds of black laborers but had promised the BML that "he would do nothing to disturb local conditions; that he merely wanted to give employment to the 'city' Negroes who loitered about public amusement places, etc.," and that this would not cause a shortage affecting their businesses.[45] The article went on to state, however, that this was not the case and that large numbers of black laborers were being enticed to leave, causing mills to employ women due to the shortage of men. BML suggested that, since outside agents coming from the government, Nebraska, and railroad interests were in Phillips County to solicit black labor, the landowners should issue warnings against migrating—they were instructed to tell "their employees that labor conditions in the North are certainly far from being ideal, that Negroes in the South, especially in this particular locality, are not being victimized, but rather to the contrary, are as well treated as are laborers anywhere else in the world."[46] The BML's pushback against losing black laborers may have been somewhat effective, as seen in a release of 8,000 to 9,000 men from military installations returning to Helena in 1917, the same year of their outspoken contempt and protests.[47]

The local white businessmen and landowners fought to control the area's black labor, and efforts of any type to try to unionize black workers were met with harsh punishments. The *Helena World* reported in late August 1917 that Red Wiggins and Roy Dramer had been tried, fined $500, and sentenced to a year in

[43] "Negro Laborers Leave for Omaha," *Helena World,* August 7, 1917.
[44] "Protests against Labor Deportation," *Helena World,* August 7, 1917.
[45] "Protests against Labor Deportation," *Helena World,* August 7, 1917.
[46] "Protests against Labor Deportation," *Helena World,* August 7, 1917.
[47] "Surplus Labor to Be Available," *Helena World,* August 10, 1917.

jail for their attempt to unionize seventeen black men on a job site. It was alleged that Wiggins and Dramer had threatened the black laborers with violence when they could not get the men to unionize and pay a union fee.[48] They were further criticized for scheming to cause disruption between the black laborers and their white employers. Another article stated that in bypassing "certain well-defined and legitimate channels," Wiggins and Dramer were spreading the idea of unionizing as a means by which to "wring from corporations and employers of all sorts a higher wage and better working conditions," adding that "so far as the laboring man himself is concerned, there are doubtless many extenuating circumstances but for the officious walking delegate and the professional agitator there can be no excuse whatever."[49] The men were painted as money-hungry trouble-makers who could have been charged with treason for their actions in a time of war, despite the fact that the BML had protested the Department of Labor specifically for using the area's black laborers for wartime efforts. It was very important to the white elites of Phillips County to maintain their control over the black labor for their interests. Still, the rising price of cotton was allowing black laborers and tenant farmers to eke out enough to change their position within this socioeconomic stronghold. Therefore, the BML turned its attention to the market and crop pricing.

By 1919, members of the BML were focused on controlling the amount of land used for planting cotton—and, therefore, the market price for the crops once harvested. If the price of cotton was rising in the market, then a smaller supply of cotton would create an even higher demand, thereby making the crop that much

---

[48] The tone used by the press was degrading to the black laborers, with statements such as Wiggins and Dramer were "unable to induce any of the negroes to part with a dollar and sign up for the union," and "Every man who works for wages (salary, if you feel snobbish and think 'wages' a degrading word!)." See "Negroes Feared Threats of Men," *Helena World*, August 30, 1917.

[49] "A Risky Business," *Helena World*, August 30, 1917.

more profitable. This price gouging by members of the BML was justified in the local newspaper, the *Helena Herald*, and even praised for taking "every chance incident to the industry" because the government did not guarantee a set base price for the cotton crop, and therefore these men's "only recourse…is organization against disaster and intelligent handling of acreage."[50] The move was exalted as a solution to a problem faced by the white land-owners even though the crop's price had steadily risen for nearly five years. The acceptable view of these actions by the white elite power holders in Phillips County was that they were, according to the *Helena Herald*, "determined to protect their own interests, and the world will applaud them."[51]

The PFHUA was formed largely to help black workers in the Arkansas Delta to break free from this planned and systematic oppression by the white landowners. Locked in cyclical peonage, this debt labor system kept black laborers shackled to their land-lords. Walter White—an investigator and later executive secre-tary of the National Association for the Advancement of Colored People (NAACP)—detailed in *The Nation* how the sharecropping system disenfranchised blacks:

> In practice the system for the past fifty years has worked out in such manner that the crop, when gathered, is taken by the landowner and sold by him, and settlement is made with the sharecropper whenever and at whatever terms the landown-er chooses to give. Instead of an itemized statement of the supplies received, in most cases only a statement of the total is given. Since there is an unwritten law which is rigidly ob-served that no Negro can leave a plantation until his debt is paid, the owner, by padding the accounts of Negroes to the point where the "balance due" always exceeds the value of the crop, can assure his labor supply for the following year.[52]

[50] "Falling in Line," *Helena World*, February 20, 1919.
[51] "Falling in Line," *Helena World*, February 20, 1919.
[52] White, "'Massacring Whites' in Arkansas," 716.

This exploitation made it nearly impossible for black share-croppers to establish any sense of economic freedom. To seek justice through the courts with white judges and juries was typically unfruitful, to say the least—such actions could be met with violence. Therefore, as White explains, "[o]rganization was imperative, for there have been numerous lynchings when Negroes have dared to protest as individuals against such practices."[53]

The PFHUA was formed to organize blacks from within this state of servitude and break from white economic dominance, legal suppression, and the threat of violence. The PFHUA sought to organize as a union and exercise the rights of sharecroppers in seeking legal action against their abusers. Before Hill established the PFHUA in 1918, there had already been formal complaints made against the white landowners for having exploited black laborers and tenant farmers. Attorney Ulysses S. Bratton, who had previously prosecuted white planters in violation of peonage laws, was hired by the PFHUA to "represent the members in their effort to secure the market price for their cotton, to arrange for better contracts, to adjust their accounts with the landowners and generally to safeguard their interests."[54] However, the PFHUA's actions were perceived as acts of aggression by the white landowners. Black fraternal organizing had proven to be successful for other black communities in Arkansas and elsewhere in the country. The black community of Phillips County had numbers on their side, being that the county was over 78 percent black, outnumbering whites four to one.[55] However, their efforts for mere independence and dignity would spark a white backlash that would claim the lives of perhaps hundreds of people and ensure that the dream

[53] White, "'Massacring Whites' in Arkansas," 716.
[54] Ida B. Wells-Barnett, "The Arkansas Race Riot" (Chicago: Hume Job Print, 1920), 54, online at https://archive.org/details/TheArkansasRaceRiot (accessed November 9, 2017).
[55] White listed Phillips County's racial demographic figures as being 7,176 white and 26,354 black in 1919. White, "'Massacring Whites' in Arkansas," 715.

of black freedom remained dead for another generation.

The PFHUA was blamed for what happened at Elaine, with white planters and politicians alleging that Hill and the PFHUA were insurrectionists who had met in secret to plan a massacre of whites in Phillips County.[56] Reports made by investigators of the NAACP found that members of the PFHUA were being false-ly accused and that blacks were being arrested in the hundreds even in the midst of white mob violence. Ida B. Wells-Barnett, NAACP co-founder and journalist who shined a light on lynching in America, noted that the "terrible crime these men had commit-ted was to organize their members into a union for the purpose of getting the market price for their cotton, to buy land of their own and to employ a lawyer to get settlements of their accounts with their white landlords."[57]

The elite white class that blacks were unionizing against in-cluded the eventual members of the Elaine Committee of Sev-en: Chairman Sebastian Straus, Judge H. D. Moore, Sheriff F. F. Kitchens, Mayor J. G. Knight, E. M. A. Lien, J. E. Horner, and T. W. Keese.[58] This committee was formed from the area's elite white powerhouse, which had a vested interest in keeping the bulk of black labor and subsequent wealth for themselves. After the events at Elaine, Arkansas governor Charles H. Brough tasked the Committee of Seven with determining what led to the so-called race riot, and they reported that the riot resulted from the PFHUA spreading anti-white propaganda, radicalizing the ar-ea's black community against whites, and inciting PFHUA mem-bers with said propaganda to massacre whites.

Just days before the Elaine Massacre began, Hill had given a speech at the PFHUA lodge in Elaine on September 25, followed by one the next day at the Ratio lodge, telling members that he

[56] White, "'Massacring Whites' in Arkansas," 716; Wells-Barnett, "The Arkansas Race Riot," 54.
[57] Wells-Barnett, "The Arkansas Race Riot," 7.
[58] Scipio A. Jones, "Arkansas Peonage," *The Crisis* 23 (December 1921): 73.

was traveling to Little Rock to hire "a white lawyer…who would protect them and see that they got their rights."[59] Opposing whites discovered that the PFHUA was hiring Ulysses S. Bratton "to represent them with their landlords, or…to institute legal proceedings to protect their interests," and when Bratton's son arrived as an agent of the firm, he was arrested and charged with murder, and "hardly escaped being mobbed."[60]

The union was demonized as a bloodthirsty, clandestine order of blacks seeking to commit mass murder against whites. After the union's destruction, Robert L. Hill left Arkansas, never to return. He wrote a letter for the press in which he stated he was surprised at the false accusations and insisted that neither the PFHUA nor its members were inciting violence against whites. Hill went on to say that "to my white friends…we negroes love you all and could not do without you. We helped you fight the Germans, and are ready to help you fight the next fellows that get after you, but we want to be treated fairly."[61] Statements recorded by the NAACP from arrested blacks testified that at no point had Hill called for any harm to be done to the area's whites, nor did the PFHUA's constitution contain any language pertaining to violence of any sort.[62] The organization had, like many fraternal bodies before it, made efforts to better black citizens' situations. In this instance, their efforts had backfired in the worst way possible.

Conclusion

The problematic relationship described by MTA Grand Master Chester W. Keatts between Southern whites and Southern blacks, between the former master and former slave, continued and grew

---

[59] C. M. Walser and C. R. Maxey Report. Investigative Case Files of the Bureau of Investigation, 1908–1922. NARA: publication number M1085, case number 373159, roll 820: 23.
[60] Jones, "Arkansas Peonage," 75.
[61] "Alleged Note Received from Robt. L. Hill," *Helena World*, December 17, 1919.
[62] Wells-Barnett, "The Arkansas Race Riot," chapter 4.

even more troubled. Black political engagement had flourished immediately following the close of the Civil War, but this came to a halt once the Reconstruction period was over and federal oversight was removed from Southern states. Regressive legislation, starting in the states and eventually reaching the federal government, had all but made blacks second-class citizens with few rights. The promises of Reconstruction had been broken.

The idea of blacks having an equal footing in the country they helped to build, enrich, and defend as their own was largely diminished under the oppressive boot of Jim Crow, but African Americans nonetheless persisted in their quest for dignity and independence through fraternal orders such as the Prince Hall Masons, the Mosaic Templars of America, and the Progressive Farmers and Household Union of America. This quest, however, was tempered by an increase in extralegal violence, perhaps best symbolized by the Ku Klux Klan, which was itself modeled after white fraternal organizations, though the concept of community it offered its members and the broader public was a vision of unrepentant white supremacy.

The PFHUA's black farmers and laborers sought socioeconomic mobility and the power to break from the old cycle of poverty that had dominated the lives of countless black families and communities since Reconstruction. Black mobility in this manner had long existed at this point by 1919, as seen with previously established black fraternal orders. What stands out with the PFHUA was its foundational mission to organize for the purpose of retaining legal recourse, wanting to establish black landownership in a climate of systemic poverty via sharecropping, and the extreme negative response to this black order's mobilizing efforts. The PFHUA sought to benefit its members and local black community much like other fraternal orders had. It also boasted of having good, upstanding members who were true American citizens invested in upholding this country's law—and asking, in turn, that the law be upheld for them as well. Despite the order's

modeling after older black fraternal organizations, its clear patriotism, and its simple mission to help black farmers in Arkansas,
the order was perceived as a threat, proving that black organizing
of this kind would not be tolerated in the climate of Jim Crow
and the extreme racial tensions that boiled over in multiple areas across America in 1919. If the number of black victims of
the Elaine Massacre is ever determined, Arkansas's so-called Red
Summer may be declared the deadliest such incident America has
ever seen. This disaster had its roots in black fraternal organizing
for a better quality of life in the face of oppression and the backlash against such efforts.

Chapter 6

The Attorney Who Fought for Justice: A Brief Biography of Scipio Jones

Steven Teske

Scipio Africanus Jones represented in court the twelve men who had been sentenced to execution in the aftermath of the Elaine Massacre. Hired in November 1919 by African Americans in Little Rock, Jones would remain active in the case until all twelve had been freed—the last of them in January 1925.

In the early decades of the twentieth century, African American communities that were largely self-supporting and independent had developed in the United States. The "separate but equal" provisions of the law that led to "Jim Crow" legislation codifying segregation compelled the leaders of these African American communities to band together for their common survival and success. Along West Ninth Street in Little Rock, for example, a number of African American businesses flourished, centered around the headquarters of the Mosaic Templars of America fraternal society and insurance organization, located at Ninth and Broadway. Jones was part of a group of African American leaders that also included John E. Bush, J. H. McConico, Joseph C. Corbin, Joseph A. Booker, and Elias Camp Morris.[1] Rather than attempting to change whites' attitudes toward African Americans, these leaders sought to succeed within the existing system of segregation. While they challenged overt injustice—as was the case with the Elaine Massacre—their success was based more upon cooperation and peaceful coexistence than upon resistance to racial prejudice and discrimination.

Scipio Jones was born in 1863, give or take a year, to Jemmi-

---

[1] Fon Louise Gordon, *Caste and Class: The Black Experience in Arkansas, 1880–1920* (Athens: University of Georgia Press, 1995), 78.

ma, a nineteen-year-old slave owned by Dr. Sanford Reamey of Tulip, Arkansas.[2] After the Civil War ended, Jemmima, her husband Horace, and eighteen other slaves took the last name "Jones" because they had been owned by Dr. Adolphus Jones until his death in 1858.[3] Although Horace Jones was Scipio's legal father, he was not his biological father. Census records for 1880 describe Scipio Jones as "mulatto," indicating both African American and white ancestry. Reamey was likely Scipio's biological father. He took great interest in the boy, far more than he gave to Scipio's brothers. Scipio Jones was the only member of his family to attend school. He was educated first in an all-black school in or near Tulip. When he was around eighteen years old, he moved to Little Rock, where he attended Walden Seminary (now Philander Smith College) and also what is now Shorter College in North Little Rock.[4] In 1885, Jones began teaching school in Sweet Home, southeast of Little Rock. He then began to study law. Reamey's connections enabled Jones to read law in the Little Rock offices of Judge Robert J. Lea, Judge John Martin, and Judge Henry C. Caldwell.[5] Jones passed the bar examination on June 15, 1889.[6] In 1900, he was admitted to practice before the Supreme Court of Arkansas, and in 1905 he received the same privilege from the U.S. Supreme Court.[7]

Jones's first law office was at 115 Louisiana Street in Little Rock, in partnership with J. A. Robinson.[8] Many of his clients were indigent African Americans who could not afford to pay for his services, but Jones also did legal work for fraternal organizations including the Mosaic Templars of America and the Arkan-

---

[2] Tom Dillard, "Scipio A. Jones," *Arkansas Historical Quarterly* 31 (Autumn 1972), 201.

[3] Dillard, "Scipio A. Jones," 202.

[4] Gordon, *Caste and Class*, 81.

[5] Dillard, "Scipio A. Jones," 204.

[6] Dillard, "Scipio A. Jones," 204.

[7] Gordon, *Caste and Class*, 81.

[8] Dillard, "Scipio A. Jones," 204.

sas Knights of Pythias, among several others.[9] The Blue Book—a directory of African American businesses in the Little Rock area, published in 1907—said the following of Jones:

> [Jones is] the star of the legal profession of the twin cities; and the most signally successful and unpretentious jurist of African descent of the State....Lawyer Jones communes in Bethel A. M. E. Church. He owns a splendid house at 1808 Ringo Street, where he resides with his family, Mrs. Carrie E. Jones and daughter, Miss Hazel K. Jones. He owns eight or ten other valuable houses and lots in the city. He is estimated to be worth from $15,000.00 to $20,000.00.[10]

Carrie Jones died in 1908, and Jones married Lillie M. Jackson of Pine Bluff in 1917.[11] They had no children. The family moved several times, residing at 1822 Ringo Street, 1911 Pulaski Street, and 1872 Cross Street.[12] The latter house, constructed by the Joneses in 1928, is now on the National Register of Historic Places.[13]

Jones was highly respected in the Arkansas legal community. He was selected to serve as a special judge, hearing a case in the Little Rock Municipal Court.[14] In 1926, he was made a special chancellor in the Pulaski County Chancery Court.[15] Jones was a delegate to the Republican National Convention in 1928.[16] In his last years, Jones successfully lobbied for state funds to assist Af-

[9] Dillard, "Scipio A. Jones," 205.
[10] E. M. Woods, *Blue Book of Little Rock and Argenta, Arkansas* (Little Rock: Central Printing Co., 1907), 59.
[11] Dillard, "Scipio A. Jones," 211.
[12] Dillard, "Scipio A. Jones," 211.
[13] "Scipio A. Jones House," National Register of Historic Places registration form, on file at Arkansas Historic Preservation Program, Little Rock, Arkansas, online at http://www.arkansaspreservation.com/National-Register-Listings/PDF/PU9832.nr.pdf (accessed May 2, 2017).
[14] Gordon, *Caste and Class*, 81.
[15] Dillard, "Scipio A. Jones," 206.
[16] Charles J. Rector, "Lily-White Republicanism: The Pulaski County Experience, 1888–1930," *Pulaski County Historical Review* 42 (Spring 1994): 14.

rican American students to attend institutions of higher education out of state to study medicine, law, or other professional disciplines.[17]

Following the events of the Elaine Massacre, Walter White—an assistant field manager for the National Association for the Advancement of Colored People (NAACP) based in New York—visited Little Rock on October 8, 1919.[18] Although White was African American, his skin was light colored enough for him to pass as white. Posing as an attorney, he interviewed Governor Charles Brough. White also met with Scipio Jones, who helped him learn about the conditions of black tenant farmers in Arkansas. On October 19, the *Arkansas Gazette* published a letter signed by Jones and other prominent African American citizens of Arkansas; the letter praised Governor Brough for his actions during the Elaine crisis and supported the governor.[19]

Speedy trials were held early in November, sentencing African Americans for alleged crimes during the massacre. Twelve men received the death penalty: Frank Hicks was convicted of the murder of Clinton Lee on November 3; Frank Moore, Ed Hicks, Joe Knox, Ed Coleman, and Paul Hill were convicted the same day of aiding and abetting in the murder; Alf Banks Jr. and John Martin were convicted the next day of the murder of Will Adkins; Will Wordlaw was convicted the same day of aiding and abetting that murder; also on November 4, Albert Giles and Joe Fox were convicted for the murder of James Tappan; and on November 17, Ed Ware, secretary of the Hoop Spur lodge, was convicted for planning the murder of Will Adkins.[20] On November 24, the NAACP hired the firm of Murphy, McHaney, and Dunaway to represent

---

[17] Dillard, "Scipio A. Jones," 213.

[18] Grif Stockley, *Blood in Their Eyes: The Elaine Race Massacres of 1919* (Fayetteville: University of Arkansas Press, 2001), 96.

[19] *Arkansas Gazette*, October 19, 1919.

[20] Stockley, *Blood in Their Eyes*, xxvii. Stockley renders the name of Will Wordlaw as William Wordlow; however, the decision in *Moore v. Dempsey*, along with other primary sources, gives the name as William Wordlaw. Other variations in the name also show up in other source material.

these twelve men, providing $3,000 as well as incidental expenses.[21] Meanwhile, black leaders in Little Rock raised money to pay Scipio Jones to assist in the defense; Jones cooperated with the firm of Murphy, McHaney, and Dunaway.

The speed of the trials—in many cases the juries reached a decision in less than ten minutes—and the fact that all the attorneys and all the jurors were white led most observers outside of Phillips County to recognize that the system was rigged, the trials unfair. Tension existed, however, between African Americans of the NAACP and black Arkansans, including Scipio Jones. Leaders of the NAACP wanted to challenge the entire code of segregation in Arkansas and other Southern states. They saw the defense of the so-called Elaine Twelve as an opportunity to strike a blow for equality in the South.[22] Jones, like many of his peers in Little Rock, was reluctant to take such a revolutionary approach. They had learned how to cooperate with segregation and how to thrive within its limits. Jones was friendly with the white leaders in Arkansas, as exemplified by his expressed support of Governor Brough. Rather than stepping on toes to defend the human rights of African Americans, Jones was prepared to battle injustice case by case without threatening the system that created the injustice.

While George Murphy—a former attorney general of Arkansas—officially led the legal challenge to the twelve convictions, Jones did a great deal of legal work behind the scenes.[23] He also arranged for conciliatory negotiations. On November 24, Governor Brough announced that he was prepared to commute the sentences of eleven of the defendants to imprisonment. He also announced the creation of a biracial commission to discuss race relations.[24] Brough chaired the commission, which consisted of eight white men and eight African American men. Evidence in-

[21] Stockley, *Blood in Their Eyes*, 142.
[22] Stockley, *Blood in Their Eyes*, 142–143.
[23] Stockley, *Blood in Their Eyes*, 148.
[24] "Racial Relations May Be Improved," *Arkansas Gazette*, November 25, 1919, p. 8.

dicates that the commission accomplished little beyond meeting and talking, but, as historian Grif Stockley notes, "This was the first time in the twentieth century that large numbers of blacks (all men, apparently) were asked to come to the state capitol to do anything but clean it up."[25]

Murphy and Jones filed a motion for new trials on December 20. As expected, they were immediately denied.[26] Governor Brough ordered stays of the executions until the appeals process could be completed. The appeal reached the Arkansas Supreme Court, which ruled on March 29, 1920, that six of the convictions were affirmed and six were reversed and remanded for a new trial.[27] That new trial took place in Helena May 3–11. The six defendants (Ed Ware, Will Wordlaw, Albert Giles, Joe Fox, John Martin, and Alf Banks Jr.) were again convicted.[28] Murphy and Jones indicated that the men were entitled to a jury of their peers but that the jury once again had been entirely white. They began the process of appeals again. This case reached the Arkansas Supreme Court, which again overturned the conviction on December 6 on the grounds of discrimination against African Americans, due to their absence on the jury.[29]

Meanwhile, George Murphy had died in October 1920.[30] He was replaced by his partner, Edgar McHaney, who continued to rely on Jones for most of the legal work. Charles Brough was replaced in the governor's office by Thomas McRae that winter, and in January, McRae scheduled the executions of the other six defendants (Frank Moore, Joe Knox, Frank Hall, Ed Coleman, Frank Hicks, and Ed Hicks) for July.[31] On June 8, McHaney and Jones filed a writ of habeas corpus in the state court in Little Rock.

[25] Stockley, *Blood in Their Eyes*, 145.
[26] Stockley, *Blood in Their Eyes*, 150
[27] Richard C. Cortner, *A Mob Intent on Death: The NAACP and the Arkansas Riot Cases* (Middletown, CT: Wesleyan University Press, 1988), 87.
[28] Stockley, *Blood in Their Eyes*, 174.
[29] Cortner, *A Mob Intent on Death*, 103–104.
[30] Stockley, *Blood in Their Eyes*, 176.
[31] Stockley, *Blood in Their Eyes*, 184.

(This called upon the courts to enforce the constitutional right to a fair and speedy trial.) Writ arguments were scheduled for June 12. On June 20, the Arkansas Supreme Court ruled against the defendants, and Jones and McHaney filed a writ of error in the U.S. Supreme Court.[32] Although this was denied on August 4—and Governor McRae rescheduled the executions for September 23—Jones and McHaney filed another writ of habeas corpus in federal court before Judge Jacob Trieber. Trieber granted a stay of executions and then recused himself from the case because he was a long-time resident of Helena.[33] On September 26, Judge J. H. Cotteral from Oklahoma heard the case, announcing the following day that there was probable cause to send the case to the U.S. Supreme Court.

By December, the NAACP had hired Moorfield Storey to replace McHaney, who they thought had taken his partner's case only for the money. The case, *Moore v. Dempsey*, was argued by Storey before the U.S. Supreme Court on January 11, 1923.[34] Jones had expected to appear in court, but Storey (using the material prepared by Jones, Murphy, and McHaney) said that the presence of Jones was unnecessary. On February 19, the U.S. Supreme Court ruled in favor of the defendants, sending the case back to district court.[35]

In March of that year, Jones began negotiating a plea bargain for the six men. John E. Miller, law partner of the prosecutor C. E. Yingling, assisted in the negotiations, suggesting that the men plead guilty to second-degree murder, be sentenced to five years, and be credited with time served. In July, the NAACP directed Storey to see if George Rose would use his influence to free the men. In November, Jones announced that a deal had been made—the men would plead guilty, be sentenced to twelve months in

---

[32] Cortner, *A Mob Intent on Death*, 118.
[33] Stockley, *Blood in Their Eyes*, 206.
[34] Cortner, *A Mob Intent on Death*, 152–153.
[35] Cortner, *A Mob Intent on Death*, 154.

prison, and be pardoned within one year. Governor McRae agreed to the bargain, but he delayed beyond the year of the agreement. Finally, on January 14, 1925, before leaving office, McRae granted an indefinite furlough to each of the six men, effectively releasing them from prison.[36]

While this was happening to Moore and the others, the six men whose convictions had been overturned on December 6, 1920, were also required to stand trial again. Their new trial was moved to Lee County, but the prosecutors repeatedly delayed the hearing, claiming that it was not ready to go to trial. In April 1923, McHaney finally protested that two terms of court had passed without a trial and that the defendants should be released. The judge ruled against the defendants, and the case was appealed to the Arkansas Supreme Court. On June 25, the court ordered the men freed.[37] To protect them from being lynched, they were transferred to the state penitentiary in Little Rock. The warden there refused to accept them, and they were released into the custody of Jones, ensuring their freedom.

This success was the most notable of several occasions in which Jones intervened to protect African Americans from racially motivated violence in Arkansas. In September and October 1906, violence was sparked in Argenta (now North Little Rock), beginning with a barroom brawl in which a black musician was shot and killed by a white former police officer. Violence continued at the black-owned Colum funeral home in Argenta, where local black citizens endeavored to conduct an inquest into the killing. More shootings followed, along with arson in the African American section of Argenta, and the lynching of a black restaurateur. In the midst of this violence, Jones arranged for shelter for the Colum families and also intervened legally to prevent further recriminations against black residents of Argenta.[38]

---

[36] Stockley, *Blood in Their Eyes*, 221.
[37] Cortner, *A Mob Intent on Death*, 162.
[38] Guy Lancaster, "Before John Carter: Lynching and Mob Violence in

174

Likewise, in May 1927, as Little Rock was already in turmoil due to flooding, an African American man named John Carter was seized and lynched for allegedly assaulting a white woman and her daughter.[39] Roughly 5,000 white citizens flooded the African American neighborhood around Ninth and Broadway, burning Carter's body along with furniture seized from black-owned stores and churches. Jones and others sent word through the community warning African American citizens to remain indoors and to avoid confrontation with the rioters. After three hours, the Arkansas National Guard was sent by Governor John Martineau to disperse the crowd and end the riot.[40]

The cases of the Elaine Twelve were the most famous in the long career of Scipio Jones. In addition to law and business, Jones was also active in politics. A member of the Republican Party, he began to be rebuffed by politicians who wanted an all-white Republican Party. In 1902, when the Pulaski County Republicans nominated an all-white slate for county offices, Jones responded by entering an all-black Independent Republican slate on the ballot. Few candidates on his slate garnered as much as five percent of the vote.[41] Jones ran for the Little Rock School Board the next year. Facing open opposition from the *Arkansas Gazette* because he was black, Jones lost by a vote of 2,202 to 181.[42] By 1920, the white and black factions of the Republican Party were in open opposition. By 1928, Jones had managed to negotiate an end to the hostilities, and he was rewarded with a seat at the Republican National Convention.[43]

Pulaski County, 1882–1906," in *Bullets and Fire: Lynching and Authority in Arkansas, 1840–1950*, edited by Guy Lancaster (Fayetteville: University of Arkansas Press, 2018), 183, 186.

[39] Jay Jennings, *Carry the Rock: Race, Football, and the Soul of an American City* (New York: Rodale Inc.), 49.

[40] Jennings, *Carry the Rock*, 42–43.

[41] Tom Dillard. "To the Back of the Elephant: Racial Conflict in the Arkansas Republican Party," *Arkansas Historical Quarterly* 33 (Spring 1974): 11.

[42] Dillard, "Scipio A. Jones," 215.

[43] Dillard, "To the Back of the Elephant," 13.

Scipio Jones died at home on March 28, 1943. His funeral was held at Bethel AME Church, where a section of the church was reserved for "white friends." He was buried at Haven-of-Rest Cemetery in Little Rock.[44] The City of North Little Rock honored him by renaming its school for African American children with his name.[45] That tribute stood until 1970, when the school was closed due to desegregation. A post office in Little Rock was named in honor of Jones in 2007.[46]

---

[44] Dillard, "Scipio A. Jones," 219.
[45] Steven Teske, *Unvarnished Arkansas: The Naked Truth about Nine Famous Arkansans* (Little Rock: Butler Center Books, 2012), 116.
[46] Steven Teske, "Scipio Africanus Jones," *Encyclopedia of Arkansas History & Culture*, http://www.encyclopediaofarkansas.net/encyclopedia/entry-detail.aspx?entryID=2427 (accessed May 2, 2017).

Chapter 7

Women and the 1919 Elaine Massacre

Cherisse Jones-Branch

The details surrounding the 1919 Elaine Massacre continue to resonate in twenty-first-century Arkansas. They speak volumes about Southern white power and the need to control African Americans, who were the majority of the population in rural Phillips County, Arkansas, when this racial travesty occurred. The Elaine Massacre was precipitated by rural African Americans' assertiveness in their demands for improved economic opportunities and human dignity at time when the South, and indeed the nation, determined that they did not deserve either. Yet scholarship on this struggle for human dignity has focused almost entirely on black and white men's interactions.

Women witnessed and experienced the racial terrorism of the Elaine Massacre as well. As angry and fearful whites terrorized black bodies, innocent women and children were among their victims. White women surely witnessed and likely participated in men's discussions about blacks' demands and commented on these matters privately within their female-dominated spaces and organizations. Rural black women, however, were routinely beset by low pay and impoverished living conditions and were not extended the consideration or protection granted to Southern white women. Nevertheless, they too challenged white Southern racial violence generally through the Arkansas Association of Colored Women, the National Association of Colored Women, and the National Association for the Advancement of Colored People. Furthermore, black women from outside of Arkansas participated in the struggle for justice. Anti-lynching crusader Ida B. Wells-Barnett, for example, secretly visited imprisoned black men and their families in the aftermath of the massacre and then wrote about it in the 1920 publication *The Arkansas Race Riot*. Yet women's voices in Arkansas, the South, and nationwide have received woefully little consideration in narratives about the Elaine Massacre. It is necessary to probe the particular silences that have long repressed their experiences. Heightening them serves to unearth the often ignored ways in which black women were especially vulnerable during times of intensified racism. Despite their extreme oppression, they organized locally and nationally to challenge the gender, racial, and economic limitations they faced daily.

On the occasion of the centennial commemoration of the 1919 Elaine Massacre, this chapter examines women's reactions to the racial terrorism that profoundly changed black lives in rural Arkansas. Its scope considers the gendered lens through which black Arkansas women and women nationwide understood the massacre and the importance of protesting racial violence in the years following World War I.

Author Robert Whitaker, in *On the Laps of Gods: The Red Summer of 1919 and the Struggle for Justice that Remade a Nation*, described Hoop Spur, Arkansas, as a place that had "disappeared from the maps of Phillips County, Arkansas," and that even in 1919 "consisted of little more than a railroad switching station and a small store."[1] Hoop Spur is located in the Arkansas Delta. Consisting of 692 acres, replete with rich soil for growing cotton, most of this land was dominated by white planters who relied upon black laborers or sharecroppers, who also were the majority of the population.[2] As a result, race relations were perpetually tense. Local whites lived in fear of black insurrection and relied upon a system of white supremacy bolstered by terror,

---

[1] Robert Whitaker, *On the Laps of Gods: The Red Summer of 1919 and the Struggle for Justice that Remade a Nation* (New York: Crown Publishers, 2008), 1.

[2] B. Boren McCool, *Union, Reaction, and Riot: A Biography of a Rural Race Riot* (Memphis: Bureau of Social Research, Memphis State University, 1970), 1.

intimidation, and local acquiescence to maintain control over an inexpensive and seemingly tractable labor force. African Americans, however, did not always readily succumb to oppressive conditions. Although limited in their power, they pushed back regularly by challenging the particular issues that plagued agricultural laborers, such as unfair wages and abysmal living conditions.

On September 30, 1919, rural blacks gathered at an African American church in Hoop Spur for a meeting of the Progressive Farmers and Household Union of America (PFHUA) to discuss suing their landlords for their fair share of what historian Nan Woodruff described as "the largest cotton crop in southern history."[3] Some of those who attended were women like Vina Mason, who brought her babies. Sallie Giles was present with her sons Albert and Milligan. She recalled that, by the time they reached the church in Hoop Spur at 8:00 p.m., "the house was packed." This declaration certainly underscored the importance of this clandestine meeting. Also at the meeting was Cleola Miller, wife of Hoop Spur Lodge PFHUA president Jim Miller.[4]

Women were fee-paying members of the union, as some white newspapers noted. The *St. Louis-Dispatch*, for instance, reported that "women are said to have been members of the organization which the authorities said was known as the Progressive Farmers and Household Union of America."[5] Women paid a fifty-cent membership fee, which was a dollar less than what men were charged.[6] Cleola Miller was twenty-four years old at the time she joined. She had filled out the "Orders of Washington, D.C., The Great Torch of Liberty," an examination and membership card bearing federal symbols, on which she noted that she was from

[3] Nan Woodruff, *American Congo: The African American Freedom Struggle in the Delta* (Cambridge: Harvard University Press, 2003), 84.
[4] Whitaker, *On the Laps of Gods*, 1.
[5] "Troops Set Trap for Alleged Head of Negro Rioters," *St. Louis-Dispatch*, October 6, 1919.
[6] "Not a Racial Riot, But Insurrection," *Atlanta Constitution*, October 7, 1919.

Mellwood, Arkansas (an unincorporated community approximately eight and a half miles southwest of Elaine). She was also
the mother of three children. Cleola answered affirmatively to
such questions as "Do you believe in the Almighty God?," "Do
you give due respect to all humankind?", "Do you obey the law
at all times?", and "Do you go to church?" When asked about the
state of her health, she answered "unhealthy," which was not an
unusual state among rural women and their families, who were
often in ill health as a result of poor nutrition and food insecu-
rity. It is likely that these factors may have further informed her
decision to join the PFHUA. In the end, physician and PFHUA
co-founder V. E. Powell determined that Cleola was "fit to sit in
the first Congress called by the Progressive Farmers and Household Union of America, which congress will be held in August at
Winchester, Arkansas" in 1918.[7]

As members continued to fill the church, Ed Ware, the lodge's
secretary, had not yet arrived. Ware, who had been a PFHUA
member for only a month, was prosperous compared to other African Americans in the Arkansas Delta. He owned and farmed his
own land. He also employed black families, like Sallie Giles and
her two sons. Ware was also an entrepreneur who owned a Ford
that was used as a taxi service.[8] The surplus income provided him
with a level of financial independence that permitted his activism,
but it alarmed and angered whites. His very existence undermined
a system precariously supported by white supremacy, racial terrorism, and an unyielding belief in black inferiority.

[7] "Orders of Washington, D.C., The Great Torch of Liberty," Casefile
10218-372: Investigation of Race Riot, Elaine, Arkansas, 1919, Federal
Surveillance of Afro-Americans (1917–1925): The First World War, the Red
Scare, and the Garvey Movement; O. A. Rogers Jr., "The Elaine Race Riots
of 1919," *Arkansas Historical Quarterly* 19 (Summer 1960): 146; Kieran
Taylor, "'We Have Just Begun': Black Organizing and White Response
in the Arkansas Delta, 1919," *Arkansas Historical Quarterly* 58 (Autumn
1999): 272.
[8] Grif Stockley, *Blood in Their Eyes: The Elaine Race Massacres of 1919*
(Fayetteville: University of Arkansas Press, 2001), 131.

Ware's rural activism upended a carefully constructed façade. He had previously attended a Progressive Farmers meeting in Elaine, Arkansas, three miles south of Hoop Spur. White planters, afraid of losing the political, economic, and psychological control they held over African Americans, upon whose labor they depended, had warned him not to attend any more meetings. Indeed, Ware was not going to attend the meeting in Elaine because he was unwell. His wife, Lulu, with whom he farmed 120 acres of cotton, insisted they go because he possessed the union's books and papers.[9] Lulu, like her husband, had been born in Louisiana (she in 1878), and she exemplifies how many rural black women were clearly the force behind male PFHUA members.

Scholars have often discussed how African Americans, emboldened by the democratic rhetoric of the World War I years, returned to the Arkansas Delta determined to access the benefits of citizenship to which they were rightfully entitled. They acted in a historical context that revealed a nation unnerved by social, racial, and gender upheaval. Their fear rendered many determined to restore the status quo. Much emphasis has been placed on African Americans who migrated out of the South to access wartime employment opportunities. But many consciously chose to remain and migrate within Southern spaces and agitated for much-needed change there. Black rural Arkansas residents and PFHUA members, including women, were among those who made this prescient choice when they congregated to challenge local white supremacist structures that relegated them to a circumstances that differed little from slavery.

As PFHUA members met at the Hoop Spur church in 1919, a firefight ensued between them and Phillips County law enforcement officers. During the melee, Will Adkins, a Missouri Pacific railroad employee, was killed. Charles Pratt, another white man,

---

[9] Whitaker, *On the Laps of Gods*, 2; *Ware et. al. v. State*, Docket #2414, 48 (typed), 57 (handwritten).

was wounded.[10] As the shooting continued, women and children took cover behind church benches. As Vina Mason attempted to protect her child from the deluge of bullets, she recalled,

> The house was packed and jammed, and I got down with the baby in my arms. The men, women and children were scuffling, and I raised up, and got shot in my arm. When the shooting ceased, people were jumping out the windows. I made it to the door, walking over people, but lost my hat and the baby's. When I got out, my husband took the baby, and told me to run for the house.[11]

Mason later became black Arkansas attorney Scipio Africanus Jones's star witness in May 1920 as he sought to appeal the State of Arkansas's decision to execute the twelve men it held captive in the case of *Moore v. Dempsey*.[12]

Black women's terror and bravery during the Elaine Massacre have largely gone unnoticed. Sallie Giles was concerned about the safety of her two sons.[13] In November 1919, her son Albert Giles was among those arrested for the murder of James Tappan, a former Confederate officer and a plantation owner in Phillips County.[14] When Ed Ware returned to his home to procure his weapon, a black "trusty," Kid Collins, along with a group of white men, demanded that he come outside. Lulu Ware appeared instead of her husband and asked, "What are you going to do with us women?" The subsequent exchange allowed her husband and another black sharecropper, Charles Robinson, to escape. Robinson was later felled by a bullet in his back. With her husband on

---

[10] Jeannie M. Whayne, "Low Villains and Wickedness in High Places: Race and Class in the Elaine Riots," *Arkansas Historical Quarterly* 58 (Autumn 1999): 287.

[11] Quoted in Whitaker, *On the Laps of Gods*, 84.

[12] Whitaker, *On the Laps of Gods*, 316–317.

[13] Whitaker, *On the Laps of Gods*, 316–317.

[14] Whitaker, *On the Laps of Gods*, 59, 179; Stockley, *Blood in Their Eyes*, xxvii.

the run, Lulu Ware was arrested and jailed.[15] She remained there for four weeks, performing hard labor along with other black women. At times, they were forced to sleep on the concrete floor. When they were released along with seventeen others, they were told to go back home and "work as they had always done" and "never join nothing more unless they got their lawyer's or landlord's consent." When Lulu Ware returned to her home, it had been ransacked. She saw her family's hard-earned belongings in white people's homes.[16]

As armed white men from around the region prepared to fight an imaginary race war, white women and children were sequestered in a school building for their own protection and later taken to Helena, Arkansas.[17] In the minds of terrified, paranoid, and angry whites, black women did not merit the same level of protection. They were women, but they were black first, and this factor made them a source of both fear and derision. Indeed, the *Atlanta Constitution* reported that, after Will Adkins was killed, over 150 African Americans were in the church in Hoop Spur including "women carrying automatic revolvers in their stockings."[18] When Ed Ware was questioned in the case *Ware et al. v. State*, he was asked at least twice if his wife possessed a "gun" or a "pistol." In both instances, Ware answered no.[19]

Local whites in Phillips County feared being slaughtered by armed African Americans who outnumbered them. However, black women remembered this experience very differently. They knew well that the death of a white man by a black hand in those

[15] Whitaker, *On the Laps of Gods*, 90.

[16] Ida B. Wells-Barnett, *The Arkansas Race Riot* (Chicago: Hume Job Print, 1920), 20, online at https://archive.org/details/TheArkansasRaceRiot (accessed February 23, 2018).

[17] Stockley, *Blood in Their Eyes*, xxiii, 11; "Refugees are Fired Upon By Hiding Negroes," *Pensacola Journal* (Pensacola, Florida), October 2, 1919, p. 1; Whayne, "Low Villains and Wickedness in High Places," 289.

[18] "Plot to Murder Laid to Negroes," *Atlanta Constitution*, October 6, 1919, p. 2; "Insurrection Planned to Be Begun Today," *Helena World* (Helena, Arkansas), October 6, 1919, p. 1.

[19] *Ware et al. v. State*, 1920, 49 (typed), 58 (written on page).

days almost certainly meant the wholesale extermination of African Americans. One black woman, Nina Jenkins, recalled that a boy came running down the road and informed them that "white people were coming and said they were going to kill everything that was big enough to die."[20]

Many black women were forced to take cover in the woods for their safety and survival. Some, like Nina Jenkins, were forced to abscond to the muddy and swampy Yellow Banks Bayou where thirty-year-old Frank Moore was hiding with his mother, wife, and children.[21] Moore and his wife, Mary, had farmed cotton on fourteen acres of land on a 200-acre farm managed by Bobby Archdale. He recalled that approximately 300 armed white men indiscriminately killed men, women, and children. The family remained in the bayou until the next morning when Moore delivered them to soldiers who then imprisoned them in a school house for five days. Moore was arrested and placed in jail in Helena, where he said he was "whipped nearly to death to make me tell stories on the others."[22] After her husband's incarceration for his role in the "riot," Mary Moore was driven from their farm and robbed of $678 in household goods. She was further jailed along with other black women, and according to Moore, "whipped as well as men," demonstrating that black women could never expect to be extended any protection from physical harm because of their gender.[23]

But local whites underestimated black women's strength and tenacity. When she was released from jail in Helena, Mary Moore returned to their home on the farm in Elaine to collect what was left of her family's belongings and to be paid for their crop. Everything was gone, and when she asked Archdale's wife where their possessions were, she was told that she "would get nothing"

[20] Whitaker, *On the Laps of Gods*, 89.
[21] Whitaker, *On the Laps of Gods*, 100.
[22] Wells-Barnett, *The Arkansas Race Riot*, 17.
[23] Wells-Barnett, *The Arkansas Race Riot*, 18.

of her stolen furniture and clothing so clearly on display in the Archdale home. Racism trumped any semblance of gender solidarity. Archdale further informed Moore that her husband was in jail in Helena and that he was going to be electrocuted. When Moore asked why—"Did he kill anybody?"—Archdale answered ironically, "No, but he had just come from the army and he was too bigoted."[24] Bobby Archdale informed Moore that if she did not "get out and stay out he would kill her, burn her up and no one would know where she was."

Mary Moore's husband was in jail, her home had been vandalized, and she was left unemployed with only the clothes on her back. Her fate worsened when another plantation manager, John Nelson, who ran the Wilford and White Farm and was identified as one of the members of mob, arrested her and took her back to jail in Helena, where she was kept for eight days and forced to work from three in the morning until nine or ten at night along with fifteen other black women.[25] Not coincidentally, Moore's father-in-law, James Moore, who was sixty-five years old, had also been arrested. Although there were no charges levied against him, his family, which included his wife and four young children, had everything taken from them, including the crops they had gathered, and were pushed off the farm where they had labored. Destitute, they moved to Little Rock, where the elder Moore was incarcerated.[26]

Indeed, the punishment meted out to black women resulted from their challenges to the gender and racial status quo. In the early morning hours following the PFHUA meeting and subsequent shootout, twelve Mississippi men accosted Lula Black, the mother of four children, in her home, dragged her outside, and asked her if she was a member of the PFHUA. When she responded affirmatively, she was then asked why. Black said, "Because

[24] Wells-Barnett, *The Arkansas Race Riot*, 20.
[25] Wells-Barnett, *The Arkansas Race Riot*, 20.
[26] Wells-Barnett, *The Arkansas Race Riot*, 20.

it would better the condition of the colored people; when they worked, it would help them to get what they worked for." Lula Black, like many rural black women, clearly understood the value of their labor and consequently the white power structure's investment in controlling them with fear and repression. Her response, however, fanned the flames of the mob's anger and fear. They knocked her down. Black was beat "over the head with their pistols," kicked all over her body, and almost killed. And then she, too, was taken to jail.[27]

This, of course, would not be the last time a rural black woman suffered for upsetting the gender, racial, and economic status quo in rural Arkansas. In 1936, for instance, Eliza Nolden, a sixty-year-old black sharecropper from Earle, Arkansas, in Crittenden County, was severely beaten by white planters "with sticks the size of axe handles" for participating in a march to protest the poor treatment of agricultural laborers. Nolden was a member of the Southern Tenant Farmers' Union, which had been founded in 1934 in Tyronza, Arkansas, in Poinsett County.[28] Nolden, who had been born in Mississippi, likely between 1878 and 1880, looked to the court system for justice for herself and other laborers.[29] She, along with Willie Sue Blagden, a white Memphis social worker who was flogged for investigating the beating of a black sharecropper, and a white minister who had also been assaulted, filed a $15,000 lawsuit against their attackers—to no avail. In the suit, Nolden alleged that she had been abducted by planters and members of the East Arkansas Planters collective

[27] Wells-Barnett, *The Arkansas Race Riot*, 21.
[28] "Farmers Seeking Dismissed Count: Seven Men Seek to Get Freedom of Flogging Charges in Appeal to Court," *Kingsport Times* (Kingsport, Tennessee), May 4, 1938, p. 12; "Trial Under Anti-Slave Law Faced by Official in Cotton Strike Sequel," *Democrat and Chronicle* (Rochester, New York), November 24, 1936, p. 1; "$15, 000 Asked by Flog Victim," *Des Moines Register* (Des Moines, Iowa), August 30, 1936, p. 4.
[29] The sources say she was 60–65 years old, in which case she was born in the 1870s. The 1930 census lists her as 43 years old and living and working on Floyd Robert's farm in Tyronza, Cross County, Arkansas.

186

John "Boss" Dulaney, H. S. Watson, Percy Magmus, and L. L. Barham in Earle's business district. The men took her to jail and then to Barham's cotton gin, where she was beaten and quite likely sexually assaulted.[30] During the trial that followed, the men all denied any knowledge of Nolden's beating. Percy Magmus described himself as "just a farmer," and L. L. Barham denied even knowing Nolden.[31] Nolden died in May 1938, presumably from her injuries, at John Gaston Hospital in Memphis, Tennessee.[32]

Back in Elaine, the mob next happened upon Frances Hall, a housekeeper known locally as a "crazy old woman." The men, clearly not seeing her as worthy of the protections of womanhood and indeed quite likely informed by stereotypes about black women's hyper-sexuality, tied her clothes over her head. As she screamed, one of them shot her in the throat.[33] Frances Hall received medical care but later died from her injuries. Her body, still exposed, was then thrown in the street, where it lay until it was removed by soldiers.[34]

In October 1919, Arkansas governor Charles Brough dispatched and accompanied 500 federal troops from Camp Pike near Little Rock to put down what many mainstream newspapers called an "insurrection." This trope had long been used by whites who lived in fear of black assertiveness, particularly in the Arkansas Delta where African Americans significantly outnumbered

---

[30] "Alleged Victim of Arkansas Floggers Files Damage Suit: Another Man and Woman Also Seek $15, 000 Damages for Floggings," *Corsicana Daily Sun* (Corsicana, Texas), August 29, 1936, p. 1; "Dies as $15,000 Suit Waits Action," *Chicago Defender*, May 28, 1938, p. 6.

[31] "Denials of the Defendants," *New York Times*, August 30, 1936, p. 12.

[32] H. L. Mitchell, *Mean Things Happening in This Land: The Life and Times of H. L. Mitchell, Co-Founder of the Southern Tenant Farmers Union* (Norman: University of Oklahoma Press, 1979, 2008), 95; "Beaten By Planters," *Anniston Star* (Anniston, Alabama), May 17, 1938, p. 1. See also Jennifer Rittenhouse, *Discovering the South: One Man's Travels through a Changing America in the 1930s* (Chapel Hill: University of North Carolina Press, 2017), 162, 168.

[33] Whitaker, *On the Laps of Gods*, 107.

[34] Wells-Barnett, *The Arkansas Race Riot*, 21.

them.[35] Racially motivated violence had served as a means to control African Americans since before the Civil War. It intensified following the war because whites feared liberated and hence uncontrolled black bodies and the possibility of a race war.[36] Black women and children were rarely spared from their atrocities.

According to one report, approximately 225 African Americans were apprehended in Elaine and held captive by the soldiers at a jail in Helena. Among them were black women who were also incarcerated and charged with murder.[37] One of them was twenty-two-year-old activist Mollie Simons. Simons, who had attended Branch Normal College—which became Arkansas Agricultural, Mechanical, and Normal College, and later the University of Arkansas at Pine Bluff in Jefferson County—told officers that she had been "composing and lecturing for the uplift of her race," a popular refrain among educated black women leaders before, during, and after World War I. Originally from Parkdale, Arkansas, in Ashley County, Simon denied advocating "social equality" because she "knew better."[38] Although the records are largely silent about this encounter, Simon may have acquiesced in an attempt to avoid the physical and sexual violence routinely inflicted on black women. This was certainly a concern for black men, who often refused to allow their female relatives to pick cotton or work

[35] Edward Passailaigue, Captain, Infantry, 3rd Ammunition Train to Assistant Chief of Staff, G-2, 3rd Division, October 7, 1919, Casefile 10218-372: Investigation of Race Riot, Elaine, Arkansas, 1919, folder 001360021-0766, Federal Surveillance of Afro-Americans (1917–1925): The First World War, the Red Scare, and the Garvey Movement; Richard C. Cortner, *A Mob Intent on Death: The Arkansas Riot Cases* (Middletown, CT: Wesleyan University Press, 1988), 21.
[36] Kay Wright Lewis, *A Curse upon the Nation: Race, Freedom, and Extermination in America and the Atlantic World* (Athens: University of Georgia Press, 2017), 176.
[37] "Troops Suppress Arkansas Riots," *Atlanta Constitution*, October 5, 1919, p. 11; *Twelfth Annual Report of the National Association for the Advancement of Colored People for the Year 1921* (New York: National Association for the Advancement of Colored People, 1922), 23.
[38] "Troops Suppress Arkansas Riots," p. 11.

for white people, particularly men, under any circumstances.[39]

Ida B. Wells-Barnett, about whom more will be said later, used newspaper articles, reports, pamphlets, and essays to protest black women's sexual violation by white men. Rape and sexual vulnerability often operated in tandem with economic oppression in black women's lives regardless of whether they lived in the North or the South.[40] Fearing reduced income-generating opportunities, and knowing they had virtually no legal recourse, black women and girls rarely reported rape and sexual assault. Activists like Wells-Barnett, however, highlighted these matters in their publications in an effort to shame white people in the communities where they lived. This focus also served as a counter narrative to assumptions about black women's hypersexuality and wantonness that were often used as an excuse for the sexual crimes perpetrated against them. It was further a clarion call to black communities nationwide to protect African American women and to pressure authorities to prosecute violators.[41]

Wells-Barnett was not alone in criticizing sexual violence against black women. The Reverend Elias Camp (E. C.) Morris—who was at various times president of the National Baptist Convention, a leader in the Arkansas Republican Party, and a member of the Commission on Race Relations—used his pulpit to admonish the soldiers who raped and sexually assaulted black women during and after the Elaine Massacre.[42] It is difficult to substantiate how many black women were victimized at the hands of white soldiers, however. Historian Darlene Clark Hine

[39] Rogers, "The Elaine Race Riots of 1919," 144.
[40] Darlene Clark Hine, "Rape and the Inner Lives of Black Women in the Middle West," *Signs* 14, no. 4 (Summer 1989): 913.
[41] Kidada Williams, *They Left Great Marks on Me: African American Testimonies of Racial Violence from Emancipation to World War I* (New York: New York University Press, 2012), 110–111.
[42] Calvin White, "It Should Be More Than Just a Simple Shout: The Life of Elias Camp ('E.C.') Morris," in John Kirk ed., *Race and Ethnicity in Arkansas: New Perspectives* (Fayetteville: University of Arkansas Press, 2014), 108–109.

has written extensively about how black women dissembled their feelings and the ways in which they engaged in "self-imposed secrecy" about their most traumatic experiences as a means to minimize the "damage to black men's sense of esteem and self-respect" in an environment where it was virtually impossible for such men to protect their wives and families.[43] Hine argues that this silence further, and more importantly, allowed them to create a "secret, undisclosed persona" or a "psychic space" to maintain their dignity and self-worth during their daily confrontations with extreme racism and sexism.[44] Middle-class black women often employed and projected the politics of morality, sexual respectability, and restraint onto poor women as a means to protect them all from sexual violation.[45] While the silences surrounding black women and sexual assault during the Elaine Massacre persisted, according to at least one source, Morris's condemnation of rape as the most "heinous of all crimes" strongly suggests that it was pervasive.[46]

In the aftermath of the melee, Governor Brough appointed the Committee of Seven, made up of Phillips County's leading white citizens, to investigate what had occurred.[47] Eventually, twelve African American men were arrested for "inciting a riot," convicted of murder, and sentenced to die in the electric chair. Sixty-seven others received long prison terms for their involvement. This story is well chronicled. However, scholars have paid woefully little

---

[43] Darlene Clark Hine, *Hine Sight: Black Women and the Re-Construction of American History* (Brooklyn: Carlson Publishing, 1994), 44.

[44] Hine, "Rape and the Inner Lives of Black Women in the Middle West," 915.

[45] Susan L. Smith, *Sick and Tired of Being Sick and Tired: Black Women's Health Activism in America, 1890–1950* (Philadelphia: University of Pennsylvania Press, 1995), 19.

[46] White, "It Should Be More Than Just a Simple Shout," 108–109; E. C. Morris, *Sermons, Addresses, and Reminiscences and Important Correspondence, With a Great Picture Gallery of Eminent Ministers and Scholars* (Nashville: National Baptist Publishing Board, 1901), 81.

[47] J. W. Butts and Dorothy James, "The Underlying Causes of the Elaine Riot of 1919," *Arkansas Historical Quarterly* 20 (Spring 1961): 99.

attention to women's reactions to this travesty of justice. Women throughout the South and the nation were shocked when the men were sentenced to death and the others given prison sentences ranging from one to twenty-one years.[48] They reached out to Arkansas's white leaders demanding justice. For example, the National Equal Rights League (NERL), a human rights organization founded in Syracuse, New York, in 1864, wrote Governor Brough asking for a stay of execution for the men. Its members included prominent African Americans like activist Wells-Barnett, who in 1914 was vice president of the organization.[49]

In the NERL's letter to Governor Brough, the committee mentioned the fact that "race riots have occurred in various parts of our country in which all races have been concerned," and that the "matter of the execution of the drastic sentence pronounced in the Elaine riot case 11 death sentences, pending an impartial investigation under your direction, in view of the present tension of public feeling."[50] The governor ultimately chose to ignore the NERL's plea, declaring that he "would not be swayed by outside influence"—and that "he was sure in his own mind that the Negroes deserved electrocution."[51]

Wells-Barnett was not deterred by the governor's rebuff. In December 1919, she published a letter in the *Chicago Defender*, calling African Americans' attention to the fact that the "riot" had occurred because black farmers refused to sell their cotton below market prices. She then urged them to use their "influence and money" to help the men who had been found guilty of murder in

---

[48] Rogers, "The Elaine Race Riots of 1919," 150.

[49] "Stay Execution," *Bisbee Daily Review* (Bisbee, Arizona), November 13, 1919, p. 5.

[50] "Equal Rights League Is Getting Active," *Arkansas Democrat*, November 13, 1919, p. 11; "League Seeks Respite for 11 Doomed Blacks," *Courier-Journal* (Louisville, Kentucky), November 13, 1919, p. 9.

[51] "Brough to Disregard Outside Interference," *Natchez Democrat* (Natchez, Mississippi), November 16, 1919, p. 8; Alfreda M. Duster, ed., *Crusade for Justice: The Autobiography of Ida B. Wells* (Chicago: University of Chicago Press, 1970), 419.

the first degree."[52] Wells-Barnett further offered a threat that may very well have made her a pariah among Arkansas's white planters when she asserted that if the "men were electrocuted because they had defended themselves when fired upon," the members of the aforementioned organizations "would immediately take steps to see that thousands more of our people who had enriched the South by their labor would leave Arkansas, never to return."[53]

Ida B. Wells-Barnett, born in 1862 in Holly Springs, Mississippi, had a long history of challenging racial violence and injustice. She moved to Memphis, Tennessee, after her parents and youngest sibling died from a yellow fever epidemic that ravaged communities up and down the Mississippi Delta. It was in Memphis in 1884 that she first fought racial injustice when she was ordered by the conductor of the Chesapeake and Ohio Railroad Company to the segregated "Jim Crow" car even though she had purchased a first-class ticket. She was violently removed from the train as white passengers applauded. Wells-Barnett confronted American racism through her Memphis newspaper, the *Free Speech and Headlight*. Her boldness, which called to task the hypocrisy of Southern white supremacy and the lynching of black men under the pretense of protecting white women, eventually led to an angry mob destroying her office and banning her from returning to Memphis—or the South, for that matter—under the threat of death.[54]

But return to the South she did in 1920, to investigate on behalf of the *Chicago Defender*. Wells-Barnett spent two weeks in Arkansas gathering firsthand information about what had occurred before and during the alleged riots. Furthermore, in January 1920, after receiving a letter from one of the twelve imprisoned black

---

[52] Duster, *Crusade for Justice*, 418.
[53] Ida B. Wells-Barnett, "Condemned Arkansas Rioters Look to Chicago for Help," *Chicago Defender*, December 13, 1919, p. 20.
[54] Lee D. Baker, "Ida B. Wells-Barnett and Her Passion for Justice," http://people.duke.edu/~ldbaker/classes/AAIH/caaih/ibwells/ibwbkgrd.html (accessed February 23, 2018).

men thanking her for the "great speach [*sic*] you made throughout the country in the *Chicago Defender*," she took a train to Little Rock and then journeyed to Helena, Arkansas.[55]

Wells-Barnett chronicled her experiences in Arkansas in a sixty-two-page self-published pamphlet, *The Arkansas Race Riot*.[56] When she arrived in Helena, Wells-Barnett was disguised as a nondescript rural black woman. She was met by the prisoners' wives, mothers, and children who were visiting their loved ones.[57] As if the trauma of seeing their husbands imprisoned was not enough, Wells-Barnett learned that black women were further humiliated by having to pay the jailer a dollar, money most surely did not possess, just to visit them. She interacted with women who had long experienced difficult times. Yet, Wells-Barnett noted that these women, who had come to visit their spouses on a Sunday, were resilient and offered them unyielding support. They were further anchored by their Christian faith. She recorded that they "sang and prayed" together, thus employing a method that would be used by civil rights activists later in the twentieth century.[58]

When Wells-Barnett returned to Chicago, she continued to utilize her organizational networks on the Arkansas men's behalf. She initiated the NERL's involvement when she attended the organization's September 1920 meeting and asked if any action had been taken on the men's behalf. She recalled that when the president said they "had considered it," and that "there is nothing we can do," she declared: "We can at least protest against it and let the world know that there is one organization of Negroes which refuses to be silent under such an outrage." Wells-Barnett

[55] "Expose New Facts in ARK. Riot Case," *Chicago Defender*, February 28, 1920, p. 1; Wells-Barnett, *The Arkansas Race Riot*, 5.
[56] Patricia Ann Schechter, *Ida B. Wells-Barnett and American Reform, 1880–1930* (Chapel Hill: University of North Carolina Press, 2001), 160.
[57] Linda O. McMurray, *To Keep the Waters Troubled: The Life of Ida B. Wells* (New York: Oxford University Press, 2000), 327.
[58] Wells-Barnett, *The Arkansas Race Riot*, 6.

appointed a committee, of which she made herself chairperson, to send protest letters to the president of the United States, Illinois senator Medill McCormick, and Congressman Martin Madden, also from Illinois, asking the federal government to seek justice for the condemned men; such a letter was also sent to Arkansas governor Charles Brough.[59] The letters had been signed by the NERL's president and Oscar De Priest, president of the People's Movement Club, a civic organization he founded in 1917.[60] In 1928, De Priest became the first non-Southern African American elected to the U.S. Congress.[61]

Wells-Barnett had signed the letters in her capacity as president of the Negro Fellowship League (NFL), which she had co-founded in 1910 to help Southern blacks who had recently migrated to Illinois.[62] The NFL kept tabs on the racial violence that occurred throughout the nation following World War I. In August 1919, a women's committee was created under the NFL's auspices to raise funds to assist African Americans who had been imprisoned and charged with rioting in the aftermath of the racial unrest that had occurred in Chicago in July of the same year.[63] They quite naturally extended these resources to African Americans in Arkansas. The NFL women's committee did not operate in isolation, however. Black women in Arkansas, particularly members of the Arkan-

---

[59] Duster, *Crusade for Justice*, 417; Wells-Barnett, *The Arkansas Race Riot*, 4.
[60] "Fort Dearborn Lodge; Building Homes; The Defender Building; The People's Movement Club House," Schomburg Center for Research in Black Culture, Jean Blackwell Hutson Research and Reference Division, The New York Public Library, New York Public Library Digital Collections, http://digitalcollections.nypl.org/items/510d47de-5186-a3d9-e040-e00a18064a99 (accessed February 23, 2018).
[61] "G.O.P. Elects Chicago Negro to Congress," *Des Moines Register* (Des Moines, Iowa), November 8, 1928, p. 26.
[62] "The Negro Fellowship League's Eighth Annual Celebration," *The Broad Ax* (Salt Lake City, Utah), January 8, 1916, p. 4.
[63] "Women's Committee to Receive Funds to Aid in the Defense of Those Charged with Rioting," *The Broad Ax* (Salt Lake City, Utah), August 23, 1919, p. 4; "Chicago's Race Riots," *Times Herald* (Port Huron, Michigan), July 28, 1919, p. 4.

sas Association of Colored Women (AACW), established in 1905 and affiliated with the National Association of Colored Women (NACW), addressed racial violence nationwide and statewide during and after World War I. Black Arkansans rallied behind the cause and established the "Citizens Defense Fund." By 1920, they had raised $10,426 to support the Elaine Twelve.[64] Black club women in Little Rock, who were almost certainly affiliated with the AACW, raised over $1,000 to support the organization.[65]

Club women discussed the Elaine Twelve's predicament at the NACW's biennial convention in Tuskegee, Alabama, in 1920. One member, Mary Jackson, a Young Women's Christian Association (YWCA) industrial secretary, relayed the details of her visit to the prison in Little Rock where the men were being held at one point. She asked the NACW to send a letter to African American attorney Scipio A. Jones to support him in his efforts to have them released.[66] Also present was AACW representative Henrietta Carolina along with three other black women, including Pine Bluff's Ladye B. O'Bryant, who later headed Arkansas's chapter of the NAACP's Anti-Lynching Crusaders, founded in 1922 to raise money to support the passage of the Dyer Anti-Lynching Bill.[67] Carolina, the group's spokesperson, advocated a "very strong and heart appealing plea…for the…condemned men awaiting executing for rioting in Elaine, Ark." Each state federation was then asked to appeal to Arkansas's governor to

[64] "The Horizon," *The Crisis* 21, no. 3 (December 1920): 81.
[65] Tom Dillard, "Scipio A. Jones," *Arkansas Historical Quarterly* 31 (Autumn 1972): 207.
[66] Minutes of the Twelfth Biennial Convention of the National Association of Colored Women, July 12th to 16th, 1920, Tuskegee Institute, Alabama, National Association of Colored Women Records, reel 1.
[67] "How Did Black Women in the NAACP Promote the Dyer Anti-Lynching Bill, 1918–1922?" http://womhist.alexanderstreet.com/lynch/intro.htm (accessed July 12, 2017). The bill was first introduced into the House of Representatives in 1918 by Missouri congressman Leonidas Dyer. See also, "The Anti-Lynching Crusaders: A Million Women United to Suppress Lynching," http://womhist.alexanderstreet.com/lynch/doc7.htm (accessed February 23, 2018).

commute the men's sentences to life imprisonment.[68]

NACW members were well aware that negative coverage in mainstream newspapers often resulted in violence against African Americans. They concluded their meeting by addressing mob violence, rioting, and lynching in their recommendations:

> Since glaring headlines and detailed accounts in the press of crimes and misdemeanors committed by colored people, tend to inflame the passions of the public against members of our race, culminating often in mob violence and rioting, we urge the press of the United States to refrain from thus perpetuating such propaganda against us. We again make solemn protest against the continued prevalence of mob violence in the United States, and we pray for an enactment of a Federal statute against lynch law, with severe penalties for the violation thereof, and that such statute be enforced, if need be, by the military power of the government.[69]

Other women leaders demanded justice for the twelve wrongfully imprisoned men as well. Willa Dwiggins, for instance, vice president of the Kansas City, Kansas, NAACP, appealed to President Woodrow Wilson for clemency on the men's behalf.[70] When asked by the organization to speak against mob violence and lynching, he "demurred," and promised "to seek an opportunity to say something." His feeble effort was not particularly impactful. Segregation and racial violence increased considerably under the

---

[68] Julia Bumry Jones, "The National Convention Held at Tuskegee," *The Competitor* 2, no. 1 (July 1920): 143–144; Minutes of the Twelfth Biennial Convention of the National Association of Colored Women, July 12th to 16th, 1920, Tuskegee Institute, Alabama, National Association of Colored Women Records, reel 1.

[69] Jones, "The National Convention Held at Tuskegee," *The Competitor* 2, no. 1 (July 1920): 143–144; Minutes of the Twelfth Biennial Convention of the National Association of Colored Women, July 12th to 16th, 1920, Tuskegee Institute, Alabama, National Association of Colored Women Records, reel 1.

[70] (No title) *Kansas City Advocate* (Kansas City, Kansas), October 29, 1920, p. 4.

Republican president's administration.[71] Racial violence consistently informed black women's community work throughout the 1920s and beyond. Dwiggins was no stranger to this activism. In 1917, she and other black women in Kansas City founded "The Mother's Guard," a self-help and welfare organization to "lift up a people and a nation" and to "brighten the world."[72] In 1921, Dwiggins, who by this point was the Kansas NAACP secretary, spoke to a group of African Americans at the Chamber of Commerce in Emporia about "race problems and race riots."[73] She also met with leaders from the NAACP headquarters in New York like Mary White Ovington, who visited the Kansas City chapter in February 1921 and informed African Americans that "their own good conduct would aid materially in winning the confidence and support of those of the white race who now are [in]different to the grave questions involved in the race problem."[74]

Mary White Ovington—a white suffragist, journalist, NAACP board member, former executive secretary, and chairperson—adamantly supported the efforts in Arkansas to secure justice for the twelve black men. In August 1921, she sent $250 to Little Rock attorney E. L. McHaney to aid the "Arkansas work."[75] She, along with African American activists Ida B. Wells-Barnett and Mary Church Terrell, had been among the NAACP's founders when it was established in 1909.[76] Ovington, also a socialist and a Unitarian from Brooklyn, New York, was the only woman to sign

[71] Kenneth O'Reilly, "The Jim Crow Policies of Woodrow Wilson," *Journal of Blacks in Higher Education*, no. 17 (Autumn 1997): 121.
[72] "A New Welfare Work," *Weekly Gazette Globe* (Kansas City, Kansas), April 5, 1917, p. 1.
[73] "Hear Miss Dwiggin's [*sic*] Lecture," *Emporia Gazette* (Emporia, Kansas), August 20, 1921, p. 1.
[74] "Great Crowd Hears Miss Ovington Talk," *Kansas City Kansan*, February 10, 1921, p. 6.
[75] Mary Ovington White to E. L. McHaney, August 25, 1921, Papers of the NAACP, Part 07: The Anti-Lynching Campaign, 1912–1955, Series A: Anti-Lynching Investigative Files, 1912–1953.
[76] Mary White Ovington, *Black and White Sat Down Together: The Reminiscences of an NAACP Founder* (New York: The Feminist Press, 1995), 59.

the organization's incorporation papers and had further drafted its call and invitation list.[77] She was appointed NAACP executive secretary in 1910 and was elected chairperson in January 1919.[78]

Ovington actively campaigned to raise funds for the men's defense. In December 1919, for instance, she used her position to procure $68.25 from white supporters in New Brunswick, New Jersey.[79] However, it was her correspondence with attorneys in Arkansas that reveals much about her views regarding *Moore v. Dempsey*. In August 26, 1921, Ovington sent McHaney a telegram that stated simply, "Confident you will do everything possible to stay execution."[80] Unfortunately, serious conflict arose between McHaney and the NAACP over the amount of money he and his firm were supposed to be paid to defend the men in the case of *Moore v. Dempsey*.[81] In September 1921, McHaney resigned and advised the organization to "secure other counsel." Scipio Jones then became the principal counsel for the Arkansas cases—or "the Association's attorney in Arkansas." Ovington was particularly critical of McHaney and appreciative of Jones's work. She asserted that what "has provoked me has been that the colored lawyer seems to have been doing all the work, while the white lawyer has taken much of the money and left us at the crucial moment."[82] Ovington wrote to Jones in September 1921 and commended him on the "remarkable work which you have done in these Arkansas cases....This has been one of the most important cases relating to the Negro in the history of the United States and I am sure that we must feel very happy to have been able to

---

[77] Stockley, *Blood in Their Eyes*, 97.

[78] Stockley, *Blood in Their Eyes*, 87.

[79] "New Brunswick Folk Give to Defence [*sic*] Fund," *New York Age*, December 20, 1919, p. 2.

[80] Western Union Telegram from Mary White Ovington to E. L. McHaney, August 26, 1921, Papers of the NAACP, Part 07: The Anti-Lynching Campaign, 1912–1955, Series A: Anti-Lynching Investigative Files, 1912–1953.

[81] This is the United States Supreme Court case in which the Court ruled 6–2 in February 1923 that the defendants were denied due process, guaranteed by the Due Process Clause of the Fourteenth Amendment.

[82] Cortner, *A Mob Intent on Death*, 133.

take so important a part in it."[83] Jones thanked Ovington for her compliment, her sympathy, and her interest in the Elaine victims. He further informed her that her intention to provide additional financial assistance to help defend the imprisoned men gave their "cause new hope and inspiration."[84]

Moore v. Dempsey was settled after a six-year battle waged by the NAACP. The imprisoned Elaine men were liberated between 1923 and 1925.[85] Having their loved ones returned to them was surely a relief for their wives and families. Yet the cost for challenging rural Southern white supremacy was staggering. Most had lost everything and endured extreme poverty as a result. These rural black women and agricultural laborers, who did not have much to begin with, lost all of their worldly possessions to the whites who had ransacked their homes. The only exception was PFHUA leader Ed Hicks's wife, Arreita, who was able to retrieve some of her household items and realize some profit by selling her hogs, chickens, and a horse. But like the rest of the families of the men who had been incarcerated and accused of "rioting," she received nothing for their crops.[86]

Of greater significance, however, is women's resilience and persistence in the face of extreme adversity. Black women, during and after World War I, empathized with African Americans in Elaine because the threat of racial and sexual violence pervaded all of their lives. Support from the National Association of Colored Women and the Arkansas Association of Colored Women attests to this. Racial anxieties plagued whites who feared the

---

[83] Mary White Ovington to Scipio A. Jones, September 27, 1921, a Western Union telegram to Arkansas attorney E. L. McHaney that said simply, "Confident you will do everything possible to stay execution."
[84] Scipio A. Jones to Mary White Ovington, September 30, 1921, Papers of the NAACP, Part 07: The Anti-Lynching Campaign, 1912–1955, Series A: Anti-Lynching Investigative Files, 1912–1953.
[85] David A. Joliffe, et al., *The Arkansas Delta Oral History Project: Culture, Place, and Authenticity* (Syracuse: Syracuse University Press, 2016), 171.
[86] Wells-Barnett, *The Arkansas Race Riot*, 21; Whitaker, *On the Laps of Gods*, 12.

usurpation of their roles atop the racial hierarchy during these years. But black women in Arkansas garnered the sympathy and support of such mixed-race organizations as the NAACP. This, of course, included white women like Ovington, who headed the NAACP New York headquarters for part of the terrible ordeal the Elaine Twelve endured.

Women's experiences during the 1919 Elaine Massacre prove most profoundly that, despite severe economic privation, racism, and sexism, they spoke truth to their realities and challenged the restrictions that held sway over their lives. Racial and sexual violence did not silence or subdue them, as many white Southerners wanted—and, indeed, needed to believe. Black women demonstrated their political consciousness through their PFHUA membership and their support for their male relatives who had been falsely charged and imprisoned for asserting their right to full citizenship. They chipped away at the edifice of white supremacy that held all in the Arkansas Delta captive. And in doing so, they laid the foundation for the next generation of rural women activists.

Chapter 8

When the Depths Don't Give up Their Dead: A Discussion on New Primary Sources and How They Are Reshaping Debate on the Elaine Massacre

Brian K. Mitchell

In *The Half Has Never Been Told*, historian Edward E. Baptist described Southern slavery in shockingly disturbing terms. Baptist wrote of agrarian entrepreneurs who "pushed," through the use of brutal torture, their slaves to work faster, harder, and longer. Baptist argued that the success of capitalism and the wealth of the United States, in the South and the North, were built at the expense of black backs and lives. Like cattle or real estate, slaves could be bought, sold, mortgaged, or leased. In the minds of many of the whites who owned them, slaves were property to be used in whatsoever way they desired.[1]

This particular systemically dehumanizing exploitation of black bodies continued, uninterrupted and largely unaltered, until the passage of the Thirteenth Amendment in 1865. The abolishment of slavery, except as punishment for a crime, forced southerners, short on money but still in need of black labor, to create new systems of exploitation to obtain the labor they required. Debt peonage (of the sort common to the sharecropping system) and mass incarceration replaced chattel slavery as the preferred methods of extracting forced labor from the South's black agrarian populace.[2] Violence and intimidation were used to sustain the

---

[1] Edward E. Baptist, *The Half Has Never Been Told: Slavery and the Making of American Capitalism* (New York: Basic Books, 2014).

[2] Grif Stockley, *Blood in Their Eyes: The Elaine Race Massacres of 1919* (Fayetteville: University of Arkansas Press, 2001), 17; Douglas A. Blackmon, *Slavery by Another Name: The Re-Enslavement of Black Americans from the Civil War to World War II* (New York: Anchor Books, 2009), 5–9;

South's racial hierarchy whenever black dissenters, however aggrieved, threatened white supremacy.

In the summer of 1919, a group of black sharecroppers in Phillips County formed a union, the Progressive Farmers and Household Union of America, to demand the payment of monies that, they contended, had been unfairly denied them by planters who refused to pay fair rates for their cotton, and who kept these men and women in a state of perpetual indebtedness by maintaining inaccurate accounts of sharecroppers' debts.[3] On the evening of September 30, 1919, while meeting in a small church a few miles outside of Elaine, union members were fired upon by sheriff deputies, who later claimed to have been ambushed by the sharecroppers after the deputies interrupted their meeting. During the melee, W. A. Adkins, a special agent of the Missouri Pacific Railroad Co., was killed, and Charles W. Pratt, a Phillips County deputy sheriff, was wounded. The massacre of black farmers that began the following morning was an act of retaliation, not only for the alleged attack on Adkins and Pratt, but also for daring to assault white authority in the county.[4]

Although nearly a century has elapsed since the shooting at the Hoop Spur church, researchers have been unable to reach a consensus on the number of individuals killed in the Elaine Massacre.[5] The lack of a death toll is in no way an indication of shoddy

Pete Daniel, *The Shadow of Slavery: Peonage in the South 1901–1969* (London: Oxford University Press, 1972), 19–42.

[3] Robert Whitaker, *On the Laps of Gods: The Red Summer and the Struggle for Justice That Remade a Nation* (New York: Crown Publishers, 2008), 7–10; Richard C. Cortner, *A Mob Intent on Death: The NAACP and the Arkansas Riot Cases* (Middletown, CT: Wesleyan University Press, 1988), 27; Stockley, *Blood in Their Eyes*, x.

[4] Cortner, *A Mob Intent on Death*, 8–9; Stockley, *Blood in Their Eyes*, xvi–xvii, 194–195; Robert T. Kerlin, *Voice of the Negro 1919* (New York: E. P. Dutton and Co., 1920), 89.

[5] The Elaine Massacre's death toll varies drastically by source. The most conservative accounts of the dead maintain that as few as seventeen blacks were killed in the riot. See "The Death Toll in the Arkansas Riot is 22, including Five Whites," *Taylor Daily Press*, October 3, 1919. However, several accounts of the massacre place the death toll from 100 to several

research or hastily completed manuscripts. Instead, the missing bodies and their identities are part of an enigma that has fueled consistent debate on the topic. Without evidence of the scale of the atrocity, the massacre has failed to attract local and national recognition commensurate to the event's historical importance.

While the location of the remains and identities of those slain remain a mystery, there are other unanswered questions that are equally perplexing. How long had landowners known about their tenant farmers' proposed litigation? How were the white planters made of aware of the Hoop Spur meeting? Which farmers were members of the Progressive Farmers and Household Union, and what happened to the incarcerated union members after they were released from prison following the massacre? These questions have puzzled researchers of the massacre for decades, as the answers are hidden, not preserved in the court records and federal reports investigating the massacre.

The absence of these essential details could be attributed to a number of sources and motives. It was in the interest of the posse members and the courts seeking to prosecute union members that the bodies of women and children not be recovered. After all, they had argued that the violence used was essential to securing the safety of the white community in Phillips County.[6] The maintenance of that argument secured Southern honor and made heroes of all who had answered the call in the community's hour of need. Noted attorney and author of *Blood in Their Eyes* Grif Stockley, who is a native of the Arkansas Delta, attributed the absence of basic information, such as the lack of an accurate accounting of the slain, to the pragmatism of Scipio Jones, the black attorney representing the sharecroppers standing trial for the murder of the five whites killed during the massacre. Stockley maintained that Jones knew "blacks had been slaughtered by the mobs and soldiers" but did "whatever was needed for the survival of his cli-

---

hundred individuals. See Whitaker, *On the Laps of Gods*, 327–329.
[6] Cortner, *A Mob Intent on Death*, 8–9.

ents and community." There was no benefit for the black farmers facing execution in provoking the ire of the governor or judge.[7] Jones thought it more prudent to address the interests of his clients than to try to shame the white populace of Phillips County by assailing their honor.

While Jones's willingness to ignore the scale of the atrocity might excuse his own lack of inquiry as to the names of the dead and location of their burials, it does little to explain why Military Intelligence, the Federal Bureau of Investigation's investigators, the county coroner, the courts, and the local newspapers found little interest in identifying the dead. Similarly still in question are the identities of the members of the union and how the men sent to Hoop Spur were made aware of the gathering of the sharecroppers.

This chapter explores primary sources that show promise in filling the gaps in the historical record relating to the Elaine Massacre. These include the correspondence of Governor Henry Allen of Kansas regarding his refusal to extradite Robert Hill, founder of the Phillips County branch of the Progressive Farmers and Household Union; minutes of the inaugural state convention of the Arkansas Department of the American Legion (Little Rock, October 8–9, 1919); an interview of Chief Deputy A. F. James of Phillips County (New Orleans States Item, November 10, 1919); and the Phillips County Indictment Book (entries regarding the Elaine Race Massacre Arrests and Charges). These are analyzed and reviewed below for their historical significance and ability to answer pertinent questions about the massacre.

The Correspondence to and from Governor Henry Allen of Kansas Regarding the Extradition of Robert Hill Back to Arkansas to Stand Trial

Although he was the founder and president of the Progressive

---

[7] Stockley, *Blood in Their Eyes*, 233.

204

Farmers and Household Union, Robert Lee Hill was not at the Hoop Spur meeting on the night of the shooting. When he was informed of the events at the church the following day, he fled, assured that the posses would come looking for him. Hill's flight from Arkansas took him to Boley, Oklahoma, then to South Dakota before he was finally apprehended in Topeka, Kansas, in January 1920. Hill was held in Topeka's jail on warrants for nightriding and first-degree murder. On January 21, 1920, Governor Charles H. Brough of Arkansas issued a requisition requesting the extradition of Hill back to Arkansas to stand trial for the aforementioned charges.[8] In his bail hearing, Hill maintained his innocence and pleaded not to be returned to Arkansas, "claiming that should he be returned he would be met with violence."[9] In fighting his extradition, he gained the support of Kansas's senators, Arthur Capper and Charles Curtis, and that of Henry Allen, governor of Kansas. As a show of support for Hill and protest against Brough's demands, on the insistence of James Weldon Johnson, Capper joined the National Association for the Advancement of Colored People (NAACP) and accepted a position on the organization's board of directors. Governor Allen also refused the extradition of Hill. Allen's refusal was applauded by blacks and advocates for civil rights throughout the nation and was denounced by those who called for Hill's return.

Among the records held by the Kansas Historical Society are a collection of Governor Allen's letters relating to Hill's extradition. This collection encompasses nearly a hundred letters, both to and from Allen, in regard to Hill. While the bulk of these letters are in support of the governor's decisions, there are several important letters and telegrams in opposition.

---

[8] Cortner, *A Mob Intent on Death*, 55–59; "Head of the Arkansas Night Riding Society Arrested," *Louisville Courier-Journal*, January 22, 1920, p. 5; John Gruber, "Robert Lee Hill," *Railroad History* 211 (Fall–Winter 2014): 58–59.
[9] "Alleged Riot Leader Held," *Evening Kansan-Republican*, January 21, 1920, p. 1

The letters and telegrams provide an account of the debate. In the earliest of telegrams, Governor Brough urged Allen to return Hill, pledging, "A fair trial is absolutely guaranteed and where there is no danger of lynching."[10] On the same day, Allen responded to Brough, maintaining that he had no fear that Hill would be lynched, but he did fear an "equally unfortunate thing" that Hill might be "tried by passion and racial bitterness."[11] Not all the correspondence was as civil in tone as that between the two governors. One letter sent from an anonymous resident of Phillips County addressed Allen as the "Kansas Nigger Lover" and informed the governor that it was too bad that he was not at Elaine during the riot and had his "white liver shot out by some of your beloved brethren."[12]

The collection also holds several letters from E. M. Allen, president of the Business Men's League of Helena, Arkansas, and a member of the Committee of Seven appointed by Governor Brough to investigate the events in Elaine. In the first of E. M. Allen's letters, he sought to build a degree of confidence and trust with Governor Allen by describing the planters and, in two instances, foremen from the plantations where the dissenting sharecroppers had farmed. In each instance, he distanced the owners from the Southern agrarian elite by portraying several as transplanted northerners and outsiders. In his brief biographical sketches, he noted that the men accused of debt peonage were from Illinois, New Jersey, Michigan, and Kansas, and several were described as "staunch Republicans." In one account, E. M. Allen maintained that the father of one planter, Harry E. Kelley,

---

[10] Western Union Telegram from Governor Charles H. Brough to Governor Henry Allen dated April 20, 1920, Governor Henry Allen Collection, Correspondence Files 1919–1923, Kansas Historical Society.

[11] Western Union Telegram from Governor Henry Allen to Governor Charles H. Brough dated April 20, 1920, Governor Henry Allen Collection, Correspondence Files 1919–1923, Kansas Historical Society.

[12] Letter from Anonymous Sender to Kansas Nigger Lover (Governor Henry Allen) postmarked March 24, 1920, Governor Henry Allen Collection, Correspondence File 1919–1923, Kansas Historical Society.

had fought with a Union regiment from Kansas during the Civil War and noted that another planter, J. N. Moore, and the manager of the Lambrook Plantation, C. W. L. Armour, had attended universities in Kansas. Allen went on to explain that he and a contingent of soldiers had escorted the sharecroppers condemned to execution to the Helena courthouse, noting that although a crowd of several hundred whites stood outside, "no attempt was made to harm the prisoners." In his closing paragraph, Allen added that Hill could obtain "a fair trial in Helena" and contended that Arkansans were "inflamed" and humiliated by Governor Allen's refusal of Governor Brough's requisition for the extradition of Hill.[13]

Nearly two weeks later, the governor received yet another letter from E. M. Allen. In this letter, Allen contended that Hill, if returned, deserved to be punished, "not because of his own participation in the insurrection, but because of the important part he played in bringing it about." Allen alleged that he had been informed, before the shooting at Hoop Spur, of Hill's meetings by "a few friendly negroes" who acted as informants, reporting to whites "what was going on" within the union. This revelation proved that the deputies' presence at the Hoop Spur church was no matter of happenstance. If, in fact, Allen and the white planters had informants, as he claimed, then they were fully aware of not only when meetings occurred but also who was in attendance and what was said.[14]

On May 21, 1920, Governor Allen replied to E. M. Allen's pleas for the extradition of Hill, noting his suspicions in regard to the "persistent charges in connection to the Hill case" and "the anxiety to secure the return of Hill" to merely give testimony

---

[13] Letter from E. M. Allen to Governor Henry Allen dated April 23, 1920, Governor Henry Allen Collection, Correspondence Files 1919–1923, Kansas Historical Society.

[14] Letter from Governor Henry Allen to E. M. Allen dated May 9, 1920, Governor Henry Allen Collection, Correspondence Files 1919–1923, Kansas Historical Society.

against the lawyers who were representing the union. Governor Allen wrote the Helena businessman, "I have gained some rather strong impressions touching both white and colored folks down in Phillips County district. The broadest charge probably is that there exists down there, with the deliberate knowledge of all respectable people, a system of peonage. I have not the idea, of course, that all are indulging in that, but that it is a general practice. Your very intelligent letters upon these matters are helping my record in this case."[15]

E. M. Allen, taking offense at the governor's suspicions regarding the prevalence of peonage in the county, vigorously denied that there was even a "single instance of peonage" in the area. In support of his allegation, he contended that Southern planters often carried sharecroppers' debts to their own detriment, arguing that plantation owners often went entire planting seasons without receiving payment from their tenant farmers and losing as much as $10,000 per year on tenant farmers' accounts. Conversely, he presented a glowing assessment of the state of sharecroppers in the region, maintaining, quite miraculously, that while white planters were losing money in their enterprises, fifty tenant farmers were worth between $5,000 and $25,000. Moreover, Allen insisted that white planters encouraged "all negroes to own their own farms and sales [of land] are made with long time payments of small amounts." He went on to list three black locals—Tom Robinson, Mose Proffit, and Charley Proctor—who, he alleged, had risen from the ranks of tenant farmers to become substantial landowners with net worths ranging from $50,000 to $150,000.[16] In his letter, E. M. Allen revealed that he also owned

---

[15] Letter from Governor Henry Allen to E. M. Allen dated May 21, 1920, Governor Henry Allen Collection, Correspondence Files 1919–1923, Kansas Historical Society.

[16] Letter from E. M. Smith to Governor Henry Allen dated May 24, 1920, Governor Henry Allen Collection, Correspondence Files 1919–1923, Kansas Historical Society. The 1920 U.S. Decennial Census for Phillips County lists two black males named Tom Robinson, and both men are indicated to have been renters, not landowners. Mose Proffit is listed as a resident of

a farm dependent upon sharecropper labor for its operation. In his admission, he stated that some of the tenants on his farm were "born on the place thirty and thirty-five years ago and in no doubt would die there." However, he attributed their lifelong residence not to peonage, but instead to loyalty and the fair wages he paid to them. Before the closing of the letter, the Helena businessman eroded any notion of benevolence or magnanimity he had cultivated through his strenuous arguments as to how well planters had treated their black tenants. If Governor Allen had been swayed by E. M. Allen's descriptions of the just treatment and fairness given to blacks in the county, the Helena businessman's pronouncement that "the only thing the white people [of Phillips County] demand here is white control" likely reassured the governor that the convicted sharecroppers' assessments of their exploitation was not far from the truth.[17]

Not all the letters from white Arkansans condemned Governor Allen's decision to withhold Hill from being forcibly returned to Arkansas. Several letters sent by the family of Benjamin Freeman, editor of the *Green Mountain News*, requested the governor's assistance in obtaining Freeman's release from a warrant calling for his arrest.[18] Freeman was charged with contempt of court after writing an article praising Allen's decision not to return Hill to the county for trial. In the article, the editor had noted, "We know the condition of that section [of the state], pretty well and we know the judge that tried the other negroes, therefore, we do not hesitate to say that we do not believe that Hill could

Helena's Ward 3; however, he is recorded as the proprietor of a home rental business, not a farmer. There was no record of a Charley Proctor in Phillips County in the 1920 Census.

[17] Letter from E. M. Smith to Governor Henry Allen dated May 24, 1920, Governor Henry Allen Collection, Correspondence Files 1919–1923, Kansas Historical Society.

[18] Letter from Mary Freeman to Governor Henry Allen dated May 6, 1920, Governor Henry Allen Collection, Correspondence Files 1919–1923, Kansas Historical Society; Letter from S. E. Freeman to Governor Henry Allen dated May 26, 1920, Governor Henry Allen Collection, Correspondence Files 1919–1923, Kansas Historical Society;

get a fair and impartial trial there and he is certainly entitled to that."[19] The sentencing judge, Judge J. M. Jackson, cited Freeman for contempt on the basis that he had assailed and impugned the honor and integrity of the court. Fearing that he would be lynched and having no money to bail himself out of jail, Freeman wrote to Governor Allen in hopes that the governor could send funds, not only to cover Freeman's bond, but also to fund the writing of an article revealing "the truth" about the Phillips County riot.[20]

In a letter following the publication of Freeman's article, Allen praised Freeman, noting that his editorial stood out "alone as the only kindly word I have heard from Arkansas." The governor added:

> The flood of anonymous and filthy letters which come, added to the intemperate statements of people who sign their names and the unreliable interview given out by the attorney general upon his return to Arkansas, all convince me that my judgement was correct in the presumption that the atmosphere there is so inflamed with passion as the natural result of the riot that the Hill case would not have received the proper consideration in an atmosphere of judicial calmness which should surround every man on trial for his life.[21]

Among the letters pertaining to Freeman is one of the most heart-wrenching in the collection. On May 6, 1920, the eldest of Freeman's five children, his thirteen-year-old daughter Mary Freeman, penned a letter to Governor Allen. In her letter, Mary expressed her fear that if her father were arrested and forced to go to Phillips County, he would be lynched. Attributing her father's

[19] "Green Forest Editor Cited on Contempt Charge," *Arkansas Democrat*, April 27, 1920, p. 1

[20] Letter from Ben Freeman to Governor Henry Allen dated May 5, 1920, Governor Henry Allen Collection, Correspondence Files 1919–1923, Kansas Historical Society.

[21] Letter from Governor Henry Allen to Ben Freeman dated April 1, 1920, Governor Henry Allen Collection, Correspondence Files 1919–1923, Kansas Historical Society.

warrant to the compliment he made supporting the governor's decision, she begged Allen to "remember the piece that papa had in the paper" before pleading with Allen to intercede on her father's behalf.[22]

The Freemans' letters provide evidence as to the lengths to which Phillips County's leadership was willing to go to present a unified white narrative in support of Hill's return. Freeman's warrant and the family's fear of violent reprisal suggest that people who disputed the narrative of a black insurrection would not be tolerated, even if the dissenting voices were those of whites. In the end, Mary would not see her father go to jail or be subjected to the lynch mob. Rather than risk incurring either fate, Freeman fled the state and the warrant for his arrest. It was likely no surprise to the white residents of Phillips County that, in selecting his place of refuge, Freeman followed the model of Robert Lee Hill, choosing Kansas for sanctuary.[23]

One of the most important letters in the collection is a handwritten two-page letter from Robert L. Hill, wherein Hill thanks Governor Allen for his refusal to extradite him back to Arkansas and describes his flight from Phillips County and the arrest of his mother after the Hoop Spur shooting.[24] Most of the remaining letters were sent from a network of institutions and professionals who rallied to show support for Governor Allen's controversial decision to protect Hill. The letters of thanks and appreciation, praising Allen for his courageous stand, came from civic leagues, industrial schools, NAACP chapters, equal rights leagues, and private citizens from all corners of the nation. Those letters illustrate the grassroots efforts that the NAACP called upon to fund

[22] Letter from Mary Freeman to Governor Henry Allen dated May 6, 1920, Governor Henry Allen Collection, Correspondence Files 1919–1923, Kansas Historical Society.
[23] "Arkansas Editor Disappears," *St. Louis Dispatch*, May 19, 1920, p. 2; "Has Come to Pittsburg?" *The Sun*, May 20, 1920, p. 2.
[24] Letter from Robert L. Hill to Governor Henry Allen dated April 19, 1920, Governor Henry Allen Collection, Correspondence Files 1919–1923, Kansas Historical Society.

the defense of the sharecroppers on death row, and they also bear testimony to connectedness of black communities throughout the nation following the riots of the Red Summer.[25]

Minutes of the Inaugural State Convention of the Arkansas Department of the American Legion (Little Rock, October 8–9, 1919) and an Interview of Chief Deputy A. F. James of Phillips County (New Orleans States Item, November 10, 1919)

The first annual convention of the Arkansas Department of the American Legion was held at the Marion Hotel in Little Rock, Arkansas, on October 8 and 9, 1919. The convention, held just days after the massacre in Phillips County, was opened with an address made by Governor Brough. The governor was followed by the master of ceremonies, Chaplin John W. Inzer, who was the Southern Field Representative for the American Legion of Mobile, Alabama. Inzer's speech to the attendees espoused three core ideals: the evils of Bolshevism, the threat of radicalism in America, and the maintenance of one-hundred-percent Americanism.

As the minute book noted: "On the following day, heated discussion arose over the formation of negro posts. J. G. Lyford of Helena protested the formation of separate negro posts, citing Phillips County with two-thirds of the veteran population comprising negro veterans. A resolution was adopted favoring state's rights, limiting posts to white veterans with outposts for negro veterans."[26] Later that day, the convention's delegates commended the Helena post for "its service during the Elaine race riots."[27] While the minutes give few details of the services rendered, in an

---

[25] Governor Henry Allen Collection, Correspondence Files 1919–1923, Kansas Historical Society.
[26] Minutes of the Inaugural State Convention of the Arkansas Department of the American Legion (Little Rock, Oct. 8–9, 1919), Annual Convention Minute book, Arkansas American Legion Auxiliary.
[27] Minutes of the Inaugural State Convention of the Arkansas Department of the American Legion (Little Rock, Oct. 8–9, 1919)

interview he gave to the *New Orleans States Item*, Chief Deputy A. F. James of Phillips County furnished insight into how the legion members were used. In his interview, James recalled the events that led to the massacre, noting that after the shooting at Hoop Spur, a posse was mustered, but upon reaching the cabin of one of the union members, Ed Ware, they discovered that "there were too many to tackle." Realizing that they were outnumbered, the deputies returned and "swore in a bunch of Legion men." James estimated that about seventy-five men were deputized and noted that, when they returned to the cabin, the sharecroppers were still congregating outside. The chief deputy said that a fierce gunfight ensued, and even though he maintained that the "negro gang," presumably the members of the union, was broken up after ten minutes, he contended that several skirmishes sprang up during the course of the day despite the apprehension of these union members. James estimated the death toll at between fifty and one hundred blacks, most of whom were killed after the arrest of those sharecroppers who had attended the Hoop Spur meeting; he noted that only five whites were killed.[28]

Despite its brevity, the American Legion's minute book is revealing in its chronicle of the events of the organization's first annual state convention. While only briefly noting the participation of Helena's white veterans in the posse, it argues that the actions of the white men involved were heroic and laudable. In contrast, the minutes also illustrate that black veterans, despite their service to the nation, were not considered "one-hundred-percent Americans" and could therefore be deprived of the privilege of establishing their own Legion posts. The minutes expose the latent fear of the potential for violence that black soldiers represented to the whites of Phillips County, who, when stating their case for exclusion of black Legion posts, clearly expressed the terror of feeling

---

[28] "Officer Comes for Negroes Charged with Inciting Riot," *New Orleans States Item*, November 10, 1919, p. 3; "Local Police Say They Have Caught Negro Ringleader," *Times-Picayune*, November 10, 1919, pp. 1, 3.

outnumbered by their former black comrades in arms.

Chief Deputy James's interview provided a first-hand account as to how the American Legion members were recruited to assist in the massacre. His timeline closely resembles those of Stockley and Robert Whitaker, author of *On the Laps of Gods*. As a member of one of the posses and a member of the local police force, James presents a credible account of the death toll.[29]

The Phillips County Indictment Book (Entries Regarding the Elaine Massacre Arrests and Charges)

Following the raid at Ed Ware's cabin, the black sharecroppers who gathered outside of the shack throughout the night were arrested. After their arrests, each man was indicted, and the charges levied against the union members were recorded in the county's indictment book. The large leather-bound volume that recorded county arrests for close to a century was discovered in the dusty records room of the Phillips County Clerk of Court's office. Its pages, reproduced here on pages 216–237, held the names of all those arrested, identifying each by the charges filed against them, the names of their alleged victims, the date of indictment, the court case number, and the date of the violation. Review of the text revealed a long list of individuals who were indicted for violations that took place between September 25 and October 1, 1919 (see below). There were fifty-three men charged with "assault with the intent to kill" despite there being only three victims (Charles Pratt, B. J. Cunningham, and Ira Proctor), and one hundred charges of "unlawfully and feloniously confederating for the purpose of going forth at night armed to commit a felonious act." Commonly referred to as nightriding, the charge was most commonly associated with the actions of white terrorist groups like the Ku Klux Klan, which preyed upon the black community after the Civil War. Wearing masks and using the cover of night to

---

[29] Stockley, *Blood in Their Eyes*, xxiii–xxiv; Whitaker, *On the Laps of Gods*, 327.

hide their advance, retreat, and identity, members of these groups burned black churches and schools and intimidated and murdered members of the black community with near impunity. There were sixty-seven charges of murder in the first degree despite there being only four murder victims: James Tappan, Clinton Lee, W. A. Adkins, and Corporal Luther D. Earls. The last charge, "Barratry," was the only charge levied against any of the white attorneys arrested (C. P. Casey, O. S. Bratton, and U. S. Bratton). More frequently applied in issues of maritime law, the charge was levied against ships' officers or crews who acted fraudulently or unlawfully against the interest of their employers and those who irresponsibly risked or damaged a ship or its cargo.[30]

The indictment book's entries regarding the Elaine Massacre identify the sharecroppers arrested for their involvement in the union. While the Elaine Twelve, the union members who were sentenced to death, have been identified, little is known about the remaining membership of the union. Besides providing names of the members of the Progressive Farmers and Household Union, the indictment book substantiates E. M. Smith's allegations that he had an informant within the union. Indictments for meetings held on September 25 and 27, 1919, days before the shooting at Hoop Spur, show that the meetings must have been surveilled or reported to the town's leadership by someone in attendance.[31]

On October 11, 1919, the *Arkansas Democrat* noted that Isaiah Murphy was "the first negro insurrectionist to give himself up, surrendered to a posse [led] by Joseph C. Meyers," a local plantation owner. Referring to Murphy as an informer, the article maintained that he had been responsible for surrendering the names of all the union members. The *Democrat* borrowed the verbiage of E. M. Allen and referred to Murphy not as a killer or monster, but

---

[30] The Phillips County Indictment Book (Entries regarding the Elaine Race Massacre Arrests and Charges), p. 175–294.

[31] Letter from Governor Henry Allen to E. M. Allen dated May 9, 1920, Governor Henry Allen Collection, Correspondence Files 1919–1923, Kansas Historical Society.

as a "good hard-working negro." Shortly after Murphy's surrender, he met with Governor Brough, posse members, newspapermen, and military offices from Camp Pike before he was returned to confinement with the other arrested sharecroppers.

The newspaper alleged that, in his meeting, it was Murphy who first provided the story of the insurrection that became the justification for the massacre and what the union members would be tried for. The article maintained that Murphy was afraid of the other union members, who likely suspected him to be an informant, and, fearing for his life, he escaped from his confinement area only to be shot and killed by a sentry as he tried to escape from the military stockade. The shooting of Isaiah Murphy was more than just convenient. Since Murphy had allegedly given his account of the plans of insurrection to a room full of trusted whites, his testimony could be repeated as a confession. Murphy's confession legitimized the actions of the mob, posse men, and soldiers. It was his testimony that changed the event from a "massacre" to an "insurrection," and if he was in fact the informant who led the deputies to the Hoop Spur meeting, the men who sent him may have felt that it was too risky to place Murphy on the stand as a witness, only to have him change his mind and reveal that the killings had been solely about suppressing the union. We may never know for certain whether or not the "tale of the squashed insurrection" was created by Murphy or created by those who killed him. In the end, the body of Isaiah Murphy, like those of all the other blacks killed in the massacre, has never been recovered.

List of Individuals Indicted in Connection to the Elaine Massacre

Page Number	Court Case Number	Defendant's Surname	Defendant's First Name	Charge	Victim	Incident Month	Incident Day
193	4498	Austin	John	Assault with Intent to Kill	B.J. Cunningham	October	1
199	4504	Austin	John	Felony—unlawfully and feloniously Confederate and band themselves for the purpose of going forth at night armed to commit a felonious act.	N/A	October	1
196	4501	Avent	Andrew	Assault with Intent to Kill	B.J. Cunningham	October	1
199	4504	Avent	Andrew	Felony—unlawfully and feloniously Confederate and band themselves for the purpose of going forth at night armed to commit a felonious act.	N/A	October	1
192	4497	Baker	Ed	Felony—unlawfully and feloniously Confederate and band themselves for the purpose of going forth at night armed to commit a felonious act.	N/A	October	1
201	4506	Baker	Ed	First Degree -Murder	Clinton Lee	October	1
260	4582	Baker	Ed	Felony—Unlawfully and Felonious unite, confederate, or band themselves together and knowingly and feloniously met or act clandestinely with the Progressive Farmer and Household Union of America which said Progressive Farmer and Household Union of America was a band or order of person who had united, confederated, or banded themselves together for the purpose of going forth armed to do a felonious act.	N/A	September	25
175	4480	Banks	Alf Jr.	First Degree -Murder	James Tappan	October	1

#	Surname	First	Charge	Name	Month	Count
177	Banks	Alf Jr.	First Degree -Murder	W.A. Adkins	October	1
183	Banks	Alf Jr.	Assault with Intent to Kill	Ira Proctor	October	1
186	Banks	Alf Jr.	Assault with Intent to Kill	Charles Pratt	October	1
189	Banks	Alf Jr.	Felony—did unlawfully and feloniously Confederate and band themselves for the purpose of doing unlawful and felonious acts in the night time and did go forth at night armed and did alarm and intimidate one Charles Pratt by assaulting him	Charles Pratt	October	1
195	Barnes	Harrison	Assault with Intent to Kill	B.J. Cunningham	October	1
200	Barnes	Harrison	Felony—unlawfully and feloniously Confederate and band themselves for the purpose of going forth at night armed to commit a felonious act.	N/A	October	1
221	Black	Charles	Felony—unlawfully and feloniously Confederate and band themselves for the purpose of going forth at night armed to commit a felonious act.	N/A	September	25
225	Bratton	O.S.	Barratry	N/A	October	1
267	Bratton	U.S.	Barratry	N/A	October	1
191	Brown	Abe	Felony—unlawfully and feloniously Confederate and band themselves for the purpose of going forth at night armed to commit a felonious act.	N/A	October	1
192	Brown	James E.	Felony—unlawfully and feloniously Confederate and band themselves for the purpose of going forth at night armed to commit a felonious act.	N/A	October	1
207	Brown	James E.	First Degree -Murder	Clinton Lee	October	1

| 4482 | 4488 | 4491 | 4494 | 4500 | 4505 | 4526 | 4530 | 4531 | 4486 | 4497 | 4512 |

210	4515	Brown	Abe	First Degree -Murder	Clinton Lee	October	1
178	4483	Burns	Will	First Degree -Murder	W.A. Adkins	October	1
185	4490	Burns	Will	Assault with Intent to Kill	Charles Pratt	October	1
189	4494	Burns	Will	Felony—did unlawfully and feloniously Confederate and band themselves for the purpose of doing unlawful and felonious acts in the night time and did go forth at night armed and did alarm and intimidate one Charles Pratt by assaulting him	Charles Pratt	October	1
224	4529	Casey	C.P.	Barratry	N/A	October	1
210	4515	Cole	Burrell	First Degree -Murder	Clinton Lee	October	1
191	4486	Cole	Burrell	Felony—unlawfully and feloniously Confederate and band themselves for the purpose of going forth at night armed to commit a felonious act.	N/A	October	1
190	4495	Coleman	Ed	First Degree -Murder	Clinton Lee	October	1
191	4486	Coleman	Ed	Felony—unlawfully and feloniously Confederate and band themselves for the purpose of going forth at night armed to commit a felonious act.	N/A	October	1
194	4499	Coleman	Bob	Assault with Intent to Kill	B.J. Cunningham	October	1
200	4505	Coleman	Bob	Felony—unlawfully and feloniously Confederate and band themselves for the purpose of going forth at night armed to commit a felonious act.	N/A	October	1
180	4485	Curry	Will Jr.	First Degree -Murder	W.A. Adkins	October	1
181	4486	Curry	Will Sr.	First Degree -Murder	W.A. Adkins	October	1

185	4490	Curry	Will Jr.	Assault with Intent to Kill	Charles Pratt	October	1
187	4492	Curry	Will Sr.	Assault with Intent to Kill	Charles Pratt	October	1
188	4493	Curry	Will Sr.	Felony—did unlawfully and feloniously Confederate and band themselves for the purpose of doing unlawful and felonious acts in the night time and did go forth at night armed and did alarm and intimidate one Charles Pratt by assaulting him	Charles Pratt	October	1
189	4494	Curry	Will Jr.	Felony—did unlawfully and feloniously Confederate and band themselves for the purpose of doing unlawful and felonious acts in the night time and did go forth at night armed and did alarm and intimidate one Charles Pratt by assaulting him	Charles Pratt	October	1
206	4511	Dale	Ernest	First Degree -Murder	Clinton Lee	October	1
191	4486	Dial	George	Felony— unlawfully and feloniously Confederate and band themselves for the purpose of going forth at night armed to commit a felonious act.	N/A	October	1
203	4508	Dial	George	First Degree -Murder	Clinton Lee	October	1
194	4499	Dixon	Felix	Assault with Intent to Kill	B.J. Cunningham	October	1
195	4500	Dixon	Tillis	Assault with Intent to Kill	B.J. Cunningham	October	1
195	4500	Dixon	Clarence	Assault with Intent to Kill	B.J. Cunningham	October	1
200	4505	Dixon	Louie	Felony—unlawfully and feloniously Confederate and band themselves for the purpose of going forth at night armed to commit a felonious act.	N/A	October	1

200	4505	Dixon	Felix	Felony—unlawfully and feloniously Confederate and band themselves for the purpose of going forth at night armed to commit a felonious act.	N/A	October	1
200	4505	Dixon	Tillis	Felony—unlawfully and feloniously Confederate and band themselves for the purpose of going forth at night armed to commit a felonious act.	N/A	October	1
192	4497	Dole	Ernest	Felony—unlawfully and feloniously Confederate and band themselves for the purpose of going forth at night armed to commit a felonious act.	N/A	October	1
192	4497	Foster	John	Felony—unlawfully and feloniously Confederate and band themselves for the purpose of going forth at night armed to commit a felonious act.	N/A	October	1
206	4511	Foster	John	First Degree -Murder	Clinton Lee	October	1
176	4481	Fox	Joe	First Degree -Murder	James Tappan	October	1
178	4483	Fox	Sikes	First Degree -Murder	W.A. Adkins	October	1
181	4486	Fox	Joe	First Degree -Murder	W.A. Adkins	October	1
184	4489	Fox	Joe	Assault with Intent to Kill	Ira Proctor	October	1
185	4490	Fox	Joe	Assault with Intent to Kill	Charles Pratt	October	1
186	4491	Fox	Sikes	Assault with Intent to Kill	Charles Pratt	October	1
189	4494	Fox	Joe	Felony—did unlawfully and feloniously Confederate and band themselves for the purpose of doing unlawful and felonious acts in the night time and did go forth at night armed and did alarm and intimidate one Charles Pratt by assaulting him	Charles Pratt	October	1

189	4494			Felony—did unlawfully and feloniously Confederate and band themselves for the purpose of doing unlawful and felonious acts in the night time and did go forth at night armed and did alarm and intimidate one Charles Pratt by assaulting him	Charles Pratt	October	1
176	4481	Giles	Albert	First Degree -Murder	James Tappan	October	1
176	4481	Giles	Mulligan	First Degree -Murder	James Tappan	October	1
179	4484	Giles	Albert	First Degree -Murder	W.A. Adkins	October	1
180	4485	Giles	Mulligan	First Degree -Murder	W.A. Adkins	October	1
184	4489	Giles	Albert	Assault with Intent to Kill	Ira Proctor	October	1
184	4489	Giles	Mulligan	Assault with Intent to Kill	Ira Proctor	October	1
187	4492	Giles	Albert	Assault with Intent to Kill	Charles Pratt	October	1
187	4492	Giles	Mulligan	Assault with Intent to Kill	Charles Pratt	October	1
188	4493	Giles	Albert	Felony—did unlawfully and feloniously Confederate and band themselves for the purpose of doing unlawful and felonious acts in the night time and did go forth at night armed and did alarm and intimidate one Charles Pratt by assaulting him	Charles Pratt	October	1
188	4493	Giles	Mulligan	Felony—did unlawfully and feloniously Confederate and band themselves for the purpose of doing unlawful and felonious acts in the night time and did go forth at night armed and did alarm and intimidate one Charles Pratt by assaulting him	Charles Pratt	October	1

191	4486	Goss	Andrew	Felony—unlawfully and feloniously Confederate and band themselves for the purpose of going forth at night armed to commit a felonious act.	N/A	October	1
210	4515	Goss	Andrew	First Degree -Murder	Clinton Lee	October	1
192	4497	Green	George	Felony—unlawfully and feloniously Confederate and band themselves for the purpose of going forth at night armed to commit a felonious act.	N/A	October	1
197	4502	Green	George	Assault with Intent to Kill	B.J. Cunningham	October	1
201	4506	Green	George	First Degree -Murder	Clinton Lee	October	1
221	4526	Griggs	Will	Felony—unlawfully and feloniously Confederate and band themselves for the purpose of going forth at night armed to commit a felonious act.	N/A	September	25
261	4583	Griggs	Will	Felony—Unlawfully and Felonious unite, confederate, or band themselves together and knowingly and feloniously met or act clandestinely with the Progressive Farmer and Household Union of America which said Progressive Farmer and Household Union of America was a band or order of person who had united, confederated, or banded themselves together for the purpose of going forth armed to do a felonious act.	N/A	September	25
190	4495	Hall	Paul	First Degree -Murder	Clinton Lee	October	1
191	4486	Hall	Paul	Felony—unlawfully and feloniously Confederate and band themselves for the purpose of going forth at night armed to commit a felonious act.	N/A	October	1

191	4486	Hampton	Will	Felony—unlawfully and feloniously Confederate and band themselves for the purpose of going forth at night armed to commit a felonious act.	N/A	October	1
203	4508	Hampton	William	First Degree -Murder	Clinton Lee	October	1
180	4485	Harris	McKenzie	First Degree -Murder	W.A. Adkins	October	1
185	4490	Harris	McKenzie	Assault with Intent to Kill	Charles Pratt	October	1
189	4494	Harris	McKenzie	Felony—did unlawfully and feloniously Confederate and band themselves for the purpose of doing unlawful and felonious acts in the night time and did go forth at night armed and did alarm and intimidate one Charles Pratt by assaulting him	Charles Pratt	October	1
194	4499	Harris	Charles	Assault with Intent to Kill	B.J. Cunningham	October	1
200	4505	Harris	Charles	Felony—unlawfully and feloniously Confederate and band themselves for the purpose of going forth at night armed to commit a felonious act.	N/A	October	1
179	4484	Hays	Dave	First Degree -Murder	W.A. Adkins	October	1
187	4492	Hays	Dave	Assault with Intent to Kill	Charles Pratt	October	1
188	4493	Hays	Dave	Felony—did unlawfully and feloniously Confederate and band themselves for the purpose of doing unlawful and felonious acts in the night time and did go forth at night armed and did alarm and intimidate one Charles Pratt by assaulting him	Charles Pratt	October	1
262	4569	Helums	Ben	First Degree -Murder	W.A. Adkins	October	1

192	4497	Hendrix	Will	Felony—unlawfully and feloniously Confederate and band themselves for the purpose of going forth at night armed to commit a felonious act.	N/A	October	1
209	4514	Hendrix	Will	First Degree -Murder	Clinton Lee	October	1
196	4501	Herbert	Clarence C.	Assault with Intent to Kill	B.J. Cunningham	October	1
199	4504	Herbert	Clarence C.	Felony—unlawfully and feloniously Confederate and band themselves for the purpose of going forth at night armed to commit a felonious act.	N/A	October	1
190	4495	Hicks	Ed	First Degree -Murder	Clinton Lee	October	1
191	4486	Hicks	Ed	Felony—unlawfully and feloniously Confederate and band themselves for the purpose of going forth at night armed to commit a felonious act.	N/A	October	1
191	4486	Hicks	Franks	Felony—unlawfully and feloniously Confederate and band themselves for the purpose of going forth at night armed to commit a felonious act.	N/A	October	1
197	4502	Hicks	Frank	Assault with Intent to Kill	B.J. Cunningham	October	1
204	4509	Hicks	Frank	First Degree -Murder	Clinton Lee	October	1
199	4504	Hobson	Felix	Felony—unlawfully and feloniously Confederate and band themselves for the purpose of going forth at night armed to commit a felonious act.	N/A	October	1
221	4526	Hollis	Henry	Felony—unlawfully and feloniously Confederate and band themselves for the purpose of going forth at night armed to commit a felonious act.	N/A	September	25

261	4583	Hollis	Henry	Felony—Unlawfully and Felonious unite, confederate, or band themselves together and knowingly and feloniously met or act clandestinely with the Progressive Farmer and Household Union of America which said Progressive Farmer and Household Union of America was a band or order of person who had united, confederated, or banded themselves together for the purpose of going forth armed to do a felonious act.	N/A	September	25
221	4526	Holloway	John M.	Felony—unlawfully and feloniously Confederate and band themselves for the purpose of going forth at night armed to commit a felonious act.	N/A	September	25
261	4583	Holloway	John M.	Felony—Unlawfully and Felonious unite, confederate, or band themselves together and knowingly and feloniously met or act clandestinely with the Progressive Farmer and Household Union of America which said Progressive Farmer and Household Union of America was a band or order of person who had united, confederated, or banded themselves together for the purpose of going forth armed to do a felonious act.	N/A	September	25
220	4525	Hooker	Eddie	Felony—unlawfully and feloniously Confederate and band themselves for the purpose of going forth at night armed to commit a felonious act.	N/A	September	27

259	4581	Hooker	Eddie	Felony—unlawfully and feloniously Confederate and band themselves for the purpose of going forth at night armed to commit a felonious act and intent to kill	W.H. McCulloch	September	27
193	4498	Hopson	Felix	Assault with Intent to Kill	B.J. Cunningham	October	1
220	4525	Hutton	Richard	Felony—unlawfully and feloniously Confederate and band themselves for the purpose of going forth at night armed to commit a felonious act.	N/A	September	27
259	4581	Hutton	Richard	Felony—unlawfully and feloniously Confederate and band themselves for the purpose of going forth at night armed to commit a felonious act and intent to kill	W.H. McCulloch	September	27
192	4497	Jackson	Robert	Felony—unlawfully and feloniously Confederate and band themselves for the purpose of going forth at night armed to commit a felonious act.	N/A	October	1
194	4499	Jackson	Will	Assault with Intent to Kill	B.J. Cunningham	October	1
194	4499	Jackson	Robert	Assault with Intent to Kill	B.J. Cunningham	October	1
197	4502	Jackson	Sullivan	Assault with Intent to Kill	B.J. Cunningham	October	1
200	4505	Jackson	Will	Felony—unlawfully and feloniously Confederate and band themselves for the purpose of going forth at night armed to commit a felonious act.	N/A	October	1

200	4505	Jackson	Robert	Felony—unlawfully and feloniously Confederate and band themselves for the purpose of going forth at night armed to commit a felonious act.	N/A	October	1
202	4507	Jackson	Robert	First Degree -Murder	Clinton Lee	October	1
182	4487	James	Charlie	First Degree -Murder	W.A. Adkins	October	1
185	4490	James	Charlie	Assault with Intent to Kill	Charles Pratt	October	1
189	4494	James	Charlie	Felony—did unlawfully and feloniously Confederate and band themselves for the purpose of doing unlawful and felonious acts in the night time and did go forth at night armed and did alarm and intimidate one Charles Pratt by assaulting him	Charles Pratt	October	1
192	4497	Jefferson	John	Felony—unlawfully and feloniously Confederate and band themselves for the purpose of going forth at night armed to commit a felonious act.	N/A	October	1
209	4514	Jefferson	John	First Degree -Murder	Clinton Lee	October	1
181	4486	Jenkins	Gilmore	First Degree -Murder	W.A. Adkins	October	1
186	4491	Jenkins	Gilmore	Assault with Intent to Kill	Charles Pratt	October	1
189	4494	Jenkins	Gilmore	Felony—did unlawfully and feloniously Confederate and band themselves for the purpose of doing unlawful and felonious acts in the night time and did go forth at night armed and did alarm and intimidate one Charles Pratt by assaulting him	Charles Pratt	October	1

192	4497	Jenkins	Gilmore	Felony—unlawfully and feloniously Confederate and band themselves for the purpose of going forth at night armed to commit a felonious act.	N/A	October	1
208	4513	Jenkins	Gilmore	First Degree -Murder	Clinton Lee	October	1
200	4505	Johnson	John	Felony—unlawfully and feloniously Confederate and band themselves for the purpose of going forth at night armed to commit a felonious act.	N/A	October	1
221	4526	Johnson	Ed	Felony—unlawfully and feloniously Confederate and band themselves for the purpose of going forth at night armed to commit a felonious act.	N/A	September	25
261	4583	Johnson	Ed	Felony—Unlawfully and Felonious unite, confederate, or band themselves together and knowingly and feloniously met or act clandestinely with the Progressive Farmer and Household Union of America which said Progressive Farmer and Household Union of America was a band or order of person who had united, confederated, or banded themselves together for the purpose of going forth armed to do a felonious act.	N/A	September	25
192	4497	Kelly	Tom	Felony—unlawfully and feloniously Confederate and band themselves for the purpose of going forth at night armed to commit a felonious act.	N/A	October	1
202	4507	Kelly	Tom	First Degree -Murder	Clinton Lee	October	1
193	4498	Keys	Lewis	Assault with Intent to Kill	B.J. Cunningham	October	1
195	4500	Keys	Chester	Assault with Intent to Kill	B.J. Cunningham	October	1

199	4504	Keys	Lewis	Felony—unlawfully and feloniously Confederate and band themselves for the purpose of going forth at night armed to commit a felonious act.	N/A	October	1
200	4505	Keys	Chester	Felony—unlawfully and feloniously Confederate and band themselves for the purpose of going forth at night armed to commit a felonious act.	N/A	October	1
190	4495	Knox	J.E.	First Degree -Murder	Clinton Lee	October	1
191	4486	Knox	J.E.	Felony—unlawfully and feloniously Confederate and band themselves for the purpose of going forth at night armed to commit a felonious act.	N/A	October	1
220	4525	Lee	James	Felony—unlawfully and feloniously Confederate and band themselves for the purpose of going forth at night armed to commit a felonious act.	N/A	September	27
259	4581	Lee	James	Felony—unlawfully and feloniously Confederate and band themselves for the purpose of going forth at night armed to commit a felonious act and intent to kill	W.H. McCulloch	September	27
178	4483	Ligon	Joe	First Degree -Murder	W.A. Adkins	October	1
187	4492	Ligon	Joe	Assault with Intent to Kill	Charles Pratt	October	1
188	4493	Ligon	Joe	Felony—did unlawfully and feloniously Confederate and band themselves for the purpose of doing unlawful and felonious acts in the night time and did go forth at night armed and did alarm and intimidate one Charles Pratt by assaulting him	Charles Pratt	October	1
193	4498	Magee	Lee	Assault with Intent to Kill	B.J. Cunningham	October	1

199	4504	Magee	Lee	Felony—unlawfully and feloniously Confederate and band themselves for the purpose of going forth at night armed to commit a felonious act.	N/A	October	1
177	4482	Martin	John	First Degree -Murder	W.A. Adkins	October	1
187	4492	Martin	John	Assault with Intent to Kill	Charles Pratt	October	1
188	4493	Martin	John	Felony—did unlawfully and feloniously Confederate and band themselves for the purpose of doing unlawful and felonious acts in the night time and did go forth at night armed and did alarm and intimidate one Charles Pratt by assaulting him	Charles Pratt	October	1
180	4485	Mason	Henny	First Degree -Murder	W.A. Adkins	October	1
187	4492	Mason	Henny	Assault with Intent to Kill	Charles Pratt	October	1
188	4493	Mason	Henny	Felony—did unlawfully and feloniously Confederate and band themselves for the purpose of doing unlawful and felonious acts in the night time and did go forth at night armed and did alarm and intimidate one Charles Pratt by assaulting him	Charles Pratt	October	1
181	4486	Mershon	Joe	First Degree -Murder	W.A. Adkins	October	1
185	4490	Mershon	Joe	Assault with Intent to Kill	Charles Pratt	October	1
189	4494	Mershon	Joe	Felony—did unlawfully and feloniously Confederate and band themselves for the purpose of doing unlawful and felonious acts in the night time and did go forth at night armed and did alarm and intimidate one Charles Pratt by assaulting him	Charles Pratt	October	1
262	4569	Miller	Will	First Degree -Murder	W.A. Adkins	October	1

182	4487	Mitchell	Ed	First Degree -Murder	W.A. Adkins	October	1
186	4491	Mitchell	Ed	Assault with Intent to Kill	Charles Pratt	October	1
189	4494	Mitchell	Ed	Felony—did unlawfully and feloniously Confederate and band themselves for the purpose of doing unlawful and felonious acts in the night time and did go forth at night armed and did alarm and intimidate one Charles Pratt by assaulting him	Charles Pratt	October	1
191	4486	Mitchell	Ed	Felony—unlawfully and feloniously Confederate and band themselves for the purpose of going forth at night armed to commit a felonious act.	N/A	October	1
212	4517	Mitchell	Ed	First Degree -Murder	Clinton Lee	October	1
179	4484	Moore	Frank	First Degree -Murder	W.A. Adkins	October	1
186	4491	Moore	Frank	Assault with Intent to Kill	Charles Pratt	October	1
187	4492	Moore	Frank	Assault with Intent to Kill	Charles Pratt	October	1
188	4493	Moore	Frank	Felony—did unlawfully and feloniously Confederate and band themselves for the purpose of doing unlawful and felonious acts in the night time and did go forth at night armed and did alarm and intimidate one Charles Pratt by assaulting him	Charles Pratt	October	1
189	4494	Moore	Frank	Felony—did unlawfully and feloniously Confederate and band themselves for the purpose of doing unlawful and felonious acts in the night time and did go forth at night armed and did alarm and intimidate one Charles Pratt by assaulting him	Charles Pratt	October	1
190	4495	Moore	Frank	First Degree -Murder	Clinton Lee	October	1

191	4486	Moore	Frank	Felony—unlawfully and feloniously Confederate and band themselves for the purpose of going forth at night armed to commit a felonious act.	N/A	October	1
197	4502	Moore	Frank	Assault with Intent to Kill	B.J. Cunningham	October	1
272	4567	Moore	Jim	First Degree -Murder	Clinton Lee	October	1
193	4498	Morgan	Cornelius	Assault with Intent to Kill	B.J. Cunningham	October	1
199	4504	Morgan	Cornelius	Felony—unlawfully and feloniously Confederate and band themselves for the purpose of going forth at night armed to commit a felonious act.	N/A	October	1
192	4497	Morris	Nathan	Felony—unlawfully and feloniously Confederate and band themselves for the purpose of going forth at night armed to commit a felonious act.	N/A	October	1
198	4503	Morris	Nathan	Assault with Intent to Kill	B.J. Cunningham	October	1
209	4514	Morris	Nathan	First Degree -Murder	Clinton Lee	October	1
212	4517	Mosely	Jesse	First Degree -Murder	Clinton Lee	October	1
191	4486	Mosley	Mat	Felony—unlawfully and feloniously Confederate and band themselves for the purpose of going forth at night armed to commit a felonious act.	N/A	October	1
191	4486	Mosley	Jesse	Felony—unlawfully and feloniously Confederate and band themselves for the purpose of going forth at night armed to commit a felonious act.	N/A	October	1
203	4508	Mosley	Mat	First Degree -Murder	Clinton Lee	October	1

192	4497	Murphy	Austin	Felony—unlawfully and feloniously Confederate and band themselves for the purpose of going forth at night armed to commit a felonious act.	N/A	October	1
208	4513	Murphy	Austin	First Degree -Murder	Clinton Lee	October	1
191	4486	Muzzle	Walter	Felony—unlawfully and feloniously Confederate and band themselves for the purpose of going forth at night armed to commit a felonious act.	N/A	October	1
203	4508	Muzzle	Walter	First Degree -Murder	Clinton Lee	October	1
192	4497	Payne	Dee	Felony—unlawfully and feloniously Confederate and band themselves for the purpose of going forth at night armed to commit a felonious act.	N/A	October	1
202	4507	Payne	Dee	First Degree -Murder	Clinton Lee	October	1
179	4484	Perkins	Will	First Degree -Murder	W.A. Adkins	October	1
186	4491	Perkins	Will	Assault with Intent to Kill	Charles Pratt	October	1
189	4494	Perkins	Will	Felony—did unlawfully and feloniously Confederate and band themselves for the purpose of doing unlawful and felonious acts in the night time and did go forth at night armed and did alarm and intimidate one Charles Pratt by assaulting him	Charles Pratt	October	
191	4486	Perkins	Will	Felony—unlawfully and feloniously Confederate and band themselves for the purpose of going forth at night armed to commit a felonious act.	N/A	October	1
197	4502	Perkins	Will	Assault with Intent to Kill	B.J. Cunningham	October	1
205	4510	Perkins	Will	First Degree -Murder	Clinton Lee	October	1

178	Ratcliffe	John	First Degree -Murder	W.A. Adkins	October	1
185	Ratcliffe	John	Assault with Intent to Kill	Charles Pratt	October	1
189	Ratcliffe	John	Felony—did unlawfully and feloniously Confederate and band themselves for the purpose of doing unlawful and felonious acts in the night time and did go forth at night armed and did alarm and intimidate one Charles Pratt by assaulting him	Charles Pratt	October	1
192	Reed	Spencer	Felony—unlawfully and feloniously Confederate and band themselves for the purpose of going forth at night armed to commit a felonious act.	N/A	October	1
200	Reed	Dave	Felony—unlawfully and feloniously Confederate and band themselves for the purpose of going forth at night armed to commit a felonious act.	N/A	October	1
207	Reed	Spencer	First Degree -Murder	Clinton Lee	October	1
200	Richardson	Young	Felony—unlawfully and feloniously Confederate and band themselves for the purpose of going forth at night armed to commit a felonious act.	N/A	October	1
195	Richardson	Dave	Assault with Intent to Kill	B.J. Cunningham	October	1
195	Richardson	Young	Assault with Intent to Kill	B.J. Cunningham	October	1
199	Richardson	Dave	Felony—unlawfully and feloniously Confederate and band themselves for the purpose of going forth at night armed to commit a felonious act.	N/A	October	1
198	Roland	Dan	Assault with Intent to Kill	B.J. Cunningham	October	1
193	Sampson	Jeff	Assault with Intent to Kill	B.J. Cunningham	October	1

				Charge	Victim	Month	Count
199	4504	Sampson	Jeff	Felony—unlawfully and feloniously Confederate and band themselves for the purpose of going forth at night armed to commit a felonious act.	N/A	October	1
191	4486	Saw	Tom	Felony—unlawfully and feloniously Confederate and band themselves for the purpose of going forth at night armed to commit a felonious act.	N/A	October	1
212	4517	Saw	Tom	First Degree -Murder	Clinton Lee	October	1
260	4582	Shelton	J.H.	Felony—Unlawfully and Felonious unite, confederate, or band themselves together and knowingly and feloniously met or act clandestinely with the Progressive Farmer and Household Union of America which said Progressive Farmer and Household Union of America was a band or order of person who had united, confederated, or banded themselves together for the purpose of going forth armed to do a felonious act.	N/A	September	25
191	4486	Smith	Alex	Felony—unlawfully and feloniously Confederate and band themselves for the purpose of going forth at night armed to commit a felonious act.	N/A	October	1
192	4497	Smith	Will	Felony—unlawfully and feloniously Confederate and band themselves for the purpose of going forth at night armed to commit a felonious act.	N/A	October	1
201	4506	Smith	Will	First Degree -Murder	Clinton Lee	October	1
203	4508	Smith	Alex	First Degree -Murder	Clinton Lee	October	1
198	4503	Stewart	Will	Assault with Intent to Kill	B.J. Cunningham	October	1

212	4517	Stewart	Will	First Degree -Murder	Clinton Lee	October	1
191	4486	Stuart	Will	Felony—unlawfully and feloniously Confederate and band themselves for the purpose of going forth at night armed to commit a felonious act.	N/A	October	1
221	4526	Swait	W.H.	Felony—unlawfully and feloniously Confederate and band themselves for the purpose of going forth at night armed to commit a felonious act.	N/A	September	25
261	4583	Swait	W.H.	Felony—Unlawfully and Felonious unite, confederate, or band themselves together and knowingly and feloniously met or act clandestinely with the Progressive Farmer and Household Union of America which said Progressive Farmer and Household Union of America was a band or order of person who had united, confederated, or banded themselves together for the purpose of going forth armed to do a felonious act.	N/A	September	25
192	4497	Thomas	John	Felony—unlawfully and feloniously Confederate and band themselves for the purpose of going forth at night armed to commit a felonious act.	N/A	October	1
201	4506	Thomas	John	First Degree -Murder	Clinton Lee	October	1
192	4497	Thompson	James	Felony—unlawfully and feloniously Confederate and band themselves for the purpose of going forth at night armed to commit a felonious act.	N/A	October	1
208	4513	Thompson	James	First Degree -Murder	Clinton Lee	October	1

192	4497	Toolie	Walter	Felony—unlawfully and feloniously Confederate and band themselves for the purpose of going forth at night armed to commit a felonious act.	N/A	October	1
207	4512	Toolie	Walter	First Degree -Murder	Clinton Lee	October	1
192	4497	Ward	Walter	Felony—unlawfully and feloniously Confederate and band themselves for the purpose of going forth at night armed to commit a felonious act.	N/A	October	1
209	4514	Ward	Walter	First Degree -Murder	Clinton Lee	October	1
192	4497	Wilson	Sam	Felony—unlawfully and feloniously Confederate and band themselves for the purpose of going forth at night armed to commit a felonious act.	N/A	October	1
206	4511	Wilson	Sam	First Degree -Murder	Clinton Lee	October	1
211	4516	Wilson	Sam	First Degree -Murder	Corporal Earls	October	2
177	4482	Wordlaw	Will	First Degree -Murder	W.A. Adkins	October	1
185	4490	Wordlaw	Will	Assault with Intent to Kill	Charles Pratt	October	1
189	4494	Wordlaw	Will	Felony—did unlawfully and feloniously Confederate and band themselves for the purpose of doing unlawful and felonious acts in the night time and did go forth at night armed and did alarm and intimidate one Charles Pratt by assaulting him	Charles Pratt	October	1

Chapter 9

Cracking Open the Door: *Moore v. Dempsey* and the Fight for Justice

William H. Pruden III

O n the morning of October 1, 1919, the residents of Elaine, Arkansas—and, indeed, the whole of Phillips County— awoke to a transformed landscape. Overnight, the county had been totally upended, exploding into a mixture of riot and massacre, of fear and fathomless violence, the roots and results of which historians are still trying to unravel almost a century later. Almost two decades into the twenty-first century, historians continue to debate aspects of the 1919 Elaine riots, ranging from fatality figures to the full range of responsible parties. Yet for all the ongoing questions, legal and political historians—with the benefit of a century of hindsight, reflection, and study—can agree that the U.S. Supreme Court's decision in *Moore v. Dempsey*, the seminal case that emerged from the incident, was a crucial if sometimes unrecognized step on the road to black equality before the law, as well as a jumping-off point for a number of critical developments in the area of criminal justice. While its immediate impact was, for all intents and purposes, the freeing of a group of six African Americans initially found guilty of murder and sentenced to be executed, in a changing American legal and political landscape, the case was much more. From the Court's decision to even hear the case to its ultimate ruling, *Moore v. Dempsey* represented a precedent-setting exercise of federal authority. It marked a new approach to the due process clause of the Fourteenth Amendment, as well as the writ of habeas corpus, thus laying the groundwork for the legal side of the civil rights movement. At same time, the Court's new interpretation of the due process guarantee would serve as a foundation for many of the criminal justice advances of the Warren Court era.

No less importantly, the outcome in *Moore v. Dempsey* played a central role in the subsequent decision of the National Association for the Advancement of Colored People (NAACP) to pursue a litigation-based approach in its effort to strike down the many legal barriers that stood between the nation's African American population and the Declaration of Independence's promise of equality. In looking back with the benefit of historical hindsight— and following the enactment of both the Civil Rights Act of 1964 and the Voting Rights Act of 1965—*Moore v. Dempsey* has come to be recognized as the first in a succession of legal victories by the NAACP that would ultimately lead to the Court's decision, three decades in the future, in the landmark school desegregation case *Brown v. Board of Education*. But in 1923, as the still-young organization became involved with Fred Moore and his fellow defendants, the NAACP was doing so in response to both a plea for help from black Arkansas attorney Scipio Jones and a report from the organization's staffer Walter White that affirmed and supported Jones's plans and efforts.[1] There was no well-articulated or defined strategy. That would come later. There was simply a desperate need for somebody or some group to address an egregious miscarriage of justice. While the NAACP's focus was on the short-term fate of a group of innocent men, its work also represented the beginning of something bigger, the ultimate impact of which could not possibly have been imagined in 1923.

An Incident in Elaine

Although the United States had emerged from World War I

---

[1] Susan D. Carle, "Re-Envisioning Models for Pro-Bono Lawyering: Some Historical Reflections," *American Journal of Gender Policy and Law* 9, no. 1 (2001): 86–87, online at http://digitalcommons.wcl.american.edu/cgi/viewcontent.cgi?article=1383&context=jgspl (accessed March 1, 2018); Megan Ming Francis, *Civil Rights and the Making of the Modern American State* (New York: Cambridge University Press, 2014), 140–145, 148.

victorious, the summer of 1919 saw both the white and the black soldiers who had fought so heroically to, as Woodrow Wilson said, "make the world safe for democracy" struggling to find their place in a nation deeply divided in the aftermath of its international foray. The nation's economy was also having considerable difficulty getting back on track following the ending of the war. The influx into the workplace of the newly discharged soldiers put a tremendous strain on a shifting labor force and an economy trying to adjust to peacetime realities. To further complicate matters, black soldiers returned to a country whose own version of democracy fell far short of its promise. Tragically, these pressures and tensions were unleashed in a string of so-called race riots that spread from coast to coast and included cities like San Francisco, California, on the West Coast and Washington DC on the East Coast. Arkansas was not immune to what came to be known as the Red Summer. By the time the air had cleared and the bodies were counted, what happened in Phillips County would be recognized as the bloodiest incident of that bloody summer.[2]

The upheaval in Elaine began on the night of September 30, 1919.[3] To this day, there remain discrepancies in the accounts of what actually happened, but that lack of consensus does not diminish the impact of a set of events that shined a bright light on the state's existing racial tension. Even motivations behind the initial gathering remain shrouded in doubt, with some white authorities maintaining, rather defensively, that the meeting represented a gathering of angry, disaffected African Americans bent on inflicting violence on the local white population, while others, including the official, documented post-riot investigations, report

---

[2] Cameron McWhirter, *Red Summer: The Summer of 1919 and the Awakening of Black America* (New York: Henry Holt, 2011) offers a comprehensive overview of the tensions and resulting actions that characterized the deadly summer of 1919. The Elaine Riots and their aftermath are given substantive attention.
[3] Grif Stockley, *Blood in Their Eyes: The Elaine Race Massacres of 1919* (Fayetteville: University of Arkansas Press, 2001), xxiii.

that the gathering at the church was simply a group of sharecroppers seeking both to organize and seek legal representation in
an effort to end the exploitive conditions under which they were
working.[4]

In the end, despite the persistent allegations and rumors about
black sharecroppers planning a campaign of vengeance, it is clear
that the gathering in the Hoop Spur church was in fact a meeting
of local black sharecroppers and representatives of the Progressive Farmers and Household Union of America. Too, the sharecroppers, frustrated and angry, tired of the exploitive practices
that the planters too often employed, were also looking into hiring
some white lawyers with an eye to suing the planters, who, they
argued, were engaging in peonage practices; ironically, they had
invited Ocier S. (O. S.) Bratton, the son of one of Arkansas's most
respected attorneys, Ulysses S. (U. S.) Bratton, a man who later
helped argue the *Moore* case before the Supreme Court.[5] Apparently, word of the meeting had gotten out, and as the sharecroppers and the union representatives discussed the situation, out-
raged whites disrupted the meeting, resulting in an exchange of
shots. At some point, a white man, W. A. Adkins, was killed.[6] And
then the whole area dissolved into a free-for-all. By all reports,
whites, including some from other states, went on the warpath.
Blacks fled their homes, often seeking refuge in the fields and
forests throughout the area, but they were indiscriminately hunted
down in the countryside, with many being killed.[7]

---

[4] While they have different perspectives, Richard C. Cortner's *A Mob
Intent on Death: The NAACP and the Arkansas Riot Cases* (Middletown,
CT: Wesleyan University Press, 1988) and Stockley's *Blood in Their Eyes*
offer the most comprehensive treatments of the Elaine Massacre/Riots—the
multi-faceted label itself a reflection of the event's different interpreta-
tions—that ultimately resulted in *Moore v. Dempsey*. Both books cover
the wide range of charges and countercharges, assertions and defenses that
continue to surround those fateful days as well as the legal actions that
followed.
[5] Stockley, *Blood in Their Eyes*, xiii–xiv.
[6] Stockley, *Blood in Their Eyes*, xv.
[7] McWhirter, *Red Summer*, 219; Robert Whitaker, *On the Laps of Gods: The*

As the violence continued, Governor Charles H. Brough got permission from the War Department to use federal troops to restore order.[8] When, after some delay, the approximately 600 U.S. Army soldiers arrived on October 2, Brough was at the head of the "parade," telling reporters that he wanted to see exactly what had happened.[9] In fact, as he ventured forth with the troops, he helped to oversee the arrests of hundreds of local blacks; those who were not arrested were reduced to having to sign out, walking the streets in their own towns only if they were in possession of a pass signed by one of the locale's reputable whites.[10] Too, numerous accounts hold that the troops actively engaged in similarly random acts of violence against the area's African American citizens, a fact enthusiastically seized upon by Arkansas officials who went to great lengths to deflect and minimize the charges by outside critics—critics who characterized the whole incident as little more than a wholesale lynching party.[11]

"Order" was finally restored after the departure of the white mobs on October 2, but to this day the exact number of the (mostly African American) dead remains unknown.[12] In addition, thousands of dollars of crops had been either destroyed or stolen from the sharecroppers by white landowners, and when those sharecroppers who had not been rounded up returned to their homes, they often found them either destroyed or simply barren, with furniture and belongings taken.[13]

Red Summer of 1919 and the Struggle That Remade a Nation (New York: Crown Publishers, 2008), 123–125.

[8] Cortner, *A Mob Intent on Death*, 11.

[9] Stockley, *Blood in Their Eyes*, xxiv–xxv, 75.

[10] Cortner, *A Mob Intent on Death*, 11.

[11] Whitaker, *On the Laps of Gods*, 218.

[12] Stockley, *Blood in Their Eyes*, xxv; Whitaker, *On the Laps of Gods*, 124–125. One of the continuing mysteries surrounding the events in Elaine is an accurate body count for both blacks and whites. Estimates, which by almost all credible accounts are vastly overblown, go as high as 856. It would appear that at least 200 African Americans lost their lives, but some credible sources place the number higher.

[13] Ida Wells-Barnett, *The Arkansas Race Riot* (Chicago, 1920) (CreateSpace Independent Publishing Platform, 2013).

Justice: Phillips County Style

With the restoration of order (such as it was) on October 2, but with federal troops still a presence, the Phillips County wheels of justice began to turn. Governor Brough gave his blessing to the formation of the Committee of Seven, a group composed of prominent local citizens, which was empowered to investigate the incident.[14] It was a task they undertook with alacrity, with their quick and arguably face-saving investigation putting the blame on the outsiders, asserting that the leaders of the Progressive Farmers and Household Union had both deceived and empowered the black sharecroppers. The committee asserted that the organization had been started by a swindler whose real goal was to get money from black members. At the same time, he had led them to think that they would be supported by the federal government in an armed effort to overthrow the white property owners.[15] According to the Committee of Seven, the plans went awry with the unexpected outbreak of violence at Hoop Spur, leading to a premature start of the insurrection.[16] Happily, or so the committee asserted, local law enforcement, aided by the military, was able to swoop in and prevent what could have been a massive black massacre of the local white population.[17]

The report did little to quell the charges and countercharges that continued to fly concerning who was responsible—and for what. It also had little effect on the local judicial process, which was to prove tone deaf to the concept of due process, but which was very responsive to the constitutional dictate of a speedy trial. Indeed, at the same time the committee was at work, local law enforcement officials, as well as the local courts, began to process the accused, and Southern justice, an oxymoron for much of the black community, began to be applied, quickly seeking to address

---

[14] Stockley, *Blood in Their Eyes*, 76–77.
[15] Cortner, *A Mob Intent on Death*, 13.
[16] Cortner, *A Mob Intent on Death*, 13.
[17] Cortner, *A Mob Intent on Death*, 13.

the status of the more than 400 local African Americans (some reports had the number exceeding 700) who had initially been taken into custody.[18]

In late October, a grand jury made up of local landowners and merchants was convened to investigate the violence. Working with testimony that later reports made clear was often coerced—either through beatings and torture or intimidation—122 indictments of blacks were returned in short order.[19] The charges ranged from murder to nightriding, but all stemmed from the alleged role of the accused in what the local papers had taken to calling a racially motivated "insurrection."[20] While Prosecuting Attorney John Miller dismissed twenty-one of the indictments for lack of evidence, the trials for the rest began on November 3, 1919, barely a month after the initial violence at Hoop Spur.[21] Those accused of murder were tried first, including the defendants whose convictions would culminate in the *Moore v. Dempsey* decision.

The proceedings, which established a pattern for all subsequent ones, were a model of judicial efficiency, if not justice. The first trial took only forty-five minutes, as the court-appointed counsel for the defense (a lawyer who was, in fact, denied advance access to his clients) failed to seek a delay or a change of venue.[22] He also failed to challenge any of the jurymen.[23] Then, once the trial had started, the attorney called no defense witnesses and also failed to give the defendants an opportunity to testify

---

[18] "The Rise and Fall of Jim Crow: Moore v. Dempsey." PBS, online at http://www.pbs.org/wnet/jimcrow/stories_events_moore.html (accessed March 1, 2018); Whitaker, *On the Laps of Gods*, 121; "February 19, 1923 – The U.S. Supreme Court Decided Moore v. Dempsey – A Seminal Step in the Enforcement of Civil Rights for Blacks," online at https://rhapsodyin-books.wordpress.com/2009/02/19/february-19-1923-%E2%80%93-the-us-supreme-court-decided-moore-v-dempsey-%E2%80%93-a-seminal-step-in-the-enforcement-of-civil-rights-for-blacks/; McWhirter, *Red Summer*, 222.

[19] Cortner, *A Mob Intent on Death*, 15.

[20] McWhirter, *Red Summer*, 223.

[21] Stockley, *Blood in Their Eyes*, 109.

[22] Richard Kluger, *Simple Justice* (New York: Alfred A. Knopf, 1976), 113; Cortner, *A Mob Intent on Death*, 16.

[23] Cortner, *A Mob Intent on Death*, 16.

on their own behalf.[24] Throughout the trial, armed mobs, ready to administer their own brand of justice, roamed the courthouse grounds.[25] The all-white jury deliberated for only eight minutes before finding Frank Hicks guilty of first-degree murder in the death of Clinton Lee.[26] And they deliberated only seven minutes to find Frank Moore, Ed Hicks, J. E. Knox, Paul Hall, and Ed Coleman guilty of murder in the first degree as accessories.[27] Later trials were just as fast, with no jury taking more than ten minutes to reach guilty verdicts; the final verdict for the twelfth defendant charged with murder and sentenced to death came after four minutes of jury deliberations.[28] These guilty verdicts for twelve defendants—who, in the words of one constitutional scholar "were at most guilty of being present when lethal shots were fired, and not even clearly of this"—established the obvious parameters of Phillips County justice in the aftermath of the Elaine riots.[29] As a result, the non-capital-case defendants still in jail rushed to secure plea bargains. A second round of dismissals by Prosecutor Miller, again for lack of evidence, reduced the number of accused to sixty-seven, and they quickly made deals that saved their lives but still resulted in prison sentences ranging from one to twenty-one years.[30] Meanwhile, execution dates for

---

[24] Stockley, *Blood in Their Eyes*, 111.

[25] Kluger, *Simple Justice*, 113.

[26] Francis, *Civil Rights*, 155, note 106. The appeals that the U.S. Supreme Court heard and decided as *Moore v. Dempsey* represented, in fact, a combined case, one that represented both the joint appeal from Frank Moore and his four fellow defendants as well as the appeal of Frank Hicks, whose initial conviction for murder had, from the beginning, been treated separately. However, by the time both cases had reached the Court the issues were identical and so, as it often does, the Court combined the cases and issued a single ruling that applied to all parties.

[27] Stockley, *Blood in Their Eyes*, xxvi–xxvii.

[28] Cortner, *A Mob Intent on Death*, 18.

[29] Michael J. Klarman, *From Jim Crow to Civil Rights: The Supreme Court and the Struggle for Racial Equality* (New York: Oxford University Press, 2004), 502, note 49.

[30] Francis, *Civil Rights*, 1; Stockley, *Blood in Their Eyes*, 130; Cortner, *A Mob Intent on Death*, 18.

the twelve convicted of murder were set for December 27, 1919, and January 2, 1920.[31]

Shining a National Spotlight

With each passing day, word of what happened in Phillips County spread, and outside civil rights groups soon began to show an interest. In the immediate aftermath of the Elaine Massacre, the NAACP dispatched its young assistant secretary Walter White to Arkansas to investigate.[32] With the ability to pass as white on account of his light skin, and with credentials from the *Chicago Daily News*, an influential black paper that had agreed to run his findings, White produced a report that not only directly rebutted the version being offered by the Committee of Seven and other local officials but also proved critical to the decision of the organization to join the legal effort and help Scipio Jones defend the twelve Elaine defendants.[33] Indeed, the publication of his reports and dispatches in the *Chicago Defender* and *The Nation*, as well as in the NAACP's own publication, *The Crisis*, did much to shine a national spotlight on the case; the *Moore* case also represented White's own debut on the national scene, the beginning of a career that would make him a central figure in the NAACP-led civil rights battles of the next four decades.

However, White's incursion into Arkansas was a risky venture. The local media had made clear that the whole event, the "riot," was a product of black anger and the embodiment of their lack of civility, demonstrating anew how the African American population was unfit for anything better than sharecropping, and certainly anyone from the outside—"outside agitator" became a popular epithet in the coming decades—who sought to counter

---

[31] Harrison Bennett, "Justice on Trial: The Phillips County Riot Cases," Arkansas State University, online at http://www.clt.astate.edu/sarahwf/elainrt/justicehb.html (accessed March 1, 2018).
[32] Cortner, *A Mob Intent on Death*, 25.
[33] Kluger, *Simple Justice*, 113; Stockley, *Blood in Their Eyes*, 97–99; Cortner, *A Mob Intent on Death*, 24–34.

the narrative was not welcome.[34] Indeed, once it was discovered that an outsider was in their midst, the local community made clear its unhappiness with his efforts. Year later, in his autobiography, White recalled how when he boarded the train from Phillips County to Little Rock, the conductor told White that he was leaving "just when the fun is going to start," because, the conductor continued, the locals had discovered that there was a "damned yellow nigger passing for white and the boys are going to get him."[35] White continued his journey, but before he left, he had gotten an eye-opening look at Phillips County justice, a view he willingly shared with allies in the North and media outlets to good effect.[36]

While White's reports cemented the NAACP's commitment to the "Elaine Twelve," as they were sometimes called, they also inspired additional engagement from the nation's African American leadership. Activist Ida B. Wells-Barnett also traveled to Arkansas and then wrote of her findings, highlighting the senseless violence and the destruction of acre upon acre of sharecroppers' land and crops that was inflicted by rampaging whites across the area, a devastation that served to all but enslave the sharecroppers whose crops had been decimated.[37] Additional efforts of leaders like William Monroe Trotter and W. E. B. Du Bois, furthered by the widespread publication of White's findings in papers like the *Boston Chronicle*, the *Pittsburgh Dispatch*, the *Baltimore Herald*, and the *Buffalo Express*, not only reinforced the efforts of White and the NAACP, but also increased public awareness and helped raise the funds needed to support the defense efforts.[38] In the end, these efforts not only provided psychological and financial sup-

---

[34] Peter de Lissovoy, "'Outside Agitator' and Other Terms of the Times: Remembering James Daniels," online at http://www.crmvet.org/nars/peter1.htm (accessed March 1, 2018); Cortner, *A Mob Intent on Death*, 34–37.

[35] Stockley, *Blood in Their Eyes*, 98; McWhirter, *Red Summer*, 230.

[36] Stockley, *Blood in Their Eyes*, 97–99.

[37] Wells-Barnett, *The Arkansas Race Riot*, 25–32; Stockley, *Blood in Their Eyes*, 49–50.

[38] McWhirter, *Red Summer*, 229–231; Francis, *Civil Rights*, 143.

port, but in raising the profile of the Elaine debacle, they shined a national spotlight on the events, a fact that may well have helped put the case on the Supreme Court's radar, increasing the chances that the justices would be willing to revisit matters they had addressed and seemingly resolved less than a decade earlier.[39]

Navigating the Local Legal Labyrinth

While national awareness of the events in Phillips County was growing, back in Arkansas, the Elaine Twelve were staring death in the face. However, although previously the victims of inadequate counsel, the two sets of six defendants suddenly found themselves the beneficiaries of the efforts of Arkansas's most prominent African American attorney, Scipio Africanus Jones, who had been retained by an Arkansas-based group, as well as the NAACP. On December 20, 1919, in the first of many legal twists and turns that would eventually lead to freedom for the twelve accused, Jones and the NAACP-designated attorney, George Murphy, filed a motion for a new trial, arguing that the defendants' right to a fair trial had been denied as a result of the mob atmosphere and the adverse publicity that had preceded the trial. The motion also asserted that their right to due process under the Fourteenth Amendment had been denied by virtue of inadequate counsel and the exclusion of black citizens from both the grand and trial court juries.[40]

The Phillips County Circuit Court was unreceptive to these arguments, with Judge J. M. Jackson denying the motion that same day.[41] However, while Jones and Murphy appealed to the Arkansas Supreme Court, Governor Brough issued a stay of execution to allow time for the appeals to be heard.[42] On March 29, 1920, the Arkansas Supreme Court issued its decisions, reversing the

---

[39] McWhirter, *Red Summer*, 229–231; Francis, *Civil Rights*, 130.
[40] Stockley, *Blood in Their Eyes*, 150.
[41] Stockley, *Blood in Their Eyes*, 150.
[42] Stockley, *Blood in Their Eyes*, 150.

convictions of the second half of the Elaine Twelve—Ed Ware, Will Wordlaw, Albert Giles, Joe Fox, Alf banks, and John Martin—ruling that there was a defect in the wording of the verdict.[43] However, the convictions of Moore and company were affirmed. From this point forward, the cases would be severed, proceeding on two very different paths.[44] Ware and his fellow defendants were quickly retried with the same result, but that conviction, too, would be overturned by the state Supreme Court because the second trial reflected clear discrimination against prospective African American jurors in violation of the Fourteenth Amendment.[45] Ultimately, this group would be freed in the early summer of 1923 after the state dragged its feet and failed to hold a third trial within the statutorily mandated time frame.[46]

In contrast, after the state Supreme Court's rejection of their appeal on behalf of Moore and his fellow defendants, lawyers Jones and Murphy were left with little but a "hail Mary" appeal to the U.S. Supreme Court, where they sought a writ of habeas corpus on behalf of Moore and his compatriots. They based their argument for the writ—in this case, an order from the court ordering the authorities to appear and explain why the defendants were being held—in their belief that their due process rights had been denied, but even more significantly, in asking for the writ, the attorneys were asking that the protections afforded by a federal writ be applied to defendants being held by a state.[47] Such a request represented largely uncharted territory, and to the degree that the Court had entertained any previous and similar cases, it had not been receptive, the most recent example being *Frank v. Magnum* decided less than a decade before.[48]

On October 11, 1920, the U.S. Supreme Court denied the

---

[43] Stockley, *Blood in Their Eyes*, 160–161.
[44] Stockley, *Blood in Their Eyes*, 161.
[45] Cortner, *A Mob Intent on Death*, 102–104.
[46] Cortner, *A Mob Intent on Death*, 161–164.
[47] Cortner, *A Mob Intent on Death*, 125–126.
[48] *Frank v. Magnum*, 237 U.S. 309 (1915).

Moore defendants' request for a writ of certiorari.[49] To further complicate matters, George Murphy died that same day.[50] While the NAACP decided to replace Murphy with Edgar McHaney, a member of Murphy's firm, the state received official word of the Supreme Court's refusal to hear the case, and soon after taking office, new Arkansas governor Thomas McRae set the execution date for the Moore Six as June 10, 1921.[51]

With time running out, on June 8, 1921, Jones and McHaney, needing to file a petition for a federal writ of habeas corpus, were unable to find the needed federal judge.[52] With no other option, they filed for a writ in state court, where Judge John Martineau signed the writ and scheduled a hearing on the petition.[53] When the Arkansas attorney general next sought to carry out the scheduled execution, the state Supreme Court refused to overturn the previously issued writ, instead scheduling a hearing and forcing the execution to again be delayed.[54] While the Arkansas Supreme Court ruled against Moore and company on June 20, Jones and McHaney slowed the march to execution by filing a writ in error in the Supreme Court.[55] That writ was denied on August 4, and a new execution date, September 23, was set by Governor Thomas McRae.[56]

Having come this far, neither Jones nor the NAACP were willing to give up. And now that he was in possession of new evidence of the extensive coercion and intimidation that had colored much of the testimony at the original trials, Jones filed a new petition with the state Supreme Court on September 21, 1921, seeking a writ of habeas corpus; pending the response by the court, the executions were postponed once again. Meanwhile, in a decision that

[49] Stockley, *Blood in Their Eyes*, 176.
[50] Stockley, *Blood in Their Eyes*, 176.
[51] Cortner, *A Mob Intent on Death*, 94; Stockley, *Blood in Their Eyes*, xxix.
[52] Stockley, *Blood in Their Eyes*, 188.
[53] Stockley, *Blood in Their Eyes*, 188.
[54] Stockley, *Blood in Their Eyes*, 190–191.
[55] Stockley, *Blood in Their Eyes*, 191.
[56] Stockley, *Blood in Their Eyes*, 192.

would have ramifications down the road, the Arkansas attorney general responded to the request for the writ of habeas corpus by accepting the statement of facts presented by the NAACP, which would bind them to accept the NAACP's version of events as fact going forward.[57] Finally, after some additional back and forth at the federal district court, Judge J. H. Cotteral stated that "there exists probable cause for an appeal in this case," a determination that, at a time when review by the court of appeals was not required, served as an impetus for the U.S. Supreme Court to decide, on this its third review, to take the case.[58] So it was that after three years of laboring to save the lives of Frank Moore and his fellow defendants, as the end of 1922 approached, Scipio Jones and his allies in the NAACP prepared to present their case to the U.S. Supreme Court.

The U.S. Supreme Court Looks at Due Process—Again

The Court's decision in the fall of 1922 to hear the appeal of Moore and company was something of a surprise—not only had the Court twice denied the *Moore* defendants a hearing, but the issue of what exactly were adequate due process protections presented in the case seemed to be same one the Court had resolved less than a decade earlier when it had decided *Frank v. Magnum*, a case arising from the infamous 1913 trial of Leo Frank for the murder of Mary Phagan in Georgia.[59] Indeed, the Court's decision in *Frank* would seem to have left little room or reason to revisit the issue, and based on the 7–2 vote, it was not even close. In that case, the Court had determined that while the *Frank* trial was likely tainted by mob domination, the fact that the state offered a corrective process (in that instance the opportunity for appeal), even one that was no more likely to achieve justice, was sufficient

---

[57] Stockley, *Blood in Their Eyes*, 206–207; Cortner, *A Mob Intent on Death*, 153.
[58] Stockley, *Blood in Their Eyes*, 206.
[59] Stockley, *Blood in Their Eyes*, 209–210; Cortner, *A Mob Intent on Death*, 140–141; *Frank v. Magnum*, 237 U.S. 309 (1915).

to satisfy the due process requirements.[60] While the Arkansas case did have a racial dimension lacking in the earlier case, there was little else in the case that would seem to have warranted a revisiting of the issue so soon after the original decision. And yet, while the core issue may have been the same, the factual circumstances, as well as the context, were different. After all, the intervening years encompassed a period that had seen the country go through the trial of a global conflict, only to see its soldiers and citizens of all colors struggle to adapt to a nation scarred not only by the war but by the resulting changed world. Indeed, from fears of outside radical influence to a recognition that, for all its effort to "make the world safe for democracy," the American version of democracy still had a ways to go, the public consciousness that served as the backdrop for the Court's deliberations in *Moore* was very different from that of *Frank*. No less important were the factors of race and religion (Frank had been Jewish)—and finally, the end result of the first case, in which final "justice" was achieved not in a courtroom, but at the end of a rope, after a mob abducted Frank from the prison in which he was being held and then proceeded to hang him in a very public ceremony.[61]

To the more astute and experienced Court observers, there were signs that a different ruling might be possible once the decision to hear the case had been made. First, there was the ever-present but seldom acknowledged matter of the Court's changing membership. While the Court has tried to present itself as a body of laws, not of men, different membership always raises the possibility of legal change. The Court that agreed in the fall of 1922 to hear the appeal in the *Moore* case was very different from the one that had decided *Frank v. Magnum* in 1915, with four new members, as well as an open seat whose previous

[60] *Frank v. Magnum*, 237 U.S. 309 (1915).
[61] Peter Jacobs, "The Lynching of a Jewish Man in Georgia 100 Years Ago Changed America Forever," *The Business Insider*, August 18, 2015.

occupant had authored the *Frank* opinion.[62]

The dynamic of the team seeking justice for Frank Moore and company had also undergone some changes. With its pocketbook and prestige both bigger than anything Scipio Jones could muster, the NAACP had taken the lead in the fight. However, it was not until shortly before the January 9 arguments that it was determined that NAACP president Moorfield Storey, accompanied by U. S. Bratton but not Jones, would actually make the argument before the Court. The decision and the accompanying communication did not represent either Storey's or the NAACP's finest hour, but by all accounts Jones, wholly focused on the pursuit of justice for the *Moore* defendants, accepted the decision with grace.[63] He was, however, concerned about having Bratton's name on the brief, a document that would be seen in advance by the Arkansas Attorney General's Office, which would be defending the state. Jones feared that some of Bratton's previous associations with the Elaine defendants might enflame local passions, and after a round of discussions involving Jones and NAACP officials, it was decided that Bratton would not be listed.[64] In the end, while some, at least early in the process, had believed that Jones would present part of the oral argument before the Court, on January 9 it was Bratton who assumed the supporting role, with that participation being seen as less of a lightning rod to the Arkansas population.[65] None of this could minimize Jones's tremendous contributions to the effort, and, ultimately, the man who had the supporting role proved to be of limited significance, for in the end, it was the embodiment of the enlightened Northern establishment, Harvard-educated Moorfield Storey, who took the lead.[66]

[62] Cortner, *A Mob Intent on Death*, 144–145.

[63] Stockley, *Blood in Their Eyes*, 213–214.

[64] Cortner, *A Mob Intent on Death*, 146–147.

[65] Cortner, *A Mob Intent on Death*, 147.

[66] William B. Hixson Jr., *Moorfield Storey and the Abolitionist Tradition* (New York: Oxford University Press, 1972) offers a comprehensive and straightforward account of one of the pillars of the late nineteenth and early twentieth-century legal community.

Interestingly, part of the reason for the delay in making the all-important decision about who would argue the case was Storey's initial reluctance to do so, a hesitation stemming from his fear that, at seventy-eight years old, he was not up to the physical demands of the case.[67] He also worried about the public reaction. While his position as the NAACP's president was a clear indication of his support for the civil rights cause, he also recognized that any effort to defend the rights of Southern blacks would likely be labeled a communist plot by Southern politicians.[68] Storey had long been aware of rumors that the Justice Department was suspicious of the NAACP, and Storey had met those rumors head on, writing to Attorney General A. Mitchell Palmer to assure him of the group's patriotism. He did despair of the more radical side of black activism, including the efforts of labor leader A. Philip Randolph and his publication, *The Messenger* (which Storey believed was a socialist periodical, although he may have been confusing it with *The Socialist*, another publication that Randolph edited); however, Storey, who as president had put the NAACP's name behind the appeals and had supported White's investigatory efforts, thought the idea that blacks were planning any kind of revolt against their white counterparts was ludicrous. Instead, in his view, the sharecroppers were seeking to defend themselves by "endeavoring to make appeals to the conscience of this country against the oppression under which they are suffering." When the dust had settled, it was this belief that ultimately carried the day, for once the Court finally agreed to hear the appeal, Storey accepted the challenge. As he wrote to his NAACP colleague James Weldon Johnson, "The Arkansas cases have always appealed to me and that carries me a great way."[69]

With that motivation and engagement, Storey and U. S. Bratton appeared before the Court on Tuesday, January 9, 1923.

[67] Hixson, *Moorfield Storey*, 183.
[68] Hixson, *Moorfield Storey*, 183.
[69] Hixson, *Moorfield Storey*, 182–183.

There, they presented a compelling argument that Moore and company had been denied due process. In a pointed fashion, they sought to paint a picture of a skewed system of justice where a trial dominated by a mob resulted in a dozen death sentences, while despite "the killing of some 200 innocent negroes...not a single indictment had been returned."[70] In the brief and in the oral argument, Storey—while arguing that there was no evidence convincing enough to warrant convictions—also made clear that the defendants' rights had been trampled upon, and that they were the victims of torture-induced testimony and a mob atmosphere that worked to convince the jury that nothing less than guilty verdicts were acceptable. In addition, Storey asserted that the appropriate corrective process, a concept that had been central to the Court's ruling in *Frank*, was wholly lacking in this instance. The supposed procedures were outweighed by the realities of processes that bowed to public pressure at the expense of due process and justice. The number of ways, as Storey noted, in which the defendants had been denied a fair trial were numerous and outrageous. From inadequate counsel to pressure-induced and perjured testimony to mob-influenced jury deliberations, the only compelling evidence was that which attested to the abridgement of the defendants' rights.[71] Complementing that effort, Bratton said that he had sought "to get a mental picture in the minds of the Court as to the exact conditions in Arkansas," adding that he had wanted to give them "an insight as to the brutality administered to the prisoners."[72]

Meanwhile, the justices had seemed very open to Storey and Bratton's arguments, with only the reliably cantankerous Justice James Clark McReynolds evincing obvious opposition to their efforts.[73] Courtroom observers left feeling that Storey and Bratton

[70] Cortner, *A Mob Intent on Death*, 153.
[71] Cortner, *A Mob Intent on Death*, 147.
[72] Cortner, *A Mob Intent on Death*, 153.
[73] Stockley, *Blood in Their Eyes*, 215.

256

had made their case to a receptive Court. Indeed, Hebert Seligmann, the NAACP's director of publicity, sent an optimistic report back to headquarters, while Walter White, although cautious,
let Scipio Jones know that they were heartened by the effort.[74]

Decision Time: Justice in Fact, Not Form

For all that had transpired between the original incident at
Elaine and the oral arguments on the ninth of January, it did not
take the Court long to render a judgment in *Moore v. Dempsey*.
On Monday, February 19, less than six weeks after Storey and
Bratton had appeared before the justices, the Court announced
its decision. Overruling the district court's dismissal of the writ
of habeas corpus, the justices by a 6–2 vote ordered the case returned to the district court for a new hearing. Justice Oliver Wen-
dell Holmes Jr.—writing for a majority that included Chief Justice William Howard Taft and Associate Justices Louis Brandeis,
Pierce Butler, Joseph McKenna, and Willis Van Devanter—all
but translated his dissent in *Frank* into a new pronouncement of
due process protections for the accused.[75] In looking at the circumstances surrounding the trial, and taking note of the mob, the
iconic jurist made clear that there must be justice not just in form,
but in fact, causing one writer to later observe that the Court ruled
that "Justice may wear a blindfold, but not a mask."[76]

Indeed, in distinguishing the case from the Court's previous
ruling in *Frank*, a case in which the Court had said that due process would be served if the state offered a corrective process—
one that in *Frank* consisted of an opportunity for appeal, without
regard to what factors the appeal considered—Holmes shifted the
Court's position, this time asserting that the mere existence of a
corrective process was not enough and that it needed to be a pro-

[74] Cortner, *A Mob Intent on Death*, 153.
[75] *Moore v. Dempsey*, 261 U.S. 86 (1923).
[76] "The Taft Court, 1921–1930." The Supreme Court Historical Society,
http://supremecourthistory.org/timeline_court_taft.html (accessed March 8,
2018).

cess that actually corrected the earlier error and thus truly ensured that a defendant's due process rights had been protected. While making clear that the U.S. Supreme Court did not correct "mere mistakes of law," he also reiterated the idea that the corrective process intended to guarantee due process actually had to *correct* the error. Holmes wrote, "But if the case is that the whole proceeding is a mask—that counsel, jury and judge were swept to the fatal end by an irresistible wave of public passion, and that the State Courts failed to correct the wrong, neither perfection in the machinery for correction nor the possibility that the trial court and counsel saw no other way of avoiding an immediate outbreak of the mob can prevent this Court from securing to the petitioners their constitutional rights."[77]

To assess its validity and, in turn, to guarantee the defendants' due process rights, Holmes asserted that the federal courts could investigate the nature of the state judicial proceedings.[78] That determination represented a major extension of federal authority and would arguably be *Moore*'s greatest legacy. And yet it was necessary at a time when Southern justice was too often a charade in the eyes of anyone not fully immersed in the distinctive Southern race-based culture. Holmes made clear his doubts about the validity of Phillips County justice when he noted that the members of the Committee of Seven had reported that a lynching party had been kept at bay when a "solemn promise was given by the leading citizens of the community that, if the guilty parties were not lynched, and let the law take its course, that justice would be done and the majesty of the law upheld."[79] With such circumstances, the Court recognized that a reliance upon professed procedures was not a guarantee of due process or the justice it was intended to achieve. After years of giving deference to proceedings that had guaranteed a two-tier system of justice in the former Confed-

---

[77] *Moore v. Dempsey*, 261 U.S. 86 (1923), 91.
[78] *Moore v. Dempsey*, 261 U.S. 86 (1923), 91.
[79] *Moore v. Dempsey*, 261 U.S. 86 (1923), 90.

eracy, Holmes and his brethren, however unintentionally, opened the door to the pursuit of a national standard of justice.

While the Holmes opinion represented a clear about-face from the Court's previous opinion in *Frank*, it also raised the question of whether the Court had, in fact, overruled *Frank* or simply distinguished it, or decided that the precedent of *Frank* would not wholly apply to the *Moore* case due to materially different facts between the two.[80] Commentators, scholars, and even Supreme Court justices have differed on that matter over time. In his dissent, Justice James Clark McReynolds made clear his belief that, in issuing the *Moore* decision, the Court was dispensing with *Frank*, while Holmes argued, perhaps a bit disingenuously, that he had distinguished, but not overruled, *Frank*.[81] At the same time, the mere fact that the Court had been willing to review the same due process question that had seemingly been laid to rest in *Frank* seemed a clear indication that the justices were not wholly satisfied with that decision, although the attorneys for the State of Arkansas rested their case on the part of *Frank* that said that a writ would not be granted if the state offered a mechanism that could correct the original defective process.[82] But, in fact, it was the refusal to accept the mere existence of a corrective process, and the requirement that the corrective process actually ensured due process, that differentiated the *Moore* ruling from the decision in *Frank*. While the question of whether *Moore* actually overturned *Frank* may remain open to debate, there is no denying the fact that, at the very least, it distinguished it in a very stark and far-reaching manner.

Of course, the establishment of that more tightly drawn distinction raises the question of why the Court changed its position

---

[80] Whitaker, *On the Laps of Gods*, 293.

[81] Cortner, *A Mob Intent on Death*, 186.

[82] J. S. Waterman and E. E. Overton, "Federal Habeas Corpus Statutes and Moore v. Dempsey," *University of Chicago Law Review* 1, no. 2 (1933): 313, online at http://chicagounbound.uchicago.edu/uclrev/vol1/iss2/8/ (accessed March 1, 2018).

on the larger question of what constitutes appropriate due process. Here, too, scholars and commentators have been split. Some have argued that the nature of the changes—including changes made by three Harding-appointed conservatives—offered no new allies for the cause. Consequently, they argue, the shift—especially given the fact that two justices changed sides—must be explained by the impact of shifting public opinion, a change that was best illustrated in the political landscape as it related to racial issues.[83] This change was clearly illustrated in the increased sensitivity to lynching and the receptivity—at least in the House of Representatives—to a federal anti-lynching law.[84] In the end, while raising the timeless question of how attuned the Supreme Court is to political currents, these observers posit that changing public opinion was the major reason why the Court changed from its earlier stance in *Frank*.

At the same time, those who put more stock in the impact of personality on the Court have noted that one of the major changes since the *Frank* decision was the ascension of William Howard Taft to the position of chief justice. While very much the conservative, Taft was also a devoted advocate of justice, a trait that caused him to look at the plight of the *Moore* defendants through a lens that made it hard to uphold the lower court's decision. In addition, although he was in only his second year on the High Court, the once feckless chief executive had already begun to distinguish himself as a strong and persuasive chief justice, one whom his liberal colleagues Holmes and Brandeis very much believed capable of bringing others along with him.[85] Given the parallel timing between congressional consideration of a federal anti-lynching law and the Court's consideration of habeas corpus as a protection in mob-dominated cases, proceedings that some saw

---

[83] Francis, *Civil Rights*, 130.

[84] Francis, *Civil Rights*, 130.

[85] Robert M. Cover, "The Left, the Right and the First Amendment: 1918–1928," *Maryland Law Review* 40, no. 3 (1981): 355–356, online at http://digitalcommons.law.yale.edu/fss_papers/2703/ (accessed March 1, 2018).

as little more than judicially sanctioned lynchings, Taft—who before joining the High Court had been active in trying to get the
Senate to investigate some of the postwar lynchings—may well
have been the key to the Court's shift from *Frank* to *Moore*.[86] In
the end, the Court ruling in *Moore* represented not just a surprising about-face, but also the advent of a new era.

The Effects of the Court's Decision on the State and Nation

The U.S. Supreme Court's decision did not represent the end
of the legal journey for the six defendants, for the High Court had
in fact only ordered a hearing by the district court.[87] However, that
hearing never took place. Instead, while the other six defendants,
the ones whose case had been overturned by the Arkansas court
only to be retried and again overturned, were ultimately released
due to the state's failure to follow through on a directive to hold
an additional trial, Moore and his fellow defendants remained in
jail, with a retrial of their own a very real possibility.

But the redoubtable Scipio Jones had not fought all the way to
the U.S. Supreme Court only to see Moore and company fail to
achieve a better result. Rather, his unrelenting efforts ultimately
proved successful when, on November 3, 1923, Arkansas governor Thomas McRae commuted the original death sentence to
twelve years, a term which, when coupled with the time the defendants had already served over the course of the appeals, made
them eligible for parole.[88] However, the wheels of justice continued to work slowly, and while an order was entered in the federal
district court on March 1, 1924, to dismiss the case for lack of
prosecution, it was not until January 14, 1925, that the six *Moore*
defendants were actually released, ultimately the beneficiaries of
an indefinite furlough—one never revoked—that was issued by

[86] Cover, "The Left, the Right and the First Amendment: 1918–1928," 357;
Francis, *Civil Rights*, 158.
[87] *Moore v. Dempsey*, 261 U.S. 86 (1923).
[88] Cortner, *A Mob Intent on Death*, 181.

Governor McRae.[89] By that time, despite all that had transpired, life had returned to "normal" in a region whose economic instability was matched by a similarly unsteady racial situation.

Yet while the Arkansas legal system's response to the Supreme Court's decision had been a slow one, the reaction in the nation at large was quick and powerful, with observers at both ends of the political spectrum recognizing the impact, both immediate and potential, of the ruling. Respected constitutional attorney Louis Marshall, who had unsuccessfully argued the *Frank* case, called the decision "a great achievement in constitutional law," predicting that it could become the "cornerstone" of future advancements in the pursuit of justice.[90] Meanwhile, *The Crisis* termed it "a milestone in the Negro's fight for justice, an achievement that is as important as any event since the signing of the Emancipation Proclamation."[91] In the American heartland, the *Toledo Times* expressed the belief that the *Moore* ruling would "spur state courts to conduct trials fairly."[92] But while the *New Republic*, the ACLU, and the *Nation*, not to mention countless black newspapers, enthusiastically applauded the decision, the *Louisville Courier* offered as trenchant an assessment as could be found when it observed, "The principle that the Federal Government may constitute itself a reviewer of the decisions of the criminal courts of States, overruling the authority of state courts of last resort, will, if established, constitute a change hardly less than revolutionary."[93] The Arkansas press also recognized the tremendous change that the case might represent, with an *Arkansas Gazette* editorial observing that *Moore* could mean that "the pow-

---

[89] Cortner, *A Mob Intent on Death*, 182–183; John S. Waterman and Edward E. Overton, "The Aftermath of Moore v. Dempsey," *Washington University Law Review* 18, no. 2 (1933): 123, online at http://openscholarship.wustl.edu/cgi/viewcontent.cgi?article=4642&context=law_lawreview (accessed March 1, 2018).
[90] Whitaker, *On the Laps of Gods*, 292.
[91] Whitaker, *On the Laps of Gods*, 292.
[92] Whitaker, *On the Laps of Gods*, 292–293.
[93] Whitaker, *On the Laps of Gods*, 292–293.

262

ers of the state courts will in large measure be nullified."[94] At the same time, the *Little Rock Daily News* headline accompanying its report noted that the "U.S. High Court Orders Fair Trials," an acknowledgment, however unintentional, that such treatment had not previously been the norm.[95] Thanks to *Moore v. Dempsey*, the impact of the Elaine Massacre would long endure, for while the event would ultimately fade in people's memories, the 1923 decision by the U.S. Supreme Court would stand as a powerful reminder of what could happen when the federal government got involved in local matters.

The Impact and Legacy of *Moore v. Dempsey*: Opening the Door to the Pursuit of Justice

The impact of *Moore* has, not surprisingly, been a subject of considerable debate. Despite the precedent-setting effect of the ruling, one commentator asserted that it would be hard to call the case "a turning point," arguing that "after 1923 southern courts continued to hold their trials much as they always had, with all white juries and amid persisting reports that mobs continued to crowd courtrooms, intimidating juries and court personnel."[96] Such an assessment, while arguably true, would seem akin to saying that *Brown v. Board of Education* was not a turning point because segregated schools remained a reality of American life for a considerable time after the ruling. Such analysis misses the fact that *Moore* gave civil rights activists a new and powerful tool with which to pursue their efforts. The idea that the federal government could oversee and intervene in state court operations marked a drastic departure from previous practices, all but erasing a longtime, seemingly immutable state/federal line of demar-

[94] Whitaker, *On the Laps of Gods*, 293.
[95] Whitaker, *On the Laps of Gods*, 293.
[96] Becca Walton, "On Violence in the South: Criminal Justice Through the Civil Rights Era," Center for the Study of Southern Culture, July 16, 2016, online at: http://southernstudies.olemiss.edu/on-violence-in-the-south-criminal-justice/ (accessed March 1, 2018).

cation. It was not going to happen all at once, but the door was open, and at a time when the legislative efforts to enact a federal anti-lynching law had all but come to an end, unable to break through the wall of Southern opposition in the Senate, *Moore v. Dempsey* specifically, along with the litigation-based strategy it encouraged, marked a major turning point in the struggle for equal justice.

While the victory in *Moore v. Dempsey* would ultimately jumpstart the NAACP's decision to develop a full-scale litigation strategy as part of its civil rights effort, the decision to adopt that approach was not made in a vacuum or immediately. Rather, its timing was complemented by the organization's most active and ongoing effort at the time, the campaign to secure passage of a federal anti-lynching law. While the efforts were basically separate, in an argument that goes to the heart of the never-ending debate about the influence of public opinion on the Court, some assert that the increased publicity and public awareness generated by the anti-lynching campaign contributed to the Court's approach toward its previous ruling in *Frank*.[97] At the same time, the challenges the organization faced in its anti-lynching campaign likely helped push the NAACP even more in the direction of a litigation-based campaign, for while its anti-lynching efforts had found a receptive audience in the House of Representatives, the recalcitrant, filibuster-wielding Southern bloc in the Senate made it clear that success in the national legislative arena was highly unlikely.[98] Coming off the victory in *Moore*, the courts increasingly looked like an alternative route to legislative efforts, offering a greater possibility for success.

Thus it was that under the leadership of Charles Hamilton Houston, beginning in the 1930s, the NAACP undertook a step-

---

[97] Francis, *Civil Rights*, 157.
[98] Robert L. Zangrando, *The NAACP Crusade Against Lynching, 1909–1950* (Philadelphia: Temple University Press, 1980) offers a comprehensive look at the NAACP's long-running but ultimately unsuccessful effort to secure passage of a federal anti-lynching law.

by-step, case-by-case campaign of attacking the legal underpin-
nings of segregation and inequality.[99] Using the precedent for federal intervention established in *Moore* as a major tool, Houston
and his protégé Thurgood Marshall methodically won victories
in *Missouri ex. rel. Gaines v. Canada* (1938), *Smith v. Allwright*
(1944), *Shelley v. Kraemer* (1948), *Sipuel v. Board of Regents
of the University of Oklahoma* (1948), *McLaurin v. Oklahoma*
(1950), and *Sweatt v. Painter* (1950).[100] These cases, all bricks in
the road to *Brown v. Board of Education*, ended the white primary,
restrictive covenants, and segregated graduate and professional
schools.

Meanwhile, in the area of criminal justice, *Moore v. Dempsey*
became the foundation upon which an expansion of due process
protections, as well as the writ of habeas corpus, was based. The
first instance was *Powell v. Alabama*, more commonly known as
the case of the Scottsboro Boys.[101] There, the U.S. Supreme Court
specifically cited *Moore*, although one scholar, apparently missing the connection, asserted that it was not until *Powell* that the
federal constitution's "usefulness as a bulwark against abuses in
state criminal procedure" was established.[102]

All the same, while *Moore*—unlike later cases, including
Gideon v. Wainwright[103] and *Miranda v. Arizona*[104]—did not es-

[99] Rawn James Jr., *Root and Branch: Charles Hamilton Houston, Thurgood Marshall, and the Struggle to End Segregation* (New York: Bloomsbury Press, 2010) offers a comprehensive look at the NAACP's litigation-based effort to end race-based segregation in the United States.
[100] *Missouri ex. rel. Gaines v. Canada*, 305 U.S. 337 (1938), *Smith v. Allwright*, 321 649 (1944), *Shelley v. Kraemer*, 334 U.S. 1 (1948), *Sipuel v. Board of Regents of the University of Oklahoma*, 332 US 631 (1948), *McLaurin v. Oklahoma*, 339 U.S. 637 (1950), *Sweatt v. Painter*, 339 U.S. 629 (1950).
[101] *Powell v. Alabama*, 287 U.S. 45 (1932).
[102] Henry P. Weihofen, "Supreme Court Review of State Criminal Procedure," *The American Journal of Legal History* 10, no. 3 (July 1966): 189–200, 191, online at https://www.jstor.org/stable/844290?seq=1#page_scan_tab_contents (accessed March 1, 2018).
[103] *Gideon v. Wainwright*, 372 U.S. 335 (1963).
[104] *Miranda v. Arizona*, 384 U.S. 436 (1966).

tablish an exact standard under which a defendant's due process rights were violated, its recognition that a mob-dominated trial represented an obvious denial of due process, and its broad establishment of what one scholar referred to as a "fair trial rule," were critical to the development of due process jurisprudence.[105] And from there came the subsequent development of additional, more specific standards that were intended to ensure that a fair trial was indeed accorded every time. It is these cases that show *Moore*'s influence.[106] *Powell* was soon followed by *Brown v. Mississippi*, in which a coerced confession was deemed a violation of the protections of the due process clause.[107] Tellingly, in neither of these cases did the U.S. Supreme Court draw upon the Bill of Rights protections of the Fifth and Sixth Amendments. Rather, in each instance, it based its ruling upon the due process guarantee of the Fourteenth Amendment, thus proceeding through the door that had been opened in *Moore*.

The key takeaway from *Moore* was its establishment of the power of the federal courts to review state court efforts and determine if the constitutional protections, protections that would guarantee a fair trial, had been guarded in an appropriate manner. That determination represented a redrawing of long-accepted lines of legal federalism, and it would be a touchpoint for an increasingly active federal involvement in activities relating to fairness and equality. In commenting on the *Moore* decision and federalism, noted scholar Paul Bator argued that the case eased the line between state and federal relations, with a state no longer able to reject out of hand a claim of a violation of a federal right. Rather, in the aftermath of *Moore*, in order to protect its results, the state had to show that those results were the product of "rea-

---

[105] Richard C. Cortner, "The Nationalization of the Bill of Rights, An Overview," online at http://faculty.smu.edu/jkobylka/supremecourt/Nationalization_BoRs.pdf (accessed March 1, 2018).
[106] *Powell v. Alabama*, 287 U.S. 45 (1932).
[107] *Brown v. Mississippi*, 297 U.S. 278 (1936).

soned findings rationally reached through fair procedures."[108]

Over the years, *Moore* has continued to be a touchpoint for federal protection of due process rights. In his dissent in the 1953 case *Brown v. Allen*, Justice Hugo L. Black offered a clear view of the importance civil libertarians attached to the landmark decision when he wrote, "I read *Moore v. Dempsey*, supra, as standing for the principle that it is never too late for courts in habeas corpus proceedings to look straight through procedural screens in order to prevent forfeiture of life or liberty in flagrant defiance of the Constitution."[109]

At the same time, however, no small part of *Moore*'s importance stems from the way it has served as a base for both criminal procedure and civil rights advances. Indeed, while *Moore* has served as the focus and foundational precedent for numerous advances in the law relating to criminal procedure, its erasure of the formerly strict line between state and federal judicial proceedings has also impacted the law in other areas. In fact, beyond its role as the starting point for the NAACP's litigation-based approach to attacking segregation, that now open boundary has been recognized in other cases such as 1948's *Shelley v. Kraemer*, in which the Court overturned the state court's enforcement of a restrictive covenant in a property transaction.[110]

In the winter of 1923, Ida B. Wells-Barnett was visited by a young man, one of the Elaine Twelve, who had traveled to Chicago to thank her for all she had done on their behalf. He told her that her efforts to help raise money, to focus attention on their

[108] Rae K. Inafuku, "Coleman v. Thompson—Sacrificing Fundamental Rights in Deference to the States: The Supreme Court's 1991 Interpretation of the Writ of Habeas Corpus," *Santa Clara Law Review* 34, no. 2 (1994): 637, online at http://digitalcommons.law.scu.edu/cgi/viewcontent.cgi?article=1607&context=lawreview (accessed March 2, 2018).
[109] Eric M. Freedman, "Brown v. Allen: The Habeas Corpus Revolution That Wasn't," *Alabama Law Review* 51, no. 4 (2000): 1540–1624, 1583, online at http://scholarlycommons.law.hofstra.edu/cgi/viewcontent.cgi?article=1048&context=faculty_scholarship (accessed March 2, 2018).
[110] *Shelley v. Kraemer*, 334 U.S. 1 (1948).

plight, and to visit him and his fellow defendants in jail had been invaluable and helped them maintain hope over the course of their long ordeal. The encounter, recorded by Wells-Barnett in her autobiography, was a poignant reminder of the human dimension of the precedent-setting case.[111]

---

[111] McWhirter, *Red Summer*, 259.

Contributors

Richard Buckelew is an associate professor of history at Bethune-Cookman University in Daytona Beach, Florida. He holds a PhD in American history from the University of Arkansas, where he wrote his dissertation on lynching in the state. He is currently working on a major revision of his lynching study. His most recent work appears in *Bullets and Fire: Lynching and Authority in Arkansas, 1840–1950*, edited by Guy Lancaster.

Nancy Snell Griffith is a graduate of Dickinson College (Carlisle, Pennsylvania) and Syracuse University. She is the author of numerous works on local history, including dozens of entries on racial violence for the online *Encyclopedia of Arkansas History & Culture*, and recently retired as the Archives and Special Collections librarian at Presbyterian College in Clinton, South Carolina.

Matthew Hild is a lecturer in the School of History and Sociology at the Georgia Institute of Technology, and he also teaches history courses as an instructor at the University of West Georgia. He is the author of *Greenbackers, Knights of Labor, and Populists: Farmer-Labor Insurgency in the Late-Nineteenth-Century South* (University of Georgia Press, 2007). He is also the co-editor, with Keri Leigh Merritt, of *Reconsidering Southern Labor History: Race, Class, and Power* (University Press of Florida, 2018).

Adrienne A. Jones is the research and scholarly communications archivist for the Center for Arkansas History and Culture at the University of Arkansas at Little Rock. She previously served as an archival technician at the Arkansas State Archives in Little Rock. She received her BA in history and her MA in public history at the University of Arkansas at Little Rock. She was the first undergraduate ever to complete an honors BA thesis, titled "The

Emergence of Black Nationalism and the Nation of Islam," and her master's thesis, "The Nation of Gods and Earths: Its Predecessors, Early History, and Influence in Hip Hop Culture," examined Islamic culture in black American history and its continued influence on hip hop culture. Jones, the first beneficiary of the Little Rock Nine Endowment Scholarship, has focused her research on little-known areas of the black experience in America, including Black Nationalism, Islam within black America, and the black history of Arkansas.

Kelly Houston Jones is an assistant professor of history at Austin Peay State University in Clarksville, Tennessee. A member of the executive committee of the Agricultural History Society and a trustee of the Arkansas Historical Association, she is currently at work on a book about slave life in Arkansas. Her most recent work appears in *Arkansas Women: Their Lives and Times*, edited by Cherisse Jones-Branch and Gary Edwards, and *Bullets and Fire: Lynching and Authority in Arkansas, 1840–1950*, edited by Guy Lancaster.

Cherisse Jones-Branch is the James and Wanda Lee Vaughn Professor of History and director of the ASTATE Digital Press at Arkansas State University in Jonesboro, where, since 2003, she has taught courses in American, women's, civil rights, rural, and African American history, as well as heritage studies. She received her BA and MA degrees from the College of Charleston, South Carolina, and a PhD in history from The Ohio State University, Columbus. She is the author of numerous articles on women's civil rights and rural activism and, in 2014, published *Crossing the Line: Women and Interracial Activism in South Carolina during and after World War II* (University Press of Florida). She is also the co-editor of *Arkansas Women: Their Lives and Times* (University of Georgia Press, 2018) and is working on a second monograph, *Better Living by Their Own Bootstraps: Ru-*

ral Black Women's Activism in Arkansas, to be published by the University of Arkansas Press.

Guy Lancaster (editor) holds a PhD in heritage studies from Arkansas State University in Jonesboro and serves as the editor of the online *Encyclopedia of Arkansas History & Culture*, a project of the Butler Center for Arkansas Studies at the Central Arkansas Library System. He is author of the monograph *Racial Cleansing in Arkansas, 1883–1924: Politics, Land, Labor, and Criminality* (Lexington Books, 2014), co-editor with Michael D. Polston of *To Can the Kaiser: Arkansas and the Great War* (Butler Center Books, 2015), and editor of *Bullets and Fire: Lynching and Authority in Arkansas, 1840–1950* (University of Arkansas Press, 2018).

Brian K. Mitchell is an assistant professor in the History Department and an associate faculty member at the Anderson Institute on Race and Ethnicity at the University of Arkansas at Little Rock. His interests include African American antebellum history, Free Black communities, and urban history. A native of New Orleans, Louisiana, he has been a resident of Arkansas since 2006.

William H. Pruden III is the director of civic engagement and college counselor at Ravenscroft School in Raleigh, North Carolina. A history major at Princeton University, he earned a JD from Case Western Reserve University, as well as master's degrees from Wesleyan University and Indiana University. His stints as a legislative assistant to both a state senator and a U.S. congressman have informed his over thirty years as an educator, teaching American history and government at both the collegiate and secondary levels. He has done presentations and published articles on a wide range of historical, political, and college admission–related subjects.

Steven Teske is an archivist at the Butler Center for Arkansas Studies and author or co-author of three books published by Butler Center Books: *Homefront Arkansas: Arkansans Face Wartime* (co-written with Velda B. Branscum Woody, 2009), *Unvarnished Arkansas: The Naked Truth about Nine Famous Arkansans* (2012), and *Natural State Notables: 21 Famous People from Arkansas* (2013). He has also contributed more than 400 entries to the online *Encyclopedia of Arkansas History & Culture* and a chapter to the book *To Can the Kaiser: Arkansas and the Great War* (2015). In addition, he is an ordained Lutheran minister who graduated from Coe College and Concordia Theological Seminary and who has served congregations in Chicago, southwestern Iowa, and central Arkansas. He also teaches college history classes and has published a number of works on theology.

Index

Corbin, Joseph C. 147, 153, 166
Cotteral, J. H. 172, 251
cotton 18, 20, 21, 27, 28, 30, 42, 50, 62, 129, 156, 157, 159, 160, 161, 178, 186, 201
Cotton Pickers Strike of 1891 62, 89
Courier (Natchez, Mississippi) 26
Craig, John A. 28
Creek (tribe) 22
Crisis, The 246, 261
Crittenden County 51, 52, 59, 60, 63, 119, 127, 185
Cuba 47
Cunningham, B. J. 213
Cunningham, Charles 122
Cunningham, George 61
Curtis, Charles 204
Curtis, Sam 37
Cutler, James 85

D

Dagbovie, Pera Gaglo 103
Davis, Bob 67, 68
Davis, Jeff 73
Democratic Party 50, 53, 59, 60, 65, 110, 115, 119, 120, 121, 123, 125, 126, 127, 128, 131, 132, 147
De Priest, Oscar 193
Dermott, Arkansas 154
Derrick, W. T. 63
DeWitt, Arkansas 74, 75, 76
Dickinson, Moses A. 145
Douglass, Frederick 79
Dramer, Roy 158, 159
Drew County 154
Duckett, General 69, 70, 71, 72, 79, 81, 90
Dulaney, John "Boss" 186
Dunn, Jim 66, 67, 68
Dwiggins, Willa 195, 196
Dwyer, Philip G. 95
Dyer Anti-Lynching Bill 194

E

Eagle, James P. 63, 126, 128
Earle 185, 186
Earls, Luther D. 214

Elaine, Arkansas 18, 39, 40, 54, 62, 78, 79, 82, 155, 162, 179, 180, 183, 186, 187, 198, 201, 205, 238, 240, 245, 246, 256, 262
Elaine Twelve 170, 174, 191, 194, 195, 198, 199, 214, 246, 249, 253, 266
Election Law of 1891 61, 64, 65, 128, 131
Emancipation 12, 36, 37, 43
Equal Justice Initiative 11, 12, 84
Evening Star, Arkansas 46, 69, 81
"extremely violent societies" 107, 109

F

Farmers' Alliance 59, 123, 124, 129, 132
Farris, Matthew 67
Faulkner County Wheel 131
Fayetteville, Arkansas 42
Featherston, Lewis P. 124, 126, 127
Federal Bureau of Investigation 203
Fein, Helen 105
Ferguson, Bessie 84
Ferguson, David 60
First Kansas Colored Infantry 96
Fitzpatrick, Charles 52
Fizer, Napoleon Bonaparte 128
Fletcher, John G. 122
Flood, Garrett 76
Flood, Randall 76
Florida 22, 50, 59
Flowers, Alonzo 56
Forrest City, Arkansas 64
Fort Gibson 22
Fort Smith, Arkansas 23, 145
Fort Smith Herald 42
Fort Towson 22
Fourteenth Amendment 48, 238, 248, 265
Fox, Joe 169, 171, 249
Frank, J. F. 62, 89
Frank, Leo 251
Frank v. Magnum 249, 251, 252, 255, 256, 258, 259, 260, 261, 263
free blacks 23, 24, 25, 26, 42

Printed in the USA
CPSIA information can be obtained
at www.ICGtesting.com
JSHW021346111123
51665JS00001B/5